Social Readers

Tweet about a book
"Sell" your book in 140 characters

Social Readers

Promoting Reading
in the 21st Century

Leslie B. Preddy

LIBRARIES UNLIMITED

AN IMPRINT OF ABC-CLIO, LLC
Santa Barbara, California • Denver, Colorado • Oxford, England

Library of Congress Cataloging-in-Publication Data

Preddy, Leslie.
  Social readers : promoting reading in the 21st century / Leslie B.
Preddy.
    p. cm.
  Includes bibliographical references and index.
  ISBN 978-1-59158-869-6 (pbk. : acid-free paper) — ISBN
978-1-59158-871-9 (ebook) 1. School libraries—Activity
programs—United States. 2. Children's libraries—Activity
programs—United States. 3. Reading promotion—United States. I.
Title.
  Z675.S3P745 2010
  027.8'222—dc22   2010002587

ISBN: 978-1-59158-869-6
EISBN: 978-1-59158-871-9

14 13 12 11 10   1 2 3 4 5

This book is also available on the World Wide Web as an eBook.
Visit www.abc-clio.com for details.

Libraries Unlimited
An Imprint of ABC-CLIO, LLC

ABC-CLIO, LLC
130 Cremona Drive, P.O. Box 1911
Santa Barbara, California 93116-1911

This book is printed on acid-free paper ∞
Manufactured in the United States of America

For the love of my children, Trevor and Paige.
You make life fun and I strive to be my best for you.
Your wildly opposite personalities and learning styles
inspire me to be a better parent and educator.

Contents

Preface

Reading is not traditionally thought of as a group activity, but we should ask ourselves, why not? People love to talk. People love to share experiences. People love to find things in common. As promoters and advocates of reading, it is necessary to take advantage of this human trait—and we must do it now. Inspiring the next generation to be readers requires us to socialize reading. Embracing children's and young people's need for community and socialization allows us to engage their lifelong reading habits in a more natural, habitual manner. This generation needs, and even thrives on, social interaction; reading must become social, too.

Students' minds today are attracted to entertainment and all things social. Just observe them in their natural habitat, outside of the classroom. Witness them hanging out. Study the commonality among all they do. For them, socializing is a multitasking phenomenon. Our young people watch a movie while simultaneously talking and texting. They hang out with friends while keeping a texting finger at the ready so they can Twitter. They talk on the phone while blogging and surfing social networking Web sites. Conversation is inherent to completing any task. To influence the reading attitudes of this generation, educators and librarians must become reading motivators. Our perpetual campaign must be reading. Reading and readers are what we promote, advocate, and advertise. To do this effectively, in our bag of tricks, we adapt some old and add new techniques. This allows us to meet young people—for whom technologies already existed when they were born and who thus grew up with them—where they live and breathe in the world of social interaction and social technology.

According to the Office of Education Research and Improvement's Web site (last modified March 21, 2002), evidence-based education requires the "integration of professional wisdom with the best available empirical evidence in making decisions about how to deliver instruction." Educational instinct, that gut feeling that tells us spending time promoting and advocating the importance of reading, sets us in the right direction, but today we require more proof than our professional intuition. To initiate change or validate current practices, it is also required to examine best practices and research. Examining the research about reading and literacy emphasizes the importance of reading's impact on quality of life for all children, young people, and adults.

- A person without a high school diploma or equivalent earns 98 percent less than a person with a bachelor's degree and "educational attainment is positively related to ... literacy" (Planty et al. 2008, p. vii; U.S. Department of Education, Department of Education Statistics 2007).

- A developed literacy in reading is an essential, determining factor for entry-level workplace and college readiness and success, according to the ACT Assessment (2006). College includes trade, technical, and two- and four-year colleges.

- Fifty-seven percent of prison inmates began their current incarceration without a high school diploma or equivalent and "incarcerated adults [have] lower average ... literacy than adults in the same age group living in households" (Greenberg, Dunleavy, and Kutner 2007, p. vi).

What does all this mean? Being literate and finding enjoyment in leisure reading is correlated to education success, work fulfillment, and income attained throughout a lifetime. Reading for enjoyment and information improves a person's odds for attaining an independent lifestyle. Developing a literate generation of lifelong readers is an important factor toward fostering self-sufficient adults.

The three Rs necessary to have an impact on the next generation are reading, relationships, and role models. In 2004, my school engaged in an action research project to pilot a local reading intervention program, SSR (Sustained Silent Reading) with Interventions. The program proved to improve student's reading attitudes, comprehension, and state standardized test scores. Three years after schoolwide implementation, we met Adequate Yearly Progress (AYP) for the first time. We successfully found a way to combine the need to value reading and the need to connect with this generation to make reading meaningful for them. What the educators learned was vital to developing lifelong readers. Creating a lifelong reader requires meeting young people's emotional needs through reading, developing relationships, and creating reading role models. Following is a description of the Three Rs.

The Three R's of Literacy to Impact a Generation

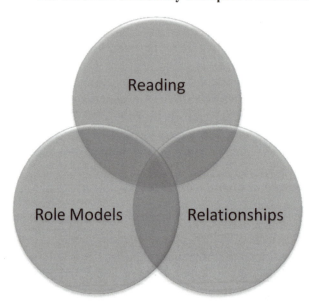

To develop a reader requires time spent reading, role models at home and school, and socialization through reading relationships.

- **Reading.** Kids today are busy. They multitask and cram a lot into one short day. They have time commitments placed on them socially and by home and school. Time is an important factor. Finding time to read together with friends, family, and throughout the school day is difficult, but it's imperative. Carving fifteen to twenty-five minutes out of a school day makes a difference. Most things in life require continual exposure and practice to gain skill, do something well, and ingrain the habit to keep doing it. Establishing time during school dedicated to pleasure reading ensures students can practice and develop the reading habit. Promoting healthy home reading habits is also vital. Spending personal time reading is important and a home reading log encourages families to continue the practice and experience at home while also giving the student reading experiences beyond the traditional school day.

- **Relationships.** Developing reading relationships gets to the heart of what children and young people cherish: socialization. They need to have discussions about what people are currently reading with teachers, peers, family, mentors, role models, and virtual friends. They need to get into the habit of sharing reading experiences and consider it as commonplace as talking about last night's game, movie, online exchange, or TV show. They need opportunities that make reading the central focus of celebrations, events, gatherings, and parties. Reading discussions do not have to be formal or lengthy; short and sweet can be just as effective, but the conversations must occur to imprint reading into this generation's hearts and minds. Talk about reading in the halls, office, cafeteria, gymnasiums, library, bus, classrooms, bathrooms, and any other place people carry on conversations. What are you reading? What can you share with others about it? What are they reading? What have they heard others are reading?

- **Role Models.** Be a reading role model. Don't just say that reading matters; show students that reading matters in everyone's life. Warm up class or a meeting by revealing something interesting you read the night before. Read aloud snippets of something you found appealing, entertaining, valuable, refreshing, educational, or downright fun. Put a sign up at your desk or door announcing to students what you are currently reading. Frequently take advantage of the time in class when everyone is completing a silent reading assignment to model reading by positioning yourself toward the front of the class and reading something in their presence. Remind students that an effective reader keeps reading material nearby. Carry reading material with you wherever you go. Develop reading and book-related advertisements—like book commercials—to share with students in a variety of venues. Reward students and classes with free reading time, and read alongside them throughout the reading reward time (Preddy 2007).

Millennial learners are a lot of fun to be around, and they are energizing to educate. Embracing the act of promoting our students' reading habits is absolutely enjoyable, and it adds life to our day as educators and reading promoters. Young people are born into a world immersed in technology. They have never experienced life without the Internet or instant gratification. They live for the moment and value people (Payne 2003/Gardiner 2005). When meeting the values, interests, and abilities of our nation's youth, we can successfully develop uninterested students into lifelong readers. Meeting their literacy needs requires a blend of entertainment, participation, control, auditory skills, and incentives. Today's educators and librarians have the joyous job of finding ways to relate reading to their values, interests, and abilities, which in itself is enjoyable and energizing. It is exciting to work with young people in a time when our job of encouraging reading includes hosting events, making and playing games, creating projects and promotions, and getting other adults to join the merriment.

To reach this generation of readers, find ways to make reading social. Find pleasure in training staff in the ways of reading engagement. Delight in finding ways to make reading socially acceptable, commonplace, entertaining, and interactive in the school and the library—for yourself, your staff, and current and future generations. Seek technologies and online resources, such as those found on my Web site: http://www.lesliepreddy.com/Authors.htm. Such resources will enrich student engagement. Read, talk, play, and have fun!

Acknowledgments

A special thanks to all who shared their ideas, inspired me, and taught collaboratively with me to create interesting opportunities for students. I am eternally grateful to all the educators who are so willing to pass on ideas to make a difference beyond their own classrooms, schools and libraries.

Lu Dayment, Greenwood Middle School, created the Author Visit Co-Op. She knew the value of working together to reduce expenses when bringing an author to town, and even when I lacked the confidence to pull off an author visit successfully, she never gave up on me. Her ability to negotiate with authors who are also engaging speakers and whose appearance fees are within our limited budget is a talent from which my students and staff reap the rewards every year.

Alison Dillman, Perry Meridian Middle School, was devastated by the sudden loss of an inspiring staff member and wanted to do something to honor her memory. Our first annual Used Book Drive was due to the inspired imaginings of Alison and her coordinated efforts with the school's Student Council.

Cheryl DiPietro, Center Grove Middle School North, mentioned in passing a project she was doing with an evening bingo night where her group gave away books. I thought it was an exciting project but knew a better fit for my school would be to try such a project during school hours. So I gratefully took her idea and transformed it into a completely different event, but with the core concept of bingo and getting books into homes.

Christy Gliva, Perry Meridian 6th Grade Academy, developed the Book Fair. When we worked together, she came to me with this inspiring idea and was ahead of the game in knowing how to reach and meet the needs of this generation. Christy is such an amazing and inspiring educator, she helped me become a better educator just by working with her, and I miss having the opportunity to work with her every day.

Judy Karty, Perry Meridian Middle School, was one of the first classroom teachers to allow me to show myself as a teacher and coteach in her classroom. The first project we did together was one I'd originally developed in college about writing and illustrating the picture book. Over the years, we revised and updated it until the Picture Book Project as it appears today was collaboratively developed and taught.

Nina Phagan, Perry Meridian Middle School, returned from a workshop one day inspired by something she learned about anticipation statements, which were explained as preparatory and post unit sets of statements. Always creative and able to see a vision beyond the obvious, Nina immediately saw how these anticipation statements could enhance our schoolwide reading projects with the adaptation of the concept into Anticipation Bookmarks.

Robyn Young, Avon High School, is one of those friends I'm grateful to have because she makes me a better school librarian simply by being around her. Whenever we get together, our conversations alone inspire thoughts and ideas to take back and make ourselves and our schools better. She was the first to share with me the idea of a school-versus-school annual Read-Off and converting digital picture frames into Booktalk Digital Picture Frames.

My humblest of apologies to anyone I have overlooked. There are so many leaders in education, within my school, state, and nationally whom I have been blessed to meet, learn from, and be inspired by. I am grateful for all the influences that motivate me to do things for the better of my school, staff, students, their families, and our community.

Introduction

Student and School

Student-centered projects are the focus of this resource. Included are ideas for encouraging, promoting, and celebrating readers, readership, and young people. Projects focus on meeting the specific needs of our youth through entertainment, active participation, control, choice, technology, and auditory means. The school building is a continually developing community. Persistently working toward creating a culture and climate of reading help students in the community develop an intrinsic desires to read. This intrinsic desire creates lifelong readers. A lifelong reader is not the only objective. We also need to create readers who share the pleasure of reading with others intuitively and without inhibition.

Students' traits can be used to our advantage. Base your projects on what is known about our learners' habits, interests, and the traits of an effective reader. Students thrive on entertainment, participation in learning, feelings of control, having choices, auditory skills, and appropriate rewards and incentives (Payne 2003/Gardiner 2005). Play to their strengths and interests to keep existing readers and gain new ones.

To develop lifelong readers, continually adapt, change, or continue successful tactics to illicit the slumbering, emerging, or successfully involved reader. This includes events, games, homemade bookmarks, clubs, sharing, interactive technology (commonly called social networking and web 2.0); other great ideas include book report alternatives, involving students in real-world applications, and designing student-centered, teacher-directed incentive and reward programs.

Entertainment: Today's youth need and demand to be entertained. As one fifth-grade intermediate school educator said to me, "they want a roller-coaster in the classroom every day." Therefore, seek ways to use the library media center as a venue to create a "reading roller-coaster" for young people.

Participation: Allow students to share book and reading experiences with peers, family, educators, and professionals. This is achieved through live, virtual, written, and interactive events, projects, communications, and displays.

Control and Choice: Feeling control over their lives means that students need freedom of choice with what they read. Young people need ways to share reading experiences without being told *exactly* what to read. Instead, youth need options, sometimes even complete freedom of choice, to be most successful. Re-create traditional ideas to fit the need to choose reading selections for oneself.

Auditory Skills: Because most students have greater listening than reading comprehension, they have excellent auditory skills (Przeclawski and Woods 2007). An added bonus for the reading promoter is that the young generation loves to listen and talk, whether it be a real conversation or a virtual chat. Incorporating social interaction adds spice to many projects and supports students' ability to comprehend and participate through listening and engaging in live, virtual, and electronic conversation.

Within the following pages, take advantage of students' interests to engage them in youth-centered projects that are tailored to their likes, habits, talents, and traits. Use the projects as they are laid out within these pages, or let them be an inspiration and modify them in ways that will be most successful for your school and community.

Promoting Reading

- ☑ Be Enthusiastic
- ☑ Set the Mood
- ☑ Be Cheesy
- ☑ Use Props
- ☑ Make Personal Connections
- ☑ Connect to Current Events
- ☑ Relate to Shared Experiences

Be creative when promoting reading, and think of simple ways to engage the intended audience.

Reading Influence: Building a Climate of Reading

Have you ever wished for ways to make a difference and build a reading influence with students, faculty, and staff? Use this resource to learn, or be reminded, about some simple ways to communicate, promote, and build a climate and culture of reading in your facility. Find out how to make reading a discovered treasure in your building. Not everything needs to be heavy and serious in school, because being a school function already has built-in weight to it. Therefore, suggestions include ideas light on "seriousness" because it is about the act of reading, sharing literacy experiences, learning to love reading for the sake of reading. Discover reading promotion methods, similar to a marketing campaign, for encouraging recreational reading to the masses. Browse to find at least one idea you can implement immediately.

The organization of this book is slightly subjective. Please do not allow the layout or location of ideas to limit your creativity and imagination for using or adapting to your needs. This is not intended to be a comprehensive list of ideas for socializing reading or building a reading community, but instead a place to start. Enjoy using the projects as they are written, or adapt them to your situation. This is a place to germinate ideas. Use the project ideas shared in this book as a springboard for your own creations.

The first time you try a project is always the most challenging, and it takes the longest to prepare. Keep that in mind when evaluating your investment in time and materials for any project. Remember to do as much as possible electronically, using word processing and desktop publishing programs so they may be saved and revised. Layout each design in a way that makes updating and reusing it simple—sometimes as easy as simply changing a date. By keeping projects organized electronically and saving electronic files, it will be easier to revise and re-create a project for future uses. Save electronic copies of signs, posters, bookmarks, registration forms, newsletter articles, advertisements, exit slips, surveys, admission slips, press releases, and anything else created electronically for future reference. Remember to archive and back up your files regularly. Creating electronic copies and backup archives anticipate potential trouble and make any project easier in the future.

All projects have certain things in common, such as cost, planning time, people (staff and volunteers needed to help accomplish the project), supplies, promotion, rewards, incentives, and evaluation. Instead of repeating these issues for each project, I review them here. Keep these factors in mind whenever planning and preparing a project.

Cost

Cost varies from project to project. Some projects cost nothing but time, using materials commonly found in schools and libraries. Others, such as an author visit, may require forethought and advance planning because of inherent expenses. Cost suggestions are just estimates, and all projects should be researched at the local level to confirm expenses before initiating a project. Creativity and substitutions with local resources often reduce, minimize, or even eliminate expenses. Expenses may vary, depending on the activity planner's desire to reduce or expand the project or gather donations. Budgets are also affected by varying regional costs and the effects of the current economy. Keep in mind that startup costs the first year are often, but not always, greater than the expense of maintaining a preexisting project. To simplify cost descriptions, use the following key:

$ = $0–$20: Free or very low cost

The financial investment for this project is minimal. Often it can be done with materials commonly found in schools and libraries.

$$ = $25–$100: Inexpensive

These projects can be done with a little bit of preparation and preplanning with an existing supply budget. Sometimes the expense can be easily reduced by contacting local merchants for donations and using materials already found on-site.

$$$ = $100–$500: Moderate

Costs for these projects may expand beyond a preexisting budget. Expenses can often be managed by requesting special funds from administration, parent teacher organizations (PTA/PTO), small grants, or local philanthropic community organizations.

$$$$ = $500–1,000: Moderately Expensive

Greater project expenses require creative funding, outside support, and advance planning. Consult administration for support and suggestions for ways to enhance the budget. Hosting a used book sale, in-house book-fair fundraiser or local bookstore fundraiser are examples of ways to augment the budget to support a variety projects.

$$$$$ = over $1,000: Expensive

Advance planning is definitely required to support these projects financially. Seek grant funding to get the project a kick-start. If successful and ongoing, consistent, annual funding will need to be sought to create an annual tradition of these projects. Once an expensive project is initiated successfully, it is often easier to get administration or PTA/PTO to commit to partial or complete annual financial support.

Planning Time

To do anything well requires forethought and advance planning. The first time something is implemented, it will take more time to plan and create. Keeping good notes and electronic files of materials created for the project will make doing it again easier and less time-consuming, allowing you to revise what you have on hand instead of creating all-new original creations. Suggested planning time is subjective because local issues need to be considered. The building policies and procedures may require certain paperwork, timelines, and protocol. The culture and climate for how things work best are unique to every school's community, students, and staff. Some people have a gift for technology or creativity and can create first-time materials with little time investment; other people need more time to create and design. Suggested planning time begins the day a decision is made to do something through to the day of cleanup and postevaluation. This does not mean that every moment of every day is spent on this project. Instead, the timeline is a part of your long-range planning and to-do list built into your work schedule. Consider basic planning questions to ask yourself:

- Within the suggested time frame, when can certain requirements fit into the work day?

- When should administrative permissions be sought?

- Where does the project fit in my calendar and the school's calendar?

- When do I ask for committee volunteers, if needed?

- When and where do we begin advertising?

- Do attendees need to register in advance so a guesstimate of attendees is known for project materials and supplies? When should preregistration begin? When does preregistration end, or can potential participants sign up to participate up to the last minute?

- If needed, when should supplies be budgeted, ordered, or purchased?

- If the work culminates in a specific event, how much set-up time is required prior to the start of the event? How much time should be scheduled for cleanup?

- When and how will the postevaluation occur? What notes or immediate changes need to be made on the basis of the postevaluations so that the next time will be even more successful?

People—Planning Involvement

People equal success. Getting other people involved is integral to developing a schoolwide culture and climate of reading. Other people committed to the project create a built-in network of promoters and advertisers. The number of people needed depends on what is being planned. Every project requires at least one person: an activity planner. Also, advance permission may be required from administration or families. Staff may need to be involved to gain buy-in. Staff members, parents, students, and administrators may need to volunteer to help plan, implement, and promote the project. A committee of staff members helps encourage participation, provides important perspectives and sharing of ideas, and reduces the amount of work for any one individual. Each concept included in this book offers an idea of how many people may be needed to plan, prepare, create, and implement a project. The number suggested is subjective and should be adjusted to fit the size of your school. Keeping the specific project in mind, also consider the project's possible global needs:

Activity Planner: To achieve success requires leadership. Depending on the school's staff, this can be the school librarian, reading specialist, administrator, or other committed staff member.

Building Administrators: Depending on the situation, the building administrator may need to approve student participation in the experience or preapprove the concept because of finances, logistics, instructional time, after-hours facility use, or the building's policies and procedures. If a contract to an outside participant is required, as would be needed for an author visit, administration will need to review and sign the contract. It may also be the administrator's responsibility to work with the activity planner to coordinate the day's schedule, especially if programming includes a convocation, large group planning, or other need to pull students from their regular schedule.

Classroom Teachers: Support from classroom teachers is often necessary for a winning program. Teachers help promote and engender schoolwide interest among staff and students. The classroom teacher may be needed as a volunteer for participation on a committee to plan, prepare and implement components of the project. Some projects may ask teachers to incorporate supporting activities into classroom instruction for building-wide events, such as "One Book, One School, One Author."

Students: It is often not necessary for students to be involved in the planning process, but including them on committees or organizing a student subcommittee for larger programs certainly increases their interest. Every student involved in planning and decision making can be counted on to share enthusiasm about what's happening and help spread the word to others.

Parents: Depending on the school policy, parent permission forms may be required for student participation as a volunteer or participant. The PTA/PTO may also be an excellent source of startup or annual costs for certain projects. Parents may volunteer to be trained to run certain projects or components of projects. For large events, parent volunteers may be solicited to help with setup, decorating, hosting, and cleanup. Involving parents also helps spread the word and increase attendance, as well as promote the school and the school library media center's special projects to other families and the community.

Supplies

Special projects require supplies. Some projects require unique supplies, but some supplies are common to many, if not all, projects. Supplies common to most projects are listed here rather than repeating them throughout the book. Whenever considering a project, consider the common supplies needed for most, if not every, project:

Computer: A computer is important for creating and archiving materials. Homemade advertising bookmarks, e-mails, signs, posters, bulletin boards, Web posts, newsletter announcements, and press releases created with a computer's word processing or desktop publishing program add a personal yet polished touch to projects.

Copier: Once documents are finalized on the computer, mass production is made simple with the addition of a printer or copier. Make inexpensive copies of bookmarks, exit slips, registration forms, and other items using regular paper, color paper, or card stock.

Digital Camera: Include a digital camera at any event. It is important to take pictures, which can be used to promote the event in library displays, newsletters, Web sites, press releases, and much more.

Exit Slips: Attendee should complete exit slips or evaluation surveys to evaluate what was successful and what requires revisions before the next time the project is attempted. Read further details in the "Evaluation" section of this Introduction.

Scissors: Scissors and/or a straight edge cutter may be helpful when trimming copy sheets into individual pieces, such as bookmarks, exit slips, and so on.

Writing Utensils: Have pencils, pens, markers, or crayons on hand for participants to complete registration, door prize slips, project activities, exit slips, and more.

Many projects can be enhanced with certain supplies, but they are not necessary for the program to function. Optional project materials are great to have if they can be found for little or no money. They set the tone and liven up the project, but the event can be sustained without them. The following are optional supplies for many projects:

- *Door Prizes and Door Prize Slips:* Everyone loves to win something. Use the registration or admission pass or have participants fill out a door prize slip. Throw them into a container, then draw winners throughout the event. Door prizes should relate to reading and school in some way. Have a variety of books, pencils, bookstore gift cards, notebooks, and other school-related supplies on hand for door prize selections.

- *Snacks and Drinks:* If an event is conducive to a party-type atmosphere, offer snacks and drinks. Even if participants just had lunch or dinner, an inexpensive gallon of punch or other beverage goes a long way toward attendees' warm memories of an event. Snacks do not need to be expensive. Packages of snack cakes, microwave popcorn, or homemade brownies may be all that's needed. Or try shopping immediately after events such as Valentine's Day, Halloween, or Christmas to buy packages of candy and snacks discounted for a quick sale after the holiday. Snacks are also helpful to have on hand for volunteers during planning meetings and work sessions.

- *Decorations:* Decorations are not necessary, but some projects that culminate in an event, such as book exchange parties, book club events, reader's café, and others are enhanced with decorations. Making the event more of a celebration for attendees with decorations, transforms an ordinary place like the library media center into a new environment. It resets the mood and tone, making the event out of the ordinary and unique. Decorating the space also makes the attendees feel special for being there, like they're part of something different from the everyday. Look for bargains and buy inexpensive, reusable table covers in the library or school's colors. Find generic party decorations that can be used for any event, maybe even invoking the theme of your school's mascot. Or, if you've found special funding or set aside supply money for it, buy themed party decorations for a particular event. For example, if hosting a genre event for science fiction and fantasy, choose an alien theme.

Promotion

Successful projects integrate advertising and promotion. Place notices or advertisements in advance in the school's family newsletter, student newspaper, Web site, and other venues available to the school library media center. Distribute pre- and post-event press releases to local news agencies.

PMMS

Instructional Media Center

Upcoming Library Events

These events have been made possible through Book Fair Fundraisers and grants from PMMS PTA and PTEF:

- **August 26** - Poetry Lovers Lunch in the Library
- **September 2** - Drama & Issues Genre Lunch in the Library (Genre Lunches are the first Wednesday of every month—the genre will change each month)
- **September 9 -** New Books Club Lunch in the Library (meets the second Wednesday of every month)
- **September 16** - Game Club Lunch in the Library (meets the third Wednesday of every month)
- **September 23** - YHBA Lunch in the Library (meets the fourth Wednesday of every month)
- **September 30** - Indianapolis-Marion County Public Library Booktalks Lunch in the Library
- **October 12-19** - Bookfair Fundraiser
- **November 17** - One Book, One School, One Author Visit with Shelley Pearsall
- **November 17, 6pm** - Family Read-In: *All Shook Up* by Shelley Pearsall (pre-register by October 8)

Please contact the Library Media Specialists at lpreddy@msdpt.k12.in.us or for more information or to sign up for any of the listed events.

Once a month or grading quarter, send home a cutout calendar of upcoming library media center events in the student newsletter.

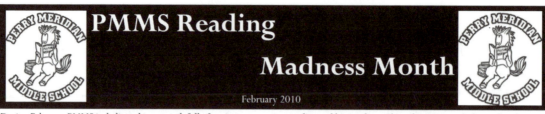

PMMS Reading
Madness Month

February 2010

During February PMMS is dedicated to a month full of projects promoting reading and having fun with reading. Research shows that the more a student reads, the better he does in school and beyond, so we want to motivate all PMMS to be lifelong readers. Throughout the month, activities will include a Read-A-Thon, Bingo for Books, Book Trivia Wednesdays, Caught Reading, READ posters, Guess Who Loves Reading, Used Book Drive, Blues for Books, and a book fair fundraiser. Participating earns students chances to win free books!

It's boys versus girls. Who can read the most minutes? Students read, fill out the home reading log, get parent initials for minutes read, then turn in the log slip for a chance to win free books and to help their team win. If the girls win, our principal will learn the true meaning of *How to Eat Fried Worms*. If the boys win, assistant principal will get the true meaning of *101 Ways to Bug Your Teacher*.

Read-Off Home Reading Log

(Remember - only count minutes spent reading outside of the school day)

Name: _____ Advisory Teacher: _____ Grade: ___ Lunch: ___
(please print first and last name)

Date	Title of Book	Pages Read	Minutes spent Reading (circle one)	Guardian Initials
Example:	*The Lightning Thief*	*Pgs 22-35*	10 20 30 40 50 60 80 90 100 110 120	*JCB*
2-1-10 Monday			10 20 30 40 50 60 80 90 100 110 120	
2-2-10 Tuesday			10 20 30 40 50 60 80 90 100 110 120	
2-3-10 Wednesday			10 20 30 40 50 60 80 90 100 110 120	
		Total Minutes Read		

- - - - - *Cut along dotted line & turn the reading log in to your SSR Advisory teacher.* - - - - -

(Remember - only count minutes spent reading outside of the school day)

Name: _____ Advisory Teacher: _____ Grade: ___ Lunch: ___
(please print first and last name)

Date	Title of Book	Pages Read	Minutes spent Reading (circle one)	Guardian Initials
Example:	*Harry Potter and the Half-Blood Prince*	*Pgs 22-35*	10 20 30 40 50 60 80 90 100 110 120	*JCB*
2-4-10 Thursday			10 20 30 40 50 60 80 90 100 110 120	
2-5-10 Friday			10 20 30 40 50 60 80 90 100 110 120	
2-6-10 Saturday			10 20 30 40 50 60 80 90 100 110 120	
2-7-10 Sunday			10 20 30 40 50 60 80 90 100 110 120	
2-8-10 Monday			10 20 30 40 50 60 80 90 100 110 120	
		Total Minutes Read		

- - - - - *Cut along dotted line & turn the reading log in to your SSR Advisory teacher.* - - - - -

Inform families and promote library-sponsored activities through the student newsletter.

Create commercials or announcements for the daily announcement program, whether televised or through the public address system. E-mail staff and advertise at staff meetings what is coming up so other staff members can help promote the event to students with whom they have personal relationships. Place homemade posters and signs in the library media center and other high-traffic locations throughout the building. Areas to consider are the main entrance, bus entrance, sports lobby, cafeteria, and library media center. If the library media center usually sets out bookmarks for students to take, create and share home-made bookmarks with student artwork or designed on the computer to help promote, remind, and advertise for the event.

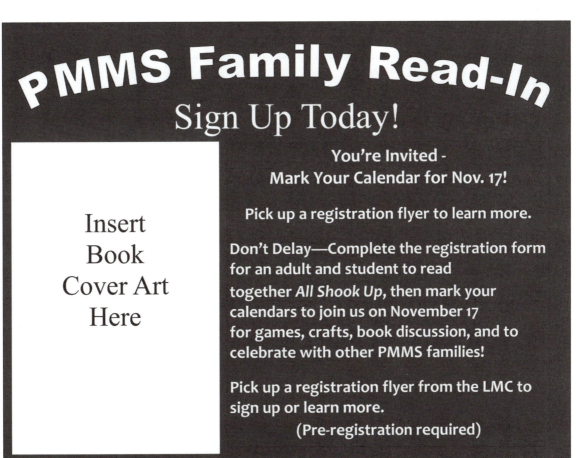

Custom posters and signs displayed throughout the school advertise upcoming reading events.

Left bookmark (front)

Next Meeting:
February 10

FUN–FICTION–FRIENDSHIP

Y.H.B.A. CLUB

February Book Club Discussion Title:
Listen! by Stephanie Tolan

Be sure to have your book read *before* the event!

READ

PMMS

Instructional Media Center
pmms.msdpt.k12.in.us/imc/index.htm

Right bookmark (back)

Young Hoosier Book Award
NOMINEES

All of the Above	by Shelley Pearsall
Bella at Midnight	by Diane Stanley
Confessions From the Principal's Chair	by Anna Myers
The Cryptid Hunters	by Roland Smith
Dark Water Rising	by Marion Hale
Double Identity	by Margaret Peterson Haddix
Firegirl	by Tony Abbott
Giving Up the Ghost	by Sheri Sinykin
Home of the Brave	by Katherine Applegate
Hurt Go Happy	by Ginny Rorby
If a Tree Falls at Lunch Period	by Jennifer Choldenko
Lawn Boy	by Gary Paulsen
Listen!	by Stephanie Tolan
The Mailbox	by Audrey Shafer
Middle School is Worse Than Meatloaf	by Jennifer L. Holm
Night of the Howling Dog	by Graham Salisbury
One-Handed Catch	by Mary Jane Auch
This is Just to Say: Poems of Apology and Forgiveness	by Joyce Sidman
Throwing Stones	by Kristi Collier
The Ultimate Weapon	by Edward T. Sullivan

Read 5 or More
Books to Vote

VOTING DAY:
April 22

Take-aways such as bookmarks help students remember and promote an event.
At left is an example of the front of a promotional bookmark. At right is an
informative back to the bookmark advertisement.

From *Social Readers: Promoting Reading in the 21st Century* by Leslie B. Preddy.
Santa Barbara, CA: Libraries Unlimited. Copyright © 2010.

If the school is connected to a social networking site, such as a moodle or blog, or announcements are televised or posted on the Web, create and post some quick commercials to advertise the upcoming program.

Reader's Rewards (aka Incentives)

Reward students—but reward appropriately. Some might argue that students shouldn't be rewarded for reading, because that is what they are supposed to do anyway. Some may argue that the real world doesn't work that way and people are not rewarded for what they are already expected to do. I argue that incentives are appropriate. The real world does offer rewards. The incentive could be a smile, praise, or objects. It could be receiving accolades from peers or administrators. It could be a thank you note or gift card. It could be a special treat for a job well done. For example, our teachers who participated in the "Share a Book You Love" event were all given a gift bag that included a free book and some snack-size treats. Reward our young people for meeting a reading or literacy goal or for participating in a reading event, but ensure that the incentive equals the task. To appropriately reward a student reader, the reward should be related to what the student needs to value (Payne 2003). If we want students to value reading, then the reward should relate to reading. Incentives could be a pass to the library, extra reading time, a free book to add to a student's home bookshelf, a gift certificate for a local bookstore, a field trip to a local bookstore, bookmarks, paperback book covers, and any other reward promoting reading or education. The internal motivation derived from the external source, if the reward is appropriate, is the encouragement this generation needs.

Evaluation

Conclude any project with formal or informal surveys or exit slips for participants to complete. Participants may include volunteers, committee members or planners, administrators, parents, and students. This will be of great help when considering how to repeat the activity in the future and what to change to improve the experience for participants. Formal surveys may be done with paper and pencil or electronically using Web-based surveys, such as surveymonkey.com. Informal surveys may be done through conversations with individuals or a group at the conclusion of the project by casually interviewing participants, volunteers, and committee members.

Name: _____ Grade:___ Lunch:___

Booktalk
Lunch in the Library
Exit Slip

A book I never heard about before today was _____
_____.

I would do this again: ___Yes   ___No

A book talked about that I now want to read is _____
_____
_____.

We should invite our guest speaker back again: ___Yes   ___No

I think we should do a *Booktalk Lunch in the Library* with this guest
speaker, book or author _____
_____.

READ
P M M S
Instructional Media Center

Name: _____ Grade:___ Lunch:___

Genre
Lunch in the Library
Exit Slip

The book I talked about today was _____.

One book somebody else talked about that I now want to read is
_____.

I would do this again: ___Yes   ___No

I had the most fun when we _____.

I think it would be fun if next time we _____
_____.

I think we should do a *Genre Lunch in the Library* with _____
_____ genre.

READ
P M M S
Instructional Media Center

**A participation evaluation may be as simple as filling out an exit slip on
a small piece of paper at the conclusion of a project.**

From *Social Readers: Promoting Reading in the 21st Century* by Leslie B. Preddy.
Santa Barbara, CA: Libraries Unlimited. Copyright © 2010.

Chapter 1
Entertainment

Entertainment is the name of the game! To keep a young person's attention or interest, find ways to make what we want them to value entertaining. Entertainment projects include events and games. Each project suggested within this chapter is independent and can be produced yearly or reproduced repeatedly within the same school year. Entertainment meets the social reading criteria because the activities help to build community.

Events

Events are productions worthy of promotion and schoolwide publicity. An event is something that takes a community to prepare for successfully, engage in, and promote. It requires forethought and preplanning to fit it into the library media center's schedule and the school calendar. Larger events deserve the school's complete focus, which requires ensuring that no other schoolwide events conflict with the event. Events invite all students to get involved or sign up to participate. The event is most successful when fellow faculty and staff members encourage and promote student involvement. Event planning culminates in a party, celebration, program, project, or convocation.

Many events are enriched by crafting simple, hands-on, themed connections. There are a lot of simple and fun craft ideas in books on the library shelves. If you can't find what you need, try browsing the following Web sites. Some sites also offer subscriptions to e-mail newsletters.

- About.com: Family Crafts—Crafts by Age: http://familycrafts.about.com/od/craftprojectsbyage/Crafts_by_Age.htm

- All Free Crafts: http://www.allfreecrafts.com/kids/index.shtml

- Craft Elf: http://www.craftelf.com

- Craftbits: http://www.craftbits.com/craft-project-categories

- Family Fun—Crafts: http://familyfun.go.com/crafts

- Free Kids Crafts: http://www.freekidcrafts.com/free_kid_craft_ideas.html

- Handcrafter's Village: http://www.handcraftersvillage.com

- The Idea Box: http://www.theideabox.com

- Kaboose—Crafts: http://crafts.kaboose.com

- Kids Craft Weekly: http://kidscraftweekly.com/printables.html

- Making Friends: http://www.makingfriends.com

- My Craftbook: http://www.mycraftbook.com

- The Toymaker: http://thetoymaker.com

Book Exchange Party

Something old can be new again with a simple change of hands. Take advantage of students' social nature and their desire to share and advise others by hosting a book exchange party. A book exchange party combines the fun of a get-together with the chance to pass on a reading experience to another person, plus the opportunity to get a book that's "new-to-you" in the bargain. This is an event that is very flexible according to the community's needs and can be sponsored during lunch, before school, after school, or in the evening as a family event.

Cost: $

This event costs nothing unless the host would like to create bookmarks, signs, or posters to promote the event; decorate; or provide drinks, snacks, or door prizes for the attendees.

Planning Time: Three Weeks

This event is simple and requires approximately three weeks to put on the calendar, promote, and host.

Planning Involvement: One to Three People

Because of the simplicity of this program, an in-school event requires only one person to plan, prepare, and host. Estimate one volunteer, staff or parent to help set up, host, and clean afterward for every ten families preregistered if planning this as an evening family event.

Suggested Supplies

- Create: admission passes, exit slips, publicity and promotional materials, sign-up forms

- Optional: decorations, reader's reward door prize, snack or dessert

- Student contribution: gently used book

- Miscellaneous: timer or stopwatch

Instructions

This event can be done any time that best fits the school calendar. It is ideal immediately before a school break when kids may soon have travel or down time reading opportunities. During initial planning, consider the time of day that best suits the patrons: before school, lunch, immediately after school, or family evening. If making this a family event, consider including exchange opportunities for younger siblings, older siblings, and parents. Decide on the maximum number of attendees.

The book exchange can be a party without limits, or it can be focused on a particular theme or genre. There are pros and cons to both. Without limits allows everyone, no matter the reading interest, to participate, but might mean somebody cannot find a matching interest to trade. A theme- or genre-related event would ensure that everyone attending shares the same interest but might exclude those not interested in that genre.

When creating materials, consider including a registration or sign-up form, admission pass, exit slip, door prize drawing ticket, and promotional materials such as bookmarks, signs, posters, or banners. Distribute the admission pass to registered students the day before or morning of the event. If it is a lunch event, this will work as a pass to get into the lunch line early and bring their lunch to the library. Passing passes out the day before helps students remember to bring the book they plan to trade to school the next day. A separate door-prize slip is not necessary if the admission pass serves a dual purpose for the door-prize drawing as well. An exit slip will help the program coordinator plan more successfully in the future. Homemade bookmarks, signs, or posters placed in strategic locations throughout the building will help to promote the upcoming event. In the promotions, be sure to emphasize that students bring a book they enjoyed but are willing to trade.

An alternative to this project is to host a book exchange event in the summer or during other long school breaks.

Three Months Before

- Select a date and time for the event.

- Design a registration or sign-up form, admission form, door prize slip, exit slip, and promotional materials.

Two Weeks Before

- Advertise registration on school announcements, the student newsletter, and to staff via e-mail.

- Begin accepting preregistrations.

- Purchase snacks, drinks, and decorations, if desired.

- Prepare an agenda. Following is an example for a thirty-minute lunchtime event:

  - 0–10 minutes: Students enter the library media center with lunch and eat.

  - 10–13 minutes: Pass out dessert or snacks and have students turn in their admission pass for door prize drawing while finishing lunch.

  - 13–25 minutes: Divide students into groups of eight to ten. Review with students the rules for giving a quick booktalk intended to get others to want to read the book. A quick booktalk includes the title, author, genre, what in the story grabbed the reader's attention, and so forth without giving away any surprises or the ending. Use the stopwatch, and give each student 45 seconds to tell why the others should want to read this book. Once everyone has had a chance to talk, make a game of trading the books. For example, the first person in each group trades his or her book with any other person in the group. This continues until everyone has had a chance to trade books with someone else in the group. No book is ever safe, and even if a book has been traded once before, the next student can still trade for it. Another example would be to use dice. Group students by genre or broad theme in groups of six (or more if the library media center has a die with more than six sides; these can be purchased online or at any local gaming store), allow all the students time to talk about their books, place the books toward the center with a number on each one, then have a student roll the dice to see which book she or he wins. Continue until all the books are won. If time permits, allow students to continue exchanging or trading privately.

- 25–30 minutes: draw for door prizes and complete exit slip evaluations.

Day before the Event

- Distribute admission passes to registered students.
- Buy or collect donated door prizes, if desired.

Day of the Event

- Have a reminder read during student announcements, if announcements occur before the event.
- Decorate and host the event.

After the Event

- Clean up area. Store extra supplies for future use.
- Review exit slips and make improvements and changes immediately in anticipation of repeating the event in the future.

Book Exchange Party

BOGO
Bring One paperback, Get One paperback
Lunch in the Library

Bring a gently used paperback to the party, then trade yours with one brought by another student to the exchange party.

Event Date: _____

	Name	Grade	Lunch Period	Team	1st Period Teacher
1					
2					
3					
4					
5					
6					
7					
8					
9					
10					
11					
12					
13					
14					
15					

While promoting the event, place a simple sign-up sheet in a public location for students to register.

Genre Brown-Bag Book Club

An alternative to the traditional book club, in which attendees all read and discuss the same books, is a themed book club event. Using a particular genre, such as mystery and detective fiction, allows students the freedom to read a book of their choosing and then share what they've read with others also interested in books from that particular genre. The double positive to this event is that students choose what they want to read and share, then they hear about other books that they may want to read based on another young person's recommendation.

Cost: $–$$

Plan a simple warm-up activity and craft for each event. The craft supplies may be items the school or library already has, such as markers and card stock to make bookmarks, or they can be donated by families or local stores. If unable to get donations or locate materials in-house, purchasing necessary supplies will be required. The activity planner may also want to purchase materials to create invitation bookmarks, signs, or posters to promote the event, decorate, or provide drinks, snacks, or door prizes for the attendees.

Planning Time: Four Weeks to One Year

One event only takes four to six weeks to prepare and host. If the host plans to sponsor more than one genre lunch throughout the school year, it is advisable to map out the year in advance, selecting dates, genres, and activities for each event so that there is no duplication and the events get on the school calendar early.

Planning Involvement: Two or Three People

The number of people necessary will depend on the number of students permitted to register for each event. The activity planner may be able to manage an event of six to eight students on his or her own but will need help with more participants. Consider one parent or teacher volunteer for every six to eight more students.

Suggested Supplies

- Craft supplies: materials needed for each individual event's craft

- Create: admission pass, agenda, craft instruction and completed samples, exit slip, publicity and promotional materials, sign-up form, warm-up activity

- Optional: decorations, dessert, reader's reward door prizes

- Student contribution: library or personal copy of book

Instructions

Although the figures included assume an event hosted during lunch, it can occur any time before, during, or after school. The example schedule offered is for a thirty-minute lunch, but this is also flexible and can be stretched to forty-five minutes or one hour, depending what fits the host's schedule. If hosting the event during lunch, it is important to remember that the event will be repeated for each individual lunch period. Create materials and collect enough supplies to cover all potential participants during every lunch period.

When planning and promoting remember students can read any book they choose within the designated genre, but it should be read before the event, and students should be encouraged to bring a copy of it to the event to show others during the discussion.

Add ambiance to the experience with themed party decorations related to the event's genre. For example:

- Action, Adventure, and Survival—Jungle

- Drama and Issues—Hollywood or the Theatre

- Friendship and Realistic Fiction—Happy Smiley Faces

- Historical Fiction, Nonfiction, Biography—Patriotic

- Horror and Suspense—Halloween Haunted

- Mystery and Detective—Police Crime Scene

- Poetry—Emoticons

- Science Fiction and Fantasy—UFOs and Aliens

- Sports Fiction, Nonfiction, Biography—Sports

Students will spend event time eating (if a lunch event), completing a warm-up activity, discussing and sharing their books, and concluding with an activity or make-it/take-it craft. Simple theme-related crafts or activities can be dreamed up by the school community, found in books, or located on free craft Web sites (see the list of these at the beginning of the chapter). Keep crafts and activities simple, with take-home instructions in case time runs out. Examples of simple craft solutions are the following:

- Adventure and Survival—animal mask bookmark

- Drama and Issues—decorate face or mardi gras mask

- Friendship and Realistic Fiction—friendship bracelet

- Historical Fiction, Nonfiction, Biography—locker picture frame

- Horror and Suspense—spider sucker

- Mystery and Detective—graffiti wall

- Poetry—locker magnets word poetry

- Science Fiction and Fantasy—paper airplane spacecraft bookmark

- Sports Fiction, Nonfiction, Biography—foam sports bookmark

While students are eating, have them complete a warm-up activity related to the genre, such as a survey, Mad Libs, or other fun mental puzzle or worksheet. When creating something yourself, make questions as gender-neutral as possible. If you're unsure how to get started and need ideas to spark the imagination, try looking at these or similar books:

Bugbird, T. *Me Myself & I.* Hertfordshire, UK: Make Believe Ideas, 2008.

Bull, Jane. *The Party Book.* New York: DK Publishing, 2005–2007.

Hainer, Michelle. *DK Girl World: Quiz Zone.* New York: DK Publishing, 2006.

—. *DK Girl World: Quiz Zone 2.* New York: DK Publishing, 2007.

Hurley, Jo. *Friends 4 Ever: Friendship 101 Quizzes and Questions.* New York: Scholastic, 2006.

Phillips, Karen. *It's All about Me!* Palo Alto, CA: Klutz, 2006.

Regan, Lisa. *What R U Like?* New York: Backpack Books, 2005.

Price, Roger, and Leonard Stern. Mad Libs series. New York: Scholastic and Price Stern Sloan, varies.

If something worth adapting to be more gender-neutral is found in a book, be sure to ask permission to adapt it and reproduce it for the purpose of the book club, which often can be done through e-mail.

When planning, calculate how many students may register for each lunch; consider six to eight students for every adult helping, including the activity planner. Include on the registration a place for each student to write the name of the book within that genre that she plans to have read prior to the event. When creating the admission slip, think about consolidating efforts. It may also be used for the door prize drawing to save paper and time. The admission slip should also give students permission to get their lunch quickly and bring food into the library media center. A bookmark can be a simple way to promote the event and the fact that students must choose a book within that genre and have read it in advance.

Preplanning

- Select a date (or dates, if doing more than one throughout the year) for the event and contact staff members, parents, or both to volunteer to help with the event.

- Design a registration or sign-up form for participants to preregister themselves and the book they will be reading.

- Create an admission pass to distribute to registered students the morning of the event, as well as a door prize slip and exit slip.

- Create handmade bookmarks, signs, or posters to promote the event.

Four to Six Weeks Before

- Advertise registration on school announcements and to staff via e-mail, and begin accepting preregistrations.

- Select a warm-up activity. Revise, print, and laminate enough copies for maximum attendance, plus a few extra.

One to Three Weeks Before

- Purchase snacks, drinks, and decorations, if needed and when convenient.

- If planning another genre lunch soon, create the preregistration form now so students may sign up during this event.

- Prepare a tentative activity timeline for guidance. An example for a thirty-minute lunchtime event follows.

  - Horror and Suspense Genre Lunch in the Library

  - Equipment and supplies: Craft paper to cover one library table, markers and crayons, laminated "Embarrassed to Death" survey and dry-erase markers, backdrop for "horrifying" photos, a digital camera, a color printer, Halloween hats and clip-on ties, homemade bookplates.

  - 0–5 minutes: Students get lunch and bring it to the library. Students turn in admission passes for the door prize drawing. Draw for door prize.

  - 5–13 minutes: Students eat, talk, and do genre-themed warm-up activity: "Embarrassed to Death" survey. Pass out candy or a snack for dessert.

  - 10–15 minutes: Begin the sharing process, and as students get finished eating, ask for volunteers to talk to the group about their book.

- 13–25 minutes: Activity—graffiti wall and make-it/take-it. Pose for a horrifying digital picture. While students continue taking turns booktalking, they decorate a portion of the craft paper with a promotion for their book, including the title and art or writing that best describes why a person should read it. One at a time, or in groups if they want to be with a buddy, pull students aside to be photographed dressed up and posing with their book. Alternate activity: have students decorate a picture frame to promote their book.

- 25–30 minutes: Students complete exit slip evaluations. An optional activity for students: sign a bookplate if they really liked their book and want to recommend it to other students. Allow students to sign up and check out books for the next genre lunch.

- After: Place signed bookplates in appropriate library books, put the "graffiti" on display in the library and print two copies of each digital photo. Deliver one copy of the photo for the student to keep and add one to the graffiti display. If using the alternate plan, put students' pictures in their frames, then deliver them to the students.

Day of the Event

- The morning of the event, distribute admission passes to registered students. The pass should work as a pass to get into the lunch line early and to bring their lunch to the library. Put a reminder on the pass for students to bring a copy of their genre book.

- Print preregistration sheets for the next genre event, and pull sample books for the upcoming genre.

- Before the event, decorate as desired, and set out all the necessary supplies.

- During the event, host and coordinate activities. Conclude with book perusal and sign-up for next genre event.

After the Event

- Clean up the area.

- Review the exit slips. Make improvements and changes immediately in anticipation of repeating this genre next year.

Horror & Suspense

Horror & Suspense Stories

Genre Brown Bag Book Club
8th Grade

Horror & Suspense Stories

When: Party **October 7th** - During lunch

How: Sign up now to order your lunch and reserve your spot. Read a horror or suspense book *before* the *Genre Brown Bag Book Club* event. Bring the book with you to share.

What: Do you like reading terror or horror stories? Do you like to be scared by what you watch or read? If you said, "Yes" to either of these questions, then this event is for you! Be sure to read the horror or suspense book *before* we meet.

Where: LMC during your lunch. Remember to bring your horror or suspense book with you!

Why: This will give you a chance to hang out, talk about books, and have fun. Hang out with people with your same interest - reading horror or suspense stories!

Hurry! Space is limited, so pre-register today!

8th Grade Genre Lunch in the Library
(Please Print)

_____ Yes, I will read a book in this genre in advance & have marked my calendar to attend.

Student's First Name: _____ Student's Last Name: _____

Team: _____ 5th Period Teacher: _____

Title of book I will read in advance & bring with me to share: _____

Lunch (circle one):   A   B   C

I understand that I will be in the library media center during lunch and...

_____ I will bring a sack lunch from home

OR

_____ I would like a cafeteria sack lunch. Please charge my lunch account number: _____

Check One: ____Hamburger   OR   ____Cheeseburger   OR   ____PBJ Uncrustable
(Lunch also includes carrot sticks & dip, fruit cup and chocolate milk)

Space is very limited!
Please return this registration form to the LMC before September 5.

Registration can be a formal invitation with a tear-off registration passed out to students (left) or a simple sign-up sheet left in a public location, like the library media center's circulation desk (right).

From *Social Readers: Promoting Reading in the 21st Century* by Leslie B. Preddy. Santa Barbara, CA: Libraries Unlimited. Copyright © 2010.

Science Fiction & Fantasy

Genre Brown Bag Book Club

Event Date (Book Read By): _____

	Name	Grade	Lunch Period	Team	1st Period Teacher	Book I will share:
1						
2						
3						
4						
5						
6						
7						
8						
9						
10						
11						
12						
13						
14						
15						

LUNCH IN THE LIBRARY

Genre:

Action, Adventure & Survival Fiction

FUN–FICTION–FRIENDSHIP

Title I'm Reading: _____
Be sure to have your book read *before* the event!

Instructional Media Center
pmms.msdpt.k12.in.us/imc/index.htm

A bookmark can act as a reminder of the date when the book needs to be read by, as well as a placeholder while the student reads the book.

Name: _____   Room: _____

MYSTERY & DETECTIVE
Genre Lunch in the Library

Time to party!

We are looking forward to seeing you! Today you will report to the LMC during lunch for the Genre party.

When your lunch begins, please be sure you bring your lunch immediately to the LMC. If you are buying your lunch, go directly to the cafeteria line and bring your tray to the LMC. Be sure to carry this pass with you to get your lunch and for admission to the party.
Be sure to bring your book with you to the party!

Reservation for Lunch Period: _____

Turn in this pass for the door prize drawing as soon as you enter the LMC.
If you cannot attend, please let the LMC staff know before 5th period.

Mystery & Detective Stories

PERRY MERIDIAN MIDDLE SCHOOL

Create an admission pass that is easy to change for other club meetings and that can work as an invitation, making students feel special and like they're about to attend a party.

Guest Booktalk Lunch in the Library

Students are often looking for reading suggestions, but educators must face the fact that it isn't always possible to be a prophet in one's own library media center. A fun solution to the library booktalk is to make an event out of it by hosting a guest booktalker. The guest could be a librarian from a neighboring school, a librarian from a nearby public library, an employee from the local bookstore, or a local literacy coach or reading coordinator. Anyone with booktalk experience and literary expertise for the appropriate grade level is a choice worth considering and contacting. For a fun twist, coordinate with a local bookstore so interested students may purchase copies of talked books for a limited time at a discount.

Cost: $–$$

This event is completely free, unless you choose to buy extra copies of the booktalked titled for the library media center or offer dessert, drinks, or door prizes to the students. It would also be appropriate to consider including a gift or gift card in the thank you note to the guest booktalker, but cost can also be eliminated with some sweat equity. In exchange for the guest's time, offer to reciprocate and help with a similar event, or other personal talent, at his or her school, library, or bookstore.

Planning Time: 4–12 Weeks

The event takes only a few weeks to promote, preregister and host, but there are other things to consider. Guest speakers may need plenty of time to arrange their schedules, select books, and prepare booktalks. The school librarian may also want enough time to ensure multiple copies of the booktalked books are ready for circulation before the big day.

Planning Involvement: One Person

This event can handle a full load of students, twenty-five to thirty, with just the activity planner and guest booktalker.

Suggested Supplies

- Books: extra copies of books for the library media center
- Create: admission pass, book order form, bookmark, exit slip, publicity and promotional materials
- Display: decorated spotlight display shelving area
- Optional: decorations, dessert, reader's reward door prize
- Miscellaneous: guest speaker

Instructions

When inviting a guest speaker, be flexible. If necessary, allow the person's availability to dictate the event date. Offer a few possible dates for the guest to choose from, but also be prepared to adjust the timeline. Some guest speakers may not know exactly what is expected of them, so provide details about what is needed. For example, explain the need to see books that are fairly new so students can learn about the latest and greatest but that are available in paperback so they are affordable for hardworking families and the library media center. Suggest the use of a theme, such as series books, so that students can continue reading if they liked the first book in a series and the library media center can easily carry more copies. Another option is to choose prolific authors so the student can be directed to other books by that author, or a genre or specialty list like the current or upcoming state student award list.

Planning might include designating a booktalk theme and month. Examples of possible theme choices are vacation reads, recent releases, award winners, state lists, or other themes or genres. Before contacting the guest speaker, selecting a month—even a short list of specific dates within that month that are viable for the library media center and school calendars—may help expedite the planning process.

Create a short list of guest booktalkers. Guests could be a children's or young adult librarian from the public library, a reading coordinator from the school district or a neighboring district, a neighboring school's library media specialist, a respected person from the state's school library professional organization, a local bookseller, or a professor from a nearby college or university. Begin by contacting the potential guests one at a time, in order of priority, inquiring as to their interest and ability to be a guest booktalker at the school for a day. Keep the phone call or e-mail brief, but provide the basic details necessary to make an informed decision: chosen theme, amount of time for each talk, length of each talk, number of times the talk will be repeated during the visit, maximum number of students in attendance for each session, and the window of time for the talks. Offer to work around her or his schedule, but offer the chosen month and ideal dates. Repeat this process as necessary, until a positive response is received. Once the guest booktalker is confirmed, allow him or her to select the books to talk but confirm that the books are in your library collection. Discuss the need to finalize the list of books two months before the event to ensure the books are in print and the library media center has copies, perhaps multiple copies, of the selected books. Share the intended audience reading level, interest level, quantity of books to talk, and the event agenda.

Preplanning

- Select a booktalk theme and potential date(s).

- Create list of potential booktalkers and contact one at a time until one is confirmed.

- Collaborate with the guest speaker to create an agenda and the book list.

Two Months Before

- Follow-up with the guest booktalker. Confirm his attendance, date, and time and ask to review his or her short list of titles.

- Verify the titles with the library media center collection. If ordering extra copies of titles, place the order.

Six Weeks Before

- Create a student sign-up process, school announcement, student newsletter advertisement, and exit slip.

- Design a display in the library media center to promote the upcoming event.

One to Three Weeks Before

- Promote the event and accept sign-ups.

- Create a bookmark keepsake for attendees that includes an annotated list of the books to be talked.

- If offering an ordering opportunity for attendees, coordinate and create a prepaid order form.

One to Seven Days Before

- Make all necessary copies.

- Make, create, or purchase a gift, if giving one to the guest speaker.

- Send a reminder to the guest speaker and confirm anticipated arrival time. Discuss which school entrance to use, the school check-in procedure, and directions for meeting the activity planner once he or she has arrived.

- Inform the office of the guest and anticipated arrival time.

- Pull library media center copies of the books being talked.

Day of the Event

- Distribute admission passes to preregistered students.

- Prepare the facility for the event.

- Greet and help the guest speaker settle in before the event. Arrange a presentation table with books on display to the speaker's satisfaction.

- Host the event. Here is an example of a thirty-minute timeline:

  - Before: On each student table, place a cup of pencils to use. At each seat, place copies of the annotated bookmark, order form, exit slip, and treat (optional).

  - 0–5 minutes: Students get lunch and bring it to the library. Students turn in their admission pass for the door prize drawing.

  - 5–7 minutes: Welcome students. Introduce the guest speaker. Draw for the door prize. Explain the bookmark and suggest that students mark books that interest them as the books are talked.

  - 7–25 minutes: Students eat and listen to booktalks, interacting with the guest speaker.

  - 25–30 minutes: Optional order form is reviewed with students, and the deadline is given for turning in prepaid orders. Point out the booktalk display area where the library media center copies of the books will be for the next few weeks. Inform students that copies of the booktalked books in the library media center will be available for checkout after all booktalk events are done at 1 P.M. Students complete exit slip evaluations, speak personally with guest speaker, or look at books as desired until the bell rings.

  - After: Confirm that the guest speaker is doing well. Share exit slips for his or her review to prepare for the next session. Reset the place setting for the next round of students.

After the Event

- Help the guest speaker pack up and escort him or her to the school exit. Hand deliver a thank you note and optional appreciation gift.

- Clean up the library media center.

- Move library media center copies of books used during the presentation to the special display area. Place extra bookmarks and order forms with the display.

- Send a follow-up e-mail to guest booktalker.

- Review students' exit slips and make immediate changes suggested by students or guest speaker, or things that you observed, for future events.Collect student prepaid order forms. Place order and distribute orders once books have arrived.

Bookmark Front

Bookmark Back

All books are available for checkout through the IMC & public library.

March 10

Indianapolis-Marion County Public Library

With

-Lunch in the Library-
Booktalks

READ
PMMS

Perry Meridian Middle School
Instructional Media Center
http://pmms.msdpt.k12.in.us/imc/index.htm

BOOKTALKS

Lunch in the Library
with
IMCPL

- **Airhead (F Cab):**
  by Meg Cabot
  After Emma gets a "whole body transplant", she finds herself changed from an excellent student who hates fashion to a world famous teen supermodel.

- **Cryptid Hunters (F Smi):**
  by Roland Smith
  Their parents have gone missing in the jungle, so twins Grace and Marty go off into the dangerous jungle in search of their missing parents.

- **Double Identity (F Had):**
  by Margaret Peterson Haddix
  Her parents suddenly disappear, she meets an aunt she didn't even know she had, and now there are secrets to be unearthed that will change everything.

- **Found (F Had):**
  by Margaret Peterson Haddix
  A plane full of babies, with absolutely no adults on board, suddenly appears. Now Jonah and Chip find out they were among those babies found all those years ago and it's a race to uncover the mystery and repair the fabric of time.

- **Hunger Games (F Col):**
  by Suzanne Collins
  In a future world, teens must compete in an annual battle for survival aired on television.

- **I'd Tell You I Love You, but Then I'd Have to Kill You (F Car):**
  by Ally Carter
  Attending a top-secret spy training boarding school has its share of danger, romance, humor, and excitement.

Give students a bookmark to help them remember the books talked to check out in the future.

From *Social Readers: Promoting Reading in the 21st Century* by Leslie B. Preddy.
Santa Barbara, CA: Libraries Unlimited. Copyright © 2010.

Barnes and Noble Bookstore
Booktalks
Lunch in the Library

Barnes & Noble Bookstore Booktalks Order Form
Orders Due: November 26

Last Period Teacher's Name: _____ Team: _____

Student's First & Last Name: _____

TITLE	ORDER NUMBER	DISCOUNT PRICE	ORDER
Twilight Series			
◊ Twilight	ISBN-13: 9780316038379	$ 7.99-20% = $ 6.39	_____
◊ New Moon	ISBN-13: 9780316024969	$10.99-20% = $ 8.79	_____
◊ Eclipse	ISBN-13: 978-0316160209	$10.99-20% = $ 8.79	_____
39 Clues			
◊ Maze of Bones	ISBN-13: 9780545060394	$12.99-20% = $10.39	_____
◊ One False Note	ISBN-13: 9780545060424	$12.99-20% = $10.39	_____
◊ Card Pack #1	ISBN-13: 9780545083423	$ 6.99-20% = $ 5.59	_____
Charlie Bone and the...			
◊ #1, Midnight...	ISBN-13: 9780439474290	$12.99-20% = $10.39	_____
◊ ...Time Twister	ISBN-13: 9780439496872	$10.99-20% = $ 8.79	_____
◊ ...Invisible Boy	ISBN-13: 9780439545266	$10.99-20% = $ 8.79	_____
◊ ...Castle of Mirrors	ISBN-13: 9780439545280	$ 9.95-20% = $ 7.96	_____
Peter and the			
◊ ...Starcatchers	ISBN-13: 9780786849079	$7.99-20% = $ 6.39	_____
◊ ...Shadow Thieves	ISBN-13: 9781423108559	$8.99-20% = $ 7.19	_____
Septimus Heap			
◊ Magyk	ISBN-13: 9780060577339	$7.99-20% = $ 6.39	_____
◊ Flyte	ISBN-13: 9780060577360	$7.99-20% = $ 6.39	_____
◊ Physik	ISBN-13: 9780060577391	$7.99-20% = $ 6.39	_____
The Name of this Book Secret			
◊ Book 1	ISBN-13: 9780316113694	$5.99-20% = $ 4.79	_____

Payment (circle one): cash OR check (made out to PMMS) Total: $ _____

Pre-paid book orders will be delivered before Winter Break.
Please visit Barnes and Noble Bookstore, the public library, or the school library media center
for these or other books by today's featured authors.

Booktalk events could include a special display in the library media center
from which students may borrow the books as well as an order form for
students to buy books to add to their home libraries.

From *Social Readers: Promoting Reading in the 21st Century* by Leslie B. Preddy.
Santa Barbara, CA: Libraries Unlimited. Copyright © 2010.

Name: _____ Grade:___ Lunch:___

Booktalk
Lunch in the Library
Exit Slip

A book I never heard about before today was _____

_____ .

I would do this again: ___Yes   ___No

A book talked about that I now want to read is _____

_____

_____ .

We should invite our guest speaker back again: ___Yes   ___No

I think we should do a *Booktalk Lunch in the Library*. We should ask
this guest speaker or include this book or author _____

_____ .

READ

P M M S

Instructional Media Center

**Exit slips for the guest booktalks might include reflecting on books and the guest
as well as an opportunity to share ideas for future booktalk events.**

From *Social Readers: Promoting Reading in the 21st Century* by Leslie B. Preddy.
Santa Barbara, CA: Libraries Unlimited. Copyright © 2010.

One Book, One School

One Book, One City events have swept across the country. Originally, many programs were geared toward adults. But imagine having a book the whole school is reading, discussing, sharing, and promoting. Turning the campus into a "One Book, One School" event allows the school community to center its focus on reading, take advantage of a successful model, and adapt it to the school setting. (See the figures included in the next section, "One School, One Book, One Author" for ideas that will also work with this project.)

Cost: $–$$$$

The cost of this event largely depends on the size of the staff and student population, as well as whether a student's family or school is paying for copies of the book. The book selected should be available in paperback to reduce expenses. Annual expenses for the school can be dropped dramatically if the school preorders copies at a deep discount and passes that discount on to students. If families buy their own copy, possibly as part of the school supply list at the beginning of the school year, expenses are shared. For most schools, it would be necessary and important to supply copies of the book to staff members to gain buy-in from those stakeholders.

Planning Time: Six to Twelve Months

Planning time begins with getting administrative permission and placing the event on the school calendar. Depending on the school and which semester is most suitable for the calendar, this process could begin as early as the prior school year.

Planning Involvement: Three or Four People

Three to four people are needed to work together and gain staff buy-in for this event. Include English/language arts teachers, but also try to include content area teachers to help with multidisciplinary connections. Including students on the committee could add a new dimension to the event with enthusiastic students creating promotions and spreading the word among their peers.

Suggested Supplies

• Books: enough copies of the selected book for staff, students, and possibly even parents; extra copies of all the author's titles for the library media center to meet increased interest and demand

• Create: basic guidelines, follow-up reminders, lesson plans, publicity and promotional materials, timeline or calendar

• Display: decorated spotlight display shelving area

• Miscellaneous: materials needed for each individual event

Instructions

This event is most successful when staff members work together to create an enriching experience. Create promotions that entice, encourage and are visible to staff, students, and parents. Keep parents informed about the event and related activities. Craft related activities and contests connected to the themes and content in the novel.

It is helpful to create a fact-finding committee. Ask administration for permission to ask for volunteers for a committee intended to look into the idea of a One Book, One School event.

As a committee, create a short list of prospective books. Confirm titles are in print and available in paperback. Establish a tentative implementation timeline. Consider incorporating family opportunities into the original plan. Include before school, lunch, and evening book discussions for students, staff, and families. As part of the analysis, contact favorite book vendors and the book's publishers to investigate discounted prices for the event. Ask about accepted methods of payment, ordering procedure, and length of time it will take from order placement to delivery.

Once the fact-finding committee has decided to pursue the event, meet with administration with a prepared budget, timeline, and a short list of possible titles. Prepare various "what-if" options for the event: if all students and staff were provided a copy of the book, if staff were provided and all students were expected to purchase a copy of the book at a discount, if the school was able to cover a portion of the cost of the book for students, and other possibilities.

When it is time to plan, some fact-finding committee members may want to continue on the committee as it morphs into the event committee. For those who don't, or if more participants are needed to spread out the work, seek new members. The new committee will work together to finalize publicity and promotion and plan implementation and the event timeline.

Invite anyone willing to read the book and help create suggested classroom activities, including content area connections and schoolwide promotions, contests, and events. Once the books arrive, distribute copies and a package of sticky notes to the committee and subcommittee members. Within one to two weeks, each volunteer should complete the book, using the sticky notes to flag pages and note questions, vocabulary, content area connections, themes, activity ideas, and so on.

Preplanning

- Request permission from administration to establish a fact-finding committee.

- Establish and complete fact-finding committee work.

- Contact book vendors for book quotes.

- Meet with administration for final approval.

- Place the event on your school calendar.

Three to Four Months Before

- Place school book order.

- Create event committee to finalize event planning.

- Keep the whole school informed through e-mails and brief presentations at staff meetings as planning continues and book-related activities and events are finalized.

- Sort books for distribution.

One to Three Weeks Before

- Committee and any subcommittees continue pre-event preparations and planning.

- Distribute copies of the book to faculty and all interested staff members.

- Promote the event and related activities through the student newsletter, Web site, public announcements, staff meetings, and more.

One to Seven Days Before

• Set up a special display in the library media center.

• Display signs and posters throughout the building.

During the Weeks or Months of One Book, One School

• Follow the committee-prepared timeline to promote, implement, and host related activities.

• Try to get feedback for each activity to find out why things were or were not successful.

After the Event

• Survey the staff.

• Send thank you notes to the committee and subcommittee members.

• E-mail families to thank them for participating at any family events.

Insert Book Cover Art Here	BEFORE		*This Side of Paradise* By Steven Layne	AFTER		Instructional Media Center
	Agree	Disagree		Agree	Disagree	
			"When you're constantly surrounded by beauty, you cease to appreciate it rather quickly."			
			Things aren't always what they seem.			
			Family can always be trusted.			
			There is a price for perfection.			
			Everyone should strive to be perfect.			
			Some people go too far in their actions on their quest for perfection.			
			There are always consequences for your actions.			

Committee volunteers create resources, such as an anticipation guide, to enrich the classroom experience.

One Book, One School, One Author Visit

A One Book, One School, One Author visit is a schoolwide event. It unifies all with building-wide activities leading up to a common event, book, and author through a "One Book, One School, One Author" visit or "One Book, One Grade, One Author" visit event. All faculty and staff are invited to read the author's books along with students. With staff and students reading the same book written by the visiting author in the months before the official day of the visit, it grows into a culturally absorbing event. Review the One Book, One School event for related programming suggestions.

One Book, One School, One Author visits cost money, so consider developing a co-op of area schools to reduce expenses. Our school was invited into an author visit co-op with a group of middle schools in the area. We bring an author in for a week. Each school gets the author for one day, with a contract to include three presentations per day, per school. One school in the co-op manages the coordination of author selection, initial contact, scheduling, contract, and travel arrangements. Because of the combined efforts, authors often reduce rates. The cost is reduced when schools divide the travel expenses and negotiate an education discount with a nearby hotel, and some authors slightly reduce the honorarium if multiple school visits can be arranged in one trip.

Cost: $$$–$$$$$

A One Book, One School, One Author visit is expensive with honorarium, travel, lodging expenses, and enough books for all students and staff to read. Costs can be reduced if a group of schools create an author visit co-op to share expenses. Costs are also often less for local and regional authors, partially because of reduced travel expenses. Author honorariums vary widely, so costs can increase or reduce dramatically on the basis of the author's fees. It is advisable to locate support to fund this event. For example, every year the school librarian requested money from the PTA, but after a few years, it had become a tradition they were so proud of supporting that the author's honorarium became a line-item in the PTA annual budget. The school librarian no longer has to ask for that money annually; it is automatic and the school knows exactly what honorarium fee we can afford. Building administration also supports the popular event and annually reserves money for the author's travel, lodging, and copies of the book for students and staff.

Books: $–$$

As discussed in "One Book, One School," the school's cost for books can range from free to moderately expensive, depending on whether parents buy the book as part of school supplies or the school provides it, the size of the student population, cost of the book (paperback versus hardback, publisher's discount), and whether classes will share copies of the book.

Planning Time: Six to Eighteen Months

The more time set aside to plan, the more successfully a One Book, One School, One Author visit will be thought out, implemented, and fit into the school calendar. Furthermore, time required will depend on how famous the author is, how busy his or her schedule is, his or her proximity to the school's location, and how quickly the school can locate funding and pull the event together. The sooner an author is contacted, the greater the school's chances of fitting into the author's schedule.

Planning Involvement: Committee of Four or More People

This event can be successfully managed by a small committee or expanded to include more for development and implementation of schoolwide promotions and instructional resources. Expanding it to include parents and students helps with promotion and planning and adds an exciting dynamic and perspective for everyone in the school community.

If working with a co-op of schools, there should be a representative from each school to work with the co-op. Most, if not all, of the author arrangements and coordination is done through e-mail, the Internet, and on the phone. Except for the occasional dinner with an author and informal conversations at conferences, it can be done without ever meeting face-to-face.

Within a school, most of the technical planning can be done by two individuals, an activity planner and an administrator. Getting the whole school engaged is more effectively done with a committee to prepare and share resources and schoolwide pre-promotional events and activities.

Suggested Supplies

- Books: Enough copies of the selected book for staff and for each student or class sets for students and classes to share; extra copies of all the author's titles for the library media center collection to meet the increased interest and demand.

- Create: basic guidelines, lesson plans, project timelines, publicity and promotional materials, reminders and schedules

- Display: decorated spotlight display shelving area

Instructions

Any school interested in a One Book, One School, One Author visit is strongly cautioned only to begin this venture if the school is willing to ensure that all students read the author's book (or have it read to them) and participate in enriching classroom activities and schoolwide promotions. This is an exciting opportunity to socialize reading, create enthusiasm, and increase interest in reading throughout the building, but it will be ineffective and a waste of time and money if all students and staff are not committed to the One Book, One School, One Author theme.

For first timers, begin working with administration and PTA a school year or more in advance to ensure support and funding. Contact fellow professionals working with the same age level and find out which authors have been most memorable and what made the author's visit so successful. Examine the range of honorarium fees authors charge and decide on an acceptable price range. Consider searching and applying for grants and contacting local community organization to support the event financially. Finding external funding and support for the first event will also give administration and PTA a chance to see how the activities cause an energizing, cooperative learning and entertainment experience throughout the building.

When meeting with administration to gain approval for the event, do research prior to the meeting. Present ideas for how the One Book, One School, One Author visit and books could be paid. Have a list of potential authors with the honorarium fee each author charges, if available. Commonly, author contracts include multiple presentations for one day, so consider how the student population would be divided, if at all, for the presentations and prepare ideas for how the school day might be adjusted for the culminating event. Upon approval, begin working with a committee, inviting all staff members to join. Encourage representation from content areas as well as language arts teachers, ensuring involvement from the whole school. Throughout the process, keep communicating with everyone, not just the committee, especially as pieces and parts are finalized and the committee creates an events activity timeline and resources for sharing. Before meeting with the committee, finalize a collection of prospective authors, their books, and potential cost. Ensure that the titles are still in print and, to keep expenses reasonable, that they are available in paperback. Once the list is drafted, meet as a committee. Review and revise the basic rules. Discuss potential authors. Consider how the school will handle the logistics of the event. As a group, agree to solutions for the following:

- Select a range of possible dates for the One Book, One School, One Author finale: the author visit.

- Prioritize a list of authors to contact first to see whether they are available within the date range the school needs and confirm they fit the budget.

- Many authors' contracts stipulate a certain number of presentations for a day's visit, which is commonly, but not always, three presentations, workshops, or community programs. Decide whether and how to divide the student population if there will be multiple presentations. Session attendees could be grouped by grade level or another way suitable to the school's interests and size.

- Staff and students will need access to the author's books. How will the library media center provide extra circulating copies of the author's books? Will the school provide class sets for each class, or will students have their own, personal copy? Can parents pay for their child's copy of the book, or will the school fund class sets for teachers to share?

- When contacting authors, or the authors' publishers, on the committee's wish list, contact one at a time in order of priority. Sometimes it may take a few days to receive a response. Contact information can often be found on the Internet and may be the author, his or her assistant, or a publisher's representative. Make the e-mail brief, but be sure to include the school demographics, how many students will attend each presentation, how many presentations are needed in a day, any special related events (for example, the author might lunch with a select group of students or stay after school for a parent or staff meet and greet), and the school's viable range of dates. Repeat this process until an author and the school agree to terms.

Preplanning

- Meet with administration for approval and initial planning.

- Seek support funding through administration, PTA, and other granting organizations or businesses.

- Create a planning committee.

- Keep all staff informed of progress and plans on a regular basis through e-mails and quick sharing opportunities at staff meetings.

Six to Eighteen Months Before

- Contact the committee's selected authors until an author and the school agree to terms.

- The principal should sign the author's contract, and both the activity planner and the administrator should keep a copy. If the PTA/PTO is a major funding partner, give them a courtesy copy as well.

- Contact vendors and the publisher to find the best deal for quantity books. Verify the wait time from the time of order to delivery.

- Order so books arrive eight to twelve weeks before the event, longer if classes will need more time to read and complete supporting activities. Allow for time to unpack, sort, and distribute the books and for classroom use.

- Committee continues to meet to locate, create, and share lessons and schoolwide book-themed promotion ideas for the selected reading and author.

- Create promotional materials.

Three Months Before

- Supervise, host, and promote scheduled schoolwide book-related events.

- Once books have arrived, schedule a meeting to distribute books to all students or class sets to participating classrooms, along with event details, resources, and reminders.

- Arrange travel and hotel accommodations, as required by the author's contract. If the author makes his or her own arrangements, contact the author for a copy of the travel itinerary.

Four to Six Weeks Before

- Coordinate airport pickup and drop-off for the author, if needed.

- Arrange for the author's transportation to and from school on the day of the visit, if needed.

- Communicate with the author to confirm presentation setup, equipment needs, and special meal requirements.

- Work with administration to create a presentation and book signing schedule for the author visit. Share that schedule with the author and staff in advance.

- Coordinate special setup and cleanup needs for the author visit day with custodial and technology staff.

- Promote the event with notices in the student newspaper, family newsletter, school announcements, homemade posters and signs, and a press release to the local news agencies.

- Make arrangements for contracted payment to be ready, as per the contracted agreement.

- In the days leading up to the event, share the One Book, One School, One Author visit schedule with staff. Answer any questions or concerns they might have.

Day of the Event

- Supervise coordination of the author's itinerary.

- Play host and handler to the author, or arrange for one or a rotation of hosts from staff or parents.

After the Event

- Gather follow-up feedback from the committee and participants, including staff and students. If your school policy permits, survey students to evaluate the event.

- Send a thank you to participating author, administration, and other appropriate supporters and funders of the event.

- If planning to host a One Book, One School, One Author event every school year, follow-up immediately to secure funding and administrative permission and begin the cycle again.

- Because staff members now have a feel for what the project is like, ask for their input for future author candidates. Allow staff the opportunity to be more involved in the selection process.

One Book, One School, One Author Book Sharing General Guidelines

TEAM/DEPARTMENT/TEACHERS:
QUANTITY REQUESTED:

Author: Wendelyn Van Draanen
Visitation: March 20, 2009

School-wide Event
- Before your team attends the author presentation, read, discuss and participate in classroom enrichment activities before the author arrival date.
  - Every student needs to actively participate in reading, being read to, and discussing the selected One Book, One School, One Author book.
  - Every team will receive one class set to share amongst the team's Language Arts teachers and classes.

Books-Temporary Class Sets
- A set of books was purchased for your team to use based on the information your team provided.
- The set of books should remain unmarked. Do not write your name, school name, team, or any other information in the book.
  - Except for your personal copy, each book will be awarded to students after being autographed by the author.
  - Each individual team may select the requirements and reward system for awarding the books.

Autographing
- Immediately prior to the author visit, return books to the library media center.
  - Just in case the author is able to personalize the autographing, place a sticky note with the winning student's first and last name on the cover of each book.
  - Return all books (be sure to have them labeled with the sticky note) to the library media center in the bag provided one week before the author's visit. Label the bag with your name, team and room number.
  - Books will be returned as soon as they are autographed by the author. Please distribute the books to winning students.

Example of book distribution and sharing guidelines.

From *Social Readers: Promoting Reading in the 21st Century* by Leslie B. Preddy. Santa Barbara, CA: Libraries Unlimited. Copyright © 2010.

When Zachary Beaver Came to Town
By Kimberly Willis Holt
http://www.kimberlywillisholt.com/

RESOURCES:
- Check the staff shared drive for resource we have created to share. Please add to the folder anything you create and email everyone to let them know.
- You can also access resources at:
  - www.zacharybeaver.com (click on "Free Teacher's Guide" for PDF download)
  - http://www.randomhouse.com/teachers/catalog/display.pperl?isbn=9780440229049&view=tg (resource guide)
  - http://www.multcolib.org/talk/guides-zachary.html (discussion questions)
  - http://www.quia.com/pop/9137.html (Quia pop quiz)
  - http://www.nancykeane.com/booktalks/holt_when.htm (booktalk)
  - http://www.enotes.com/when-zachary-qn/ (e-notes - be sure to use the 'navigate' bar to the right
  - http://www.kimberlywillisholt.com/home.html (author's official website
  - http://www.kimberlywillisholt.com/zachbookmarks.html (bookmark)
  - http://www.kimberlywillisholt.com/zachguide.html (teacher's guide)

Pre-Reading / Pre-Learning
1. Background on 70's
   - Vietnam War
   - Peace Movement (how soldiers were treated)
   - Music: Tammy Wynette, Beatles, James Taylor, "Natural Woman", "RESPECT", Carpenters
   - Clothing: tie dye shirts, KEDS, mini-skirts, high-top lace boots, cowboy boots, polyester clothing, bell bottoms,
   - T.V. Shows: Seasme Street, Mr. Rogers, Password, Let's Make a Deal, Price is Right
   - Sea Monkies
   - Foods: Granola, jello salad, coffee movement, casseroles
2. Side Shows
   - *Guinness Book of World Records*
   - Asking the question "Why do we go see or watch unusual things?"
   - History of Side Shows
   - *Ripley's Believe it or Not*
3. Brainstorm what a small town in Texas during the 70's might look like.
5. Teaching Tolerance Survey and Article (attached)
6. Bookmark

During Reading
1. Daily Journal Reflection
   - Questions for author
   - Questions dealing with abandonment
   - What would you have done questions
   - Predictions
   - Concepts
     - "rides shotgun" p.64
     - "I'm his bread and butter" p.69
     - "Tales the phone with a long extension"
2. Vocabulary Words (Throughout Novel)

As the multidisciplinary committee of volunteers meets, ideas are brainstormed, resources are found, and classroom enrichment suggestions are developed.

- Chapter One: amateurs, album, reputation
- Chapter Two: revival, suspiciously, Plexiglas
- Chapter Three: turquoise, gourmet chef, war correspondent, gawk
- Chapter Four: parallel park, hunches, twang, honky-tonk
- Chapter Five: emphysema, beehive hairdo, averts
- Chapter Six: hoots (verb)
- Chapter Seven: loan shark, casserole, baptism, draping
- Chapter Nine: shuffling

3. Write a letter giving a compliment (chapter 8)
4. Write a descriptive paragraph about what Zachary sees on his way to the drive-in. (Point-of View)
5. Toby writes a letter to Cal talking about Wayne's death. Why did he feel that he could write the letter?
6. Discussion Question: How would you feel if people were gawking at you all day long?
7. Write a persuasive essay discussing why the cafeteria should have healthier lunch choices using examples from the story.
- Why we should have P.E. in schools
8. Character Drawings
- Find excerpts from the story to defend sketches
9. Setting Drawings (Dioramas)

After Reading
1. Write a country western song "Zachary's Ballad"
2. "Project Tolerance" campaign
3. Letter to serviceperson
4. Talk Show with characters
5. Writing Suggestions
- Theme Essay
    - abandonment
    - differences
    - social status
    - loyalty
    - family
    - friendship
    - self discovery
    - peer pressure
    - diversity
    - kindness
    - hope
- Character Analysis Paper
- Select a character and analyze three main traits (3-5 Paragraph Essay)
- Three Central Characters
- Compare & Contrast Essay
- Toby versus Zachary
- Student's Life versus Cal/Zachary/Toby
- Movie versus Book
6. Movie
- Could be used as a reward for completion of novel and all work/projects
- May work as a team or grade level incentive/celebration

Please contact the library media specialist if you have any questions.

As the multidisciplinary committee of volunteers meets, ideas are brainstormed, resources are found, and classroom enrichment suggestions are developed. (*Cont.*)

From *Social Readers: Promoting Reading in the 21st Century* by Leslie B. Preddy. Santa Barbara, CA: Libraries Unlimited. Copyright © 2010.

One Book, One School, One Author
Author Visit Schedule

Please check your e-mail for suggested post-presentation discussion questions and activities.

8th Grade: 8:15–9:15

At 8:00, after announcements and attendance is taken, please escort your students to the presentation and sit with them. Students leave materials in the classroom. After the program, 1st-period teachers will escort their class back to their room. Students will remain with that teacher until dismissal at 9:30 to the 3rd period class.

Off Team: 8th graders will not have a 2nd-period class.

Teachers: If you have a 2nd period with only 8th graders, please come to the presentation to assist with supervision as some teachers need their prep. time.

7th Grade: 9:25–10:25

We will make an announcement at approximately 9:15 to have 2nd period teachers escort their students to the presentation. Please sit with your group to assist with supervision. Have students bring materials with them. We will dismiss to 4th period from the presentation.

Off Team: There will be no 3rd period for 7th graders.

Teachers: If you have a 3rd period of 7th graders only, please come to the presentation to assist with supervision as some teachers need to leave for their prep. time.

6th Grade: 1:15–2:15

At 1:00, after attendance is taken for 6th period, please escort students to the presentation. Leave materials in the classroom. We will dismiss from the presentation back to the 6th period room for dismissal. Teachers will dismiss students to buses at the normal time.

Off Team: There will be no 7th period for 6th graders.

Teachers: If you have a 7th period 6th-grade only class, please come to the presentation to assist with supervision. Some teachers need to leave for their prep time.

This sample author visit schedule shows how to give consideration to how long it will take the students to travel and settle for the convocation and the need to consider teacher prep time.

From *Social Readers: Promoting Reading in the 21st Century* by Leslie B. Preddy.
Santa Barbara, CA: Libraries Unlimited. Copyright © 2010.

P M M S

Instructional Media Center

Award Winning Author
Wendelin Van Draanen
to visit Perry Meridian!

Insert
Book
Cover
Art Here

DATE
March 20
TIMES
(tentative)
8:00 am - grade 7
9:45 am - grade 8
1:15 pm - grade 6

Insert
Book
Cover
Art Here

One Book, One School, One Author

For information
contact
Leslie Preddy
at
lpreddy@msdpt.
k12.in.us

Insert
Book
Cover
Art Here

Our author visit
was made
possible through
a grant from
PMMS/PMA
PTA.
Thank you!

Wendelin Van Draanen's Website
www.randomhouse.com/kids/vandraanen/index.html

The author will autograph books for a limited
time during the visit. If your family would like
books autographed by the author, please drop
books off before March 19 to Mrs. P at PMMS
or Mrs. G at PMA or purchase books through
the attached order form.

Create simple announcements to promote the upcoming One Book, One School, One Author
visit to parents and the community in the student newsletter. After the One Book, One School,
One Author visit, a similar post-presentation announcement would celebrate the successful event
and could also include pictures of students interacting with the author.

From *Social Readers: Promoting Reading in the 21st Century* by Leslie B. Preddy.
Santa Barbara, CA: Libraries Unlimited. Copyright © 2010.

Author Neal Shusterman
'Staff Meet & Greet'

Join us in the library media center to visit with our guest author, Neal Shusterman. He will be with us after school on Friday for an informal gathering and book signing.

Plus enjoy the library's world famous snacks and beverages!

Place: Library Media Center

Date: Friday, December 7

Time: 2:30-3:15 pm

If you would like a book signed by the author, you can bring in your own copy or the library media center has books for sale at a discounted price. See us if you would like to purchase a copy from the LMC.

Arrange with the author in advance for a meet and greet with staff.

From *Social Readers: Promoting Reading in the 21st Century* by Leslie B. Preddy. Santa Barbara, CA: Libraries Unlimited. Copyright © 2010.

One Book, One School, One Author
Post-Presentation Discussion or Writing Prompts

- How did meeting the author affect your opinion of the novel? Explain your answer.
- List three words to describe the author (appearance, personality, and/or presentation style). Explain in detail why you chose these particular words to describe her.
- Are you now interested in reading other books by the author? Why or why not? How is your opinion related to the author's presentation? How is your opinion related to the novel?
- Did the visit from the author live up to your expectations? Did she surpass your expectations? Explain your opinion.
- If you have heard other authors speak in person (as a 6th grader or 7th grader, at a bookstore, at the public library, etc.), how does this author's presentation compare? Explain.
- What do you think are some of the positive impacts of spending time with an author?
- Rate the audience's performance. How could an audience have an impact on the author's presentation (positive and negative)?

Having the students reflect on the author's presentation through discussion or writing helps reinforce the experience, meet curricular standards, and build enrichment.

From *Social Readers: Promoting Reading in the 21st Century* by Leslie B. Preddy. Santa Barbara, CA: Libraries Unlimited. Copyright © 2010.

One Book, One School, One Author

Please complete this survey and place in Mrs. P's mailbox by Friday afternoon. Thank You!

I am a (check one) _____ Parent _____ Teacher _____ Administrator _____ Support Staff

	Strongly Agree				Strongly Disagree	
This project helped us meet district reading initiative goals:	6	5	4	3	2	1
Students were excited about meeting an author:	6	5	4	3	2	1
Students were positive about the author's presentation:	6	5	4	3	2	1
Staff members were positive about the author's presentation:	6	5	4	3	2	1
After the visit, students seem more interested in reading:	6	5	4	3	2	1
After the visit, students seem more interested in writing/authoring:	6	5	4	3	2	1
This was worth a disruption to the regular school day:	6	5	4	3	2	1
We should do this again:	6	5	4	3	2	1

Did you attend the author's presentation?   yes   no

(If you attended any portion of one of the presentations, please respond to the following statements)

Student were well-behaved	6	5	4	3	2	1
Students were attentive	6	5	4	3	2	1
The author's presentation was interesting	6	5	4	3	2	1
Which grade-level presentation did you attend? 6 7 8						

Positive Comments:

Concerns:

Suggestions:

Using an online survey tool or a paper copy placed in staff mailboxes, evaluate the overall effectiveness and efficiency of the One Book, One School, One Author visit event. A separate parent survey could also be developed and published in the student newsletter or online to gather parents' feedback and input.

From *Social Readers: Promoting Reading in the 21st Century* by Leslie B. Preddy.
Santa Barbara, CA: Libraries Unlimited. Copyright © 2010.

One Book, One School, One Author · November 2009 · One Book, One School, One Author · November 2009 ·

Insert Book Cover Art Here

Perry Meridian Middle School

Shelley Pearsall

One Book, One School, One Author
November 17, 2009

PMMS Book of Records

9 events - 8 teams - 1 month - Many Winners

WHY: This school-wide project connects to the character's desire to make the Guinness Book of Records

WHAT: 9 Events - Juggling - Hula Hoop - Staring (no blinking) - Thumb War - Pin the Feather on the Turkey - Clothes Pin Drop - Balance Spoon on Nose - Tallest Card House (constructed with triangles) - Paddle Ball

WHO: Every M-U-S-T-A-N-G team

WHEN:
October - inner-team competitions
- Hold team contests for each of the 9 events. (This could be done during the extra 15 minutes in 5th period.)
- Each team will decide their own rules, procedures for selecting their finalists.
- Select 3 finalists for each event to compete in the finals
October 28—Report 3 finalists per event to the IMC before October 28.
November - PMMS Book of Records Finals
- Finals held during A, B & C lunch.
November 2-12 Finalist compete during lunch on the stage
November 13: Awards ceremony during lunch

Project leaders: Mrs. P, Mrs. F, Mrs. D
Finals MC's: Mrs. R & Mr. L
Photo/Video-grapher: Mrs. G, Mrs. H

PMMS Tetrahedron Construction

WHY: This school-wide project is in honor of the tetrahedron in the book.

WHAT: PMMS tries to construct the largest tetrahedron possible in one month. Classes use the spare 15 minutes in 5th period to glue/tape a 3D triangle together, then bag up triangles and deliver class set of triangles to the LMC.

WHO: All 5th period students and classes.

WHEN:
October 5-9
Every student constructs 1 3-dimensional triangle in 5th period
- Triangle cut-outs will be delivered October 2 for 5th period classes.
- Deliver completed 3-D triangles to the IMC by Friday, October 9.
- If you have a hard time gathering materials (glue stick, glue, or tape), let us know.
October 12-November 17 -
All teams, classes, clubs, groups, staff invited to drop by the LMC at any time to help construct the 3D triangles into a tetra as big as we can get it before the author arrives.

WHERE: Tetrahedron constructed in LMC.

Project leaders: Mrs. P & Mrs. H

STAFF "Willy's BBQ" Pitch-In

WHY: In honor of Willy's BBQ restaurant & recipes spotlighted throughout the book.

WHAT: STAFF BBQ Pitch-In
Any team, department or group may volunteer to bring in a BBQ item to share for the pitch-in. Bring in anything you want or connect it to the book:
- BBQ recipe options are on pages 30, 48, 74, 137, 220 (or one of your own creations)
- Willy Q's Chocolate Truch Cake (p. 137) "Sweet enough to make tongues start talking"
- Lemonade
WHO: Every team, department or group interested in participating and partaking of the yummy-ness.

WHEN:
A, B, C lunch on Friday, **Nov. 13**

WHERE: TBD by the Social Committee

Organizers: Social Committee

Chromatography

WHY: Recreate art project in book.
WHAT: Coffee Filter Chromatography
WHO: Option for science classes.
WHEN: Coordinate with E/LA team teacher to do it right after students read that section.
WHERE: During science class.

For interested Science classes, see Mr. K.

STUDENT BBQ Lunch

WHY: To celebrate Willy's BBQ restaurant. **WHAT:** Special Lunch Options

WHO: Available to all students   **WHEN:** A,B,C, lunch, **November 17**

WHERE:
- Chipotle line: "Willy's BBQ" (pork) sandwiches
- Extra on every tray: "Wily Q's Chocolate Truth Cake" (actually small brownie with chocolate frosting)

Publicity: Mrs. B's class
Organizers: Cafeteria Staff

The school reading community is enhanced by schoolwide team-building activities centered on the themes, characters, and events in the novel.

From *Social Readers: Promoting Reading in the 21st Century* by Leslie B. Preddy.
Santa Barbara, CA: Libraries Unlimited. Copyright © 2010.

PMMS/PMA Family Read-In

You're Invited - Mark Your Calendar for November 17!

How: Register and pre-order the book before September 30.

What: Both a significant adult and child read the book at home during the month of November. You will also receive a packet of optional activities to do together while reading the book. (Home packets will be sent home on the bus with your child in late October.)

When: November 17 - Participating adult and child join other PMMS/PMA families for a Family Read-In full of friends, activities and book discussion on November 17 at 6pm.

Where: Perry Meridian Middle School LMC (library)

Why: This will give you and your child an activity and time to spend together and have something in common—reading!

All students will meet author Shelley Pearsall during our PTA sponsored Author Visit!

Insert Book Cover Art Here

"All Shook Up is alternately wry, silly, thoughtful and laugh-out-loud funny. It will appeal to any kids who've been mortified by their parents..."
(Review: Bookpage)

All Shook Up
By Shelley Pearsall

"When 13-year-old Josh finds out he has to stay with his dad in Chicago for a few months, he's not too thrilled. But when he arrives at the airport, he's simply devastated. His father--who used to be a scatterbrained, but pretty normal, shoe salesman--has become a sideburn-wearing, hip-twisting, utterly embarrassing Elvis impersonator. Josh is determined to keep his dad's identity a secret, but on his very first day at his new school, a note appears on his locker. It's signed "Elvisly Yours, "and instead of a name, a sneering purple smiley face. The secret is out, and when his dad is invited to perform at a special 50's concert at his school. From award-winning author Shelley Pearsall comes a hilarious novel about a father and son discovering something about being who you are--and who you're not." (Books-A-Million.com)

Perry Meridian Family Read-In Registration
(Please Print)

_____ Yes, we will read the book in advance and have marked our calendar to attend 6pm, November 17.

Participating Adult's Name (First & Last): _____

Child/Student's Name (First & Last): _____

Grade (circle one): 6 7 8   Team: _____ Last Period Teacher: _____

Address:_____ Apt # _____

  Indianapolis, Indiana   Zip: _____

Participating adult's email: _____

_____ We would like to order 1 paperback copy that we will share. $ 6.00
  OR
_____ We would like to order 2 paperback copies so we can each have our own copy. $12.00
  OR
_____ We don't need to order because we already have the book at home. $ *free*

Payment (circle one): cash   OR   check made out to PMMS

Home packets and pre-paid books will be sent home on the bus with your child in late October.
Please return this registration form and payment to the LMC/Mrs. Preddy before September 30.

The school reading community is enhanced by schoolwide team-building activities centered on the themes, characters, and events in the novel. (*Cont.*)

From *Social Readers: Promoting Reading in the 21st Century* by Leslie B. Preddy.
Santa Barbara, CA: Libraries Unlimited. Copyright © 2010.

Read-In or Read-A-Thon

A Read-In or Read-A-Thon is adapted from Walk-A-Thon events. The purpose is to collectively promote reading awareness, not fundraising, although it can be done as a fundraiser. Through a Read-In, classes take turns at a reading sit-in in a prominent location in the building, like the lobby or main foyer. It could be used as a culminating event, kickoff event, or connection to another school event. Perry Meridian Middle School likes to use the Read-In as the annual kickoff event for an annual Reading Madness Month.

Cost: $

This event costs nothing but time, creativity, and supplies already available to create promotional materials.

Planning Time: Two Weeks

Only two weeks are needed to create a sign-up and register participants, promote and build enthusiasm, and run the event. If administrative permission and calendar planning are required, time in advance of the two weeks may be needed. If this is a planned school or library media center fundraiser, more organization and promotion time will be needed.

Planning Involvement: One Person

It only takes one person to get this event in motion, plan, register, remind participants, and host the event.

Suggested Supplies

• Books: short stories for students unable to remember to bring their book to the read-in station

• Create: follow-up reminder, instructions, invitation, publicity and promotional materials, schedule, sign-up

• Student contribution: book

Instructions

The Read-In is simple, takes only one day, and involves the whole school. If it's a large school, create a sign-up sheet and ask for volunteers to sign up for fifteen- to twenty-minute blocks. If the school is small and everyone can fit for a reading time in one day, ask everyone to participate. Another option for larger schools where everyone wants to participate is to stage the read-in in multiple prominent locations simultaneously.

Plan for the Read-In to be in a visible location in the building, ideally where there is a lot of traffic by visitors, staff and other students. Prime locations may be the lobby, main foyer, gym, stage, busy hallway, or other high traffic location.

Because this is a schoolwide event, coordinate with the assistance of administration, meeting to work out details and approval. Establish from the beginning whether it is a fundraiser (Read-A-Thon) or awareness campaign (Read-In). If it is a fundraiser, extra measures will need to be taken, including procedures and paperwork for accepting and collecting donations. Discuss connecting it to another event at school, using the Read-In to kickoff or wrap up that event or run simultaneously with an event that draws the community to the school that day.

Preplanning

- Meet with administration to approve the project and finalize a date for the Read-In.

- Place event on school calendar.

One Month Before

- Create a class sign-up schedule.

- Write a "coming soon" announcement for the student newsletter.

One to Three Weeks Before

- E-mail staff about the Read-In. Explain the procedure, date, and times available. Open up registration for classes to sign up for time slots.

- Follow-up at a staff meeting reminding people of the event and pass around the sign-up to fill any still-available spots. If there is still space available after this, speak to individual teachers who might be receptive and ask for their participation.

- Design and print signs, posters, or banners for the main entry or Read-In location.

- Create reminder slips to place in mailboxes the day before and the day of the event.

One Day Before

- Pull together a collection of short stories to stage at the Read-In location for students who forget to carry a book.

- Place reminder slips in mailboxes.

Day of the Event

- Hand deliver, or have student helpers deliver, a second reminder slip to participating teachers.

- Hang signs, posters, or banners.

- Stage short story collection at the Read-In location.

- Have digital pictures taken of each group as they participate.

After the Event

- Clean up Read-In area. Return short story collection to the library media center. Take down signs and store for reuse.

- Get formal or informal feedback, verbal or written, from participating classes.

- Send thank you notes to participating classes. Include in the thank you a picture of the class participating in the Read-In.

- E-mail all staff members to thank them for a great day and ask for feedback to make things better for the next time.

PMMS 2nd Annual Reading Madness Month Read-In
Please sign up your class/classes for a 20-minute block of time.

Time	Class
7:40-8:00	
8:05-8:25	
8:30-8:50	
8:54-9:14	
9:19-9:39	
9:43-10:03	
10:08-10:28	
10:32-10:52	
10:57-11:17	
11:21-11:41	
11:45-12:05	
12:09-12:29	
12:37-12:57	
1:01-1:21	
1:26-1:46	
1:50-2:10	
2: 15-2:35	

Create a sign-up, dividing the day into as many time slots as needed.

Read-A-Thon

PERRY MERIDIAN

MIDDLE SCHOOL

Reading Madness Month
Kick-Off Event in Progress

Design posters, signs, or banners to announce the event to visitors.

From *Social Readers: Promoting Reading in the 21st Century* by Leslie B. Preddy.
Santa Barbara, CA: Libraries Unlimited. Copyright © 2010.

Read-A-Thon

Thank You for volunteering to participate in the PMMS Read-A-Thon! Please be sure to have your class in the main lobby reading at your designated time.

_____   _____
DATE   TIME
You Make a Reading Difference!

Friendly reminders go a long way to ensure classes remember their commitment and show up on time.

READ Bingo

READ Bingo allows every classroom to participate in a building-wide game of bingo each day. A class with the winning BINGO card is awarded a book to add to home bookshelves for each winning student in the class. This is a simple, fun way to encourage reading, build schoolwide enthusiasm and help students develop a home bookshelf. READ Bingo will be immediately popular and one of the most recognized and remembered annual events sponsored by the library media center. The primary objective of this event is to promote class spirit, have fun promoting reading, and encourage home libraries through the reward of free books during READ Bingo.

Cost: $$

Most of the items on the supply list can be created with materials you'll already have available in the school. The bingo prizes will cost money, but with some creativity, books can be found at a discount and supplemented with school supplies donated by local stores or businesses. Immediately estimate the largest class size times the cost to provide each student in a winning class book prizes. To figure the budget, decide how many times the game will be restarted (to allow for more fun and winners) and multiply the number of winning classes by the per-class cost.

Planning Time: Three Months

The first year, more time is needed to create all the READ Bingo game boards and cut out the construction-paper markers. Laminating the game boards and including instructions to classroom teachers that the game boards and place markers will be returned for reuse will greatly reduce the preplanning time for future years.

The actual event time will vary depending on how long the bingo game will run. Run it for a month, but it could be run for one special week, or on a special day, like the 100th day of school, field day, or any other day when the whole school is celebrating.

Planning Involvement: One or Two People

This event is very easy to run after making everything the first year and does not require much to encourage classes to enjoy the fun. READ Bingo can easily be done with one person and a few student volunteers to help sort, organize, deliver, and return the bingo game boards, bag of markers, and instruction sheet.

- Create: instructions and rules sheet, laminated READ Bingo game board posters for each classroom, publicity and promotional materials, READ Bingo call key, READ Bingo call objects or cards
- Reader's Reward: new paperback books
- Miscellaneous: Plastic bag of construction paper cutout shapes to use for place markers for each classroom
- Option: poster machine

Instructions

During READ Bingo, every classroom is given a unique bingo game board, which can be blown up to poster size with a poster printer or printing, cutting and pasting a poster together using a publishing program like Microsoft Publisher. Laminate the posters and they can be collected and reused year after year. READ Bingo game boards can be custom-made with the school name, logo, mascot, or library media center logo, or use Web sites such as print-bingo.com. Make each one unique and create a few more than actually needed, just in case some are lost. Number each game board and save an electronic copy so that a damaged or lost game board can easily be replaced.

Create place markers with small shapes cut out with any commercial letter system, such as an Ellison or Cricut or individual punches sold at card-making craft stores, or by cutting or tearing triangles, squares, and other shapes out of construction paper or card stock.

Create cards, balls, or objects for each individual call that is possible, such as "B10" or "R14." These can be created from anything on hand or donated, like 3 × 5 cards or counter sample tiles from the local do-it-yourself home repair store. We happened to have a bunch of miniature rubber ducks from an old event that we repurposed for READ Bingo and wrote the calls onto the bottom of the ducks, which are fun because we draw the calls live during the televised student news broadcast.

If prizes are going to be part of the game, order enough books or school supplies for the full length of the event. Calculate by taking the largest class, multiply by the number of times you plan to play, then add one to two extra classes worth just in case there are any ties. Contact vendors and look in catalogs for bargain books, but try to order a variety of titles, genres, and reading levels so there is a nice selection for students.

A lot of the day-to-day logistics is done by guesswork until you've figured out about how many call numbers are used before getting a winner. For example, let's say a school gives out approximately fifty game boards and wants about one class to win each week for a month of READ Bingo. With the number of game boards in use, read four calls a day, which usually gets a winning classroom each week for four weeks. If wins are coming too slow or too fast, adjust the number of calls read daily as the event progresses.

Once a winner is announced, if the school plans to replay again, ask all classes to clear their game boards and prepare for the next game to start. Arrange for the winning class to visit the reward books so each child may select for him- or herself a free book to keep. If there are too many winners and book prizes are running low, stop playing early, but be sure to stop after the latest winner and not in the middle of a game.

Preplanning

- Meet with administration to gain permission and funding. Place READ Bingo on the calendar.

- If needed, locate a funding source to purchase the reward books.

Three Months Before

- Order prize books.

- Write and create promotions for READ Bingo to place in the student newsletter and announcements.

- Begin creating the READ Bingo game boards and game board call key.

Six Weeks to Two Months Before

- Begin promoting READ Bingo through the student newsletter and staff announcements.

- Print and laminate game boards and the call key.

- Create call objects or cards.

- If needed, test the game to gauge average number of calls needed for a win.

- Create instruction and rules sheet. Make one copy for each game board. Laminate for reuse.

One to Three Weeks Before

• Create storage bags with fifteen to twenty place markers in each bag for each game board.

• Bundle together one poster, instruction sheet, and storage bag in preparation for distribution.

One to Seven Days Before

• At a staff meeting or through e-mail, remind teachers of the upcoming event and how to play and win. Distribute game bundles.

• Promote the upcoming event through daily teasers on student announcements.

• The day before, remind teachers and students to be sure their game board is posted in the classroom and that they are ready to play.

During the Game

• Begin drawing and calling decided number of call cards or objects every day during student announcements. Simple examples of announcements are:

    • "READ Bingo begins today! Teachers, do you have your call markers ready? Today we'll draw three bingo calls. Ready? Today, mark your Read Bingo game board with … [draw and read the letter and number from three call cards. After announcements, put an X through the calls on the call key]" or

    • "Time for READ Bingo! Today we will draw three—are you ready? Today mark your READ Bingo game board with … [draw and read the letter and number from three call cards. After announcements, put an X through the calls on the call key]."

• Once a call card or object is called, set it aside until the game has a winner.

• When there is a winner, announce it during the next announcement, stop the game, and prepare to start a new one. For example, "Congratulations to Mr. X's class—our READ Bingo winner! Teachers, please clear your Bingo game board. We will start a new game tomorrow!" Make arrangements for the students in the winning class to pick out their prize books or school supplies. Wipe clean the call key. Set the used call cards aside to ensure other calls are made, or mix them back in before starting the next game.

• The next day, start a new game with "Time for READ Bingo! Today is a new game, and we will draw four. Are you ready? Today, mark your READ Bingo game board with …" [draw and read the letter and number from four call cards. After announcements, put an X through the calls on the call key].

• Repeat until all prizes are awarded or game time has concluded. *Be sure to stop READ Bingo for the year on a winning day.*

After the Event

• Collect all the classroom game boards and plastic baggies.

• Clean up or replace game boards as needed.

• Store READ Bingo supplies for next year.

• Send thank you notes to any volunteers or donors.

• Informally survey staff and make plans and adjustments for next year.

READ Bingo!
P.M.M.S.

R (1-15)	E (16-30)	A (31-45)	D (46-60)	S (61-75)
6	19	37	49	68
15	17	41	60	66
4	23	BOOKS	47	71
11	22	34	53	70
1	27	38	57	75

Perry Meridian Middle School   Reading Madness Month   READ Bingo Card 43

Create and number READ Bingo game boards to display and use in classrooms.

READ Bingo! Call Key

R (1-15)	E (16-30)	A (31-45)	D (46-60)	S (61-75)
1	16	31	46	61
2	17	32	47	62
3	18	33	48	63
4	19	34	49	64
5	20	35	50	65
6	21	36	51	66
7	22	37	52	67
8	23	38	53	68
9	24	39	54	69
10	25	40	55	70
11	26	41	56	71
12	27	42	57	72
13	28	43	58	73
14	29	44	59	74
15	30	45	60	75

Perry Meridian Middle School   Reading Madness Month   Bingo Call Key

Hang a laminated READ Bingo call key near where the call cards are drawn to keep track of what has already been called in the game using a dry-erase marker.

READ Bingo

Teachers:

By February 6, please post your READ Bingo game board someplace prominent in your Homeroom classroom. Beginning February 9, we will begin playing READ Bingo during announcements with your Homeroom class.

SUPPLIES for your SSR classroom: READ Bingo game board, plastic baggie of call markers.

WINNING CLASSROOMS: Each student in the winning classroom will get the chance to choose a new paperback book to keep out of the Reader's Reward cart.

RULES:
- Listen carefully to announcements every day. Multiple bingo calls will be made daily.
- Gently tape the call markers (cutout stars, hearts, etc.) provided to you on your READ Bingo game board.
- Continue playing every day.
- If you think you have "Bingo," bring your READ Bingo game board to the library media center immediately.
- The first class to notify the LMC of a winning "Bingo" will win a FREE BOOK for every Homeroom student.
- Listen carefully to announcements. The school day following a "Bingo" win, *Mustang News* will announce for all Homerooms to clear the READ Bingo game board. No bingo calls will be made that day. Instead, remove all the call markers you have gently taped to your game board in preparation for a new game to begin.
- READ Bingo will be played more than once. Listen to announcements. Following each win, after you have cleared your game board of call markers, prepare to play again!

The day's calls will be e-mailed and the call key will be posted on the Production Studio's inner door for staff members to view at any time and catch any missed calls.

When all READ Bingo activities have ended, take down and return your READ Bingo game board and plastic baggie of call markers so that we can reuse them next year.

Thanks and Good Luck!

PMMS SSR/Literacy Committee   Perry Meridian Middle School   Instructional Media Center

Along with explaining how to play the game at a staff meeting, put the instructions in writing to eliminate any confusion.

Read-Off

Hearing of a similar event from another library media center inspired the creation of our version of a Read-Off. In Perry Meridian Middle School's Read-Off, we compete with home reading minutes for a month with a nearby school, between grade levels, or boys versus girls. The team-like atmosphere this builds turns reading into a social and competitive event, much like traditional sports.

In a Read-Off, students and their parents complete and turn in a home reading log for up to a month. Collectively, students try to accrue more reading minutes than the opposing team. The objective is to win the Read-Off by spending more minutes reading. The team that reports the most minutes spent reading outside of school wins.

Portions of the reading log are collected throughout the month so that a biweekly score can be publicized and the contest will stay real to the students, fresh on their minds, and maintain the competitive nature of the event. The turned-in reading logs can also be used for daily reader's reward drawings for free books, school supplies, bookstore gift cards, or bookmarks.

Cost: $–$$

Some supplies will already be on hand, such as paper for reading logs and bookmarks for reader's rewards. Costs incurred will be prizes not already kept in stock by the school, such as giveaway books or decorative pencils.

Planning Time: Three to Six Months

This event does not take much planning time or effort prior to the event, especially once the school has experience hosting it. The reason the event requires six months to plan is so that the two schools involved have time to coordinate schedules and align guidelines. Once the event begins, it does require regularly dedicated time to tally and report reading minutes to the competing schools.

Planning Involvement: One Person per School

Each school needs an event coordinator and liaison for the event. The school representatives need to be able to communicate on e-mail and by phone to plan, prepare, and exchange updates during the event and the results.

Suggested Supplies

- A partnering school (or competing grade level in the same school)
- Create: Banners or signs for tracking reading minutes, reading logs, publicity, and promotional materials
- Optional: books for reader's reward
- Technology: Microsoft Excel or comparable program for tracking results

Instructions

When seeking permission from an administrator, create a list of potential school partners in your area and months that would work best for the school library media centers' schedule. Also discuss with administration the possibility of silly or serious rewards for the winning team, which often involves the principals' willingness to do something for the good of the cause, such as "pies" in the face or being duct-taped to a wall by the winning participants.

Students need regular feedback to maintain commitment to the event. Work with the partnering school to set biweekly dates for students to turn in sections of a reading log. It could be every Tuesday and Thursday during the competition month. On those days, tally the minutes turned in by the students and report them to the other school, as they report theirs to you. Scores are immediately and regularly announced and posted to engender and maintain enthusiasm in students and staff.

Work with the partnering school to create basic, common rules for the schools to share. Begin by discussing the following.

Is it pleasure reading only, or will reading for school assignments count?

Does during-school pleasure reading time count, like sustained silent reading, "drop everything and read," or free reading class time?

To encourage honesty, do parents need to sign off on the minutes read at home?

Can the losing school's principal come to the winning school for a day and personally congratulate the winners during lunch or on student announcements?

At a staff meeting prior to the event, review reading logs, rules, purpose, and incentives. Encourage teachers to keep their own banner or sign to track the school's success. Teachers could also decide to build their own classroom competition within the contest, like boys versus girls or Mrs. D's class versus Mrs. B's class or Team M versus Team S.

When tallying reading minutes, there are issues to consider. Each school's student population may be different and require a balance. Use a formula to equalize the population. For example, if School A's student population is 1,188 and the competitor's population is 1,053; the minutes of School A could be multiplied by .89 to level the discrepancies in population. In this scenario, the competitor's minutes would be turned in exactly as they are counted. If School A students read 14,230 minutes during that same time, those minutes would actually be reported as 12,667. If staff is included in the contest, use a similar equalizing formula.

Create reading logs for the month with tear-off sections for students to turn in pieces at a time. Encourage honest reporting by including a place on the log for parents to vouch for time spent reading at home with a parent signature or initials. To reduce frustration for students, parents, and staff, create multiple reading logs for the month; therefore, once all the tear-off slips from one reading log are turned in, another reading log will be distributed. If using the turned-in reading log slips during the event for prize drawings, keep a list of who has won so that there are no repeat winners and more students receive reader's rewards. In advance, decide how many students will be drawn every day, and if possible, break it down by grade level. This will ensure all grade levels are included and all students and teachers feel a part of something. For example, draw two students from each grade level every day. Drawings should also be from the current reading log slips, so once a new set of slips have been collected, set the old ones aside.

Preplanning

- Gain permission to host event from administration.

- Contact the first school on the list seeking a partnering Read-Off school. Continue this effort until a school is found.

- Select a month acceptable for both schools. Place event on school calendars.

Three to Six Months Before

- Collaborate with participating school to agree on common rules for the competing schools to share.

- Choose days of the week acceptable for both schools' schedules to collect reading log slips. Twice a week is preferable to keep the event's momentum.

- Create reading logs with tear-off sections. Competing schools do not need to use the exact same format for reading logs, but the turn-in dates need to be the same.

- E-mail information out to staff to keep them informed.

Six Weeks Before

- Get a list of all homeroom names, room numbers, and class sizes. Add one extra number to each class size.

- Make enough copies of each reading log for each class, plus extras to set out in the main office and library media center.

- Sort reading logs for future classroom distribution.

- E-mail reminder to staff of the event details.

One to Three Weeks Before

- Share event final details with staff through e-mail and a brief presentation at a staff meeting.

- Post a pdf of the reading logs on the school Web site for parents.

- Share information with parents in the student newsletter. If space is available, include a copy of the reading log in the newsletter.

One to Seven Days Before

- Promote the event to students during announcements.

- Distribute first set of reading logs to homerooms with instructions.

During the Event

- Keep communication open with the other school.

- Promote the event on student announcements. Announce daily reading log winners.

- Collect reading logs from classes on appropriate days.

- Update students on the competition status after every reading log slip turn-in day. Update the reading minutes counting banners or signs in the public areas.

- Distribute new reading logs to classes the day prior to distribution.

After the Event

- Announce the winning school. Have the losing school address the winning school's population to congratulate them.

- Conclude with culminating events, as planned, and a brief concluding article in the student newsletter.

- Review with students and staff and make adjustments for next year.

- Send thank you notes to partnering school's event coordinator and principal.

Perry vs. Southport Reading Log

Homeroom Teachers:

Beginning February 1, PMMS will participate in a reading challenge with SMS. Our students will be challenged and encouraged to spend time reading outside of school for recreation, log the minutes spent on our "Perry vs. Southport Reading Log," and get the minutes signed by their parent/guardian. Have them turn a portion of the log in to you every Tuesday and Thursday.

The library media center will send student assistants around after Homeroom to collect the reading logs from you every Tuesday and Thursday. The Literacy Committee will tabulate our reading minutes and post updates in the cafeteria and on *Mustang News* of our minutes read versus minutes read by SMS.

At the end of the month, the losing school's principal's punishment will be to wear the winning school's colors and spirit wear and spend student lunch periods at the winning school's cafeteria with that school's students on Read Across America Day.

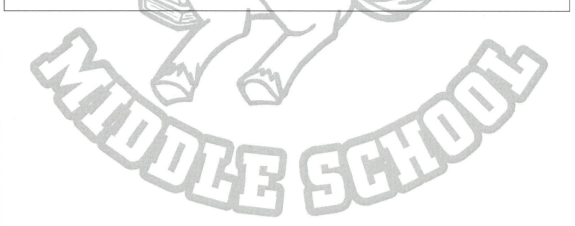

- Please pass out the attached reading logs on **February 1** to your Homeroom students. Explain to them what the reading challenge is and how to fill out the reading log.
- Encourage your students to bring their log to Homeroom every day so that they do not forget to turn it in for their minutes to count.
- Listen to announcements for reminders. We will make an announcement every Tuesday and Thursday on *Mustang News* to remind you to collect reading logs during Homeroom.
- Cut or tear along the dotted line of the reading log to collect only the completed section due that day. Students should keep the rest and continue to participate.
- You will receive new Perry versus Southport Reading Log sheets to pass out to students on **February 12** and **February 21.**
- The final day to collect reading logs will be February 28.
- Extra copies of the Perry versus Southport Reading Logs will be available in the library media center (for students who misplace their reading log).

PMMS SSR/Literacy Committee   Perry Meridian Middle School   Instructional Media Center

Create reading logs with tear-off sections to be turned in on tally days.

Perry vs. Southport Reading Log

*(Remember: only count minutes spent reading **outside of the school day**.)*

Name: _____ Teacher: _____ Period/Block: <u>Advisory</u>

(please print first and last name)

Date	Title of Book	Pages Read	Minutes spent Reading (circle one)	Guardian Initials
Example:	*Harry Potter and the Deathly Hallows*	*Pgs 22–35*	10 20 ③0 40 50 60 80 90 100 110 120	*JCB*
2-1-08 Friday			10 20 30 40 50 60 80 90 100 110 120	
2-2-08 Saturday			10 20 30 40 50 60 80 90 100 110 120	
2-3-08 Sunday			10 20 30 40 50 60 80 90 100 110 120	
2-4-08 Monday			10 20 30 40 50 60 80 90 100 110 120	

Total Minutes Read

Cut along dotted line and turn the reading log in to your SSR advisory teacher.

- -

*(Remember: only count minutes spent reading **outside of the school day**.)*

Name: _____ Teacher: _____ Period/Block: <u>Advisory</u>

(please print first and last name)

Date	Title of Book	Pages Read	Minutes spent Reading (circle one)	Guardian Initials
Example:	*Harry Potter & the Deathly Hallows*	*Pgs 22–35*	10 ②0 30 40 50 60 80 90 100 110 120	*JCB*
2-5-08 Tuesday			10 20 30 40 50 60 80 90 100 110 120	
2-6-08 Wednesday			10 20 30 40 50 60 80 90 100 110 120	

Total Minutes Read

Cut along dotted line & turn the reading log in to your SSR Advisory teacher.

- -

*(Remember - only count minutes spent reading **outside of the school day**)*

Name: _____ Teacher: _____ Period/Block: <u>Advisory</u>

(please print first and last name)

Date	Title of Book	Pages Read	Minutes spent Reading (circle one)	Guardian Initials
Example:	*Harry Potter and the Deathly Hallows*	*Pgs 22–35*	10 20 ③0 40 50 60 80 90 100 110 120	*JCB*
2-7-08 Thursday			10 20 30 40 50 60 80 90 100 110 120	
2-8-08 Friday			10 20 30 40 50 60 80 90 100 110 120	
2-9-08 Saturday			10 20 30 40 50 60 80 90 100 110 120	
2-10-08 Sunday			10 20 30 40 50 60 80 90 100 110 120	
2-11-08 Monday			10 20 30 40 50 60 80 90 100 110 120	

Total Minutes Read

PMMS SSR/Literacy Committee   Perry Meridian Middle School   Instructional Media Center

Create reading logs with tear-off sections to be turned in on tally days. (*Cont.*)

From *Social Readers: Promoting Reading in the 21st Century* by Leslie B. Preddy. Santa Barbara, CA: Libraries Unlimited. Copyright © 2010.

Sample Read-Off Student Announcements:

Day 1:

Today you should receive a blue Reading Log from your homeroom teacher. Take your log home for the weekend and begin logging personal minutes spent reading when not in school. Be sure to bring your Reading Log to HOMEROOM every day because twice a week we will collect the logs. We will count up our minutes and compare them to Southport Middle, so be sure to help us crush the Cougars by beating them in a landslide! And every time you turn in a section of your reading log, it will go in a drawing. We will draw daily for Reader's Reward winners, so listen to announcements to see if your name is called.

Sample Monday:

Do you have your PMMS versus SMS Reading Log? Did you log a lot of minutes this weekend? Hopefully you did, because the Mustangs want to beat those Cougars! Be sure to bring in your Reading Log Tuesday. Tuesday we will collect a portion of your reading log, so be sure to bring your Reading Log to HOMEROOM tomorrow. Remember, the Mustangs don't want to just beat the Cougars reading minutes, we want to blow them away!

Sample Monday/Wednesday afternoon announcement:

Perry Mustang versus Southport Cougar home reading logs will be turned in tomorrow during homeroom. Be sure to bring your reading log to homeroom tomorrow so every minute counts!

Sample Tuesday/Thursday:

Do you have your PMMS versus SMS Reading Log? Hopefully you do, because it's time to turn in a section of your reading log. Get out your reading log, fold & tear along the dashed line, then turn it in to your HOMEROOM teacher. Listen to tomorrow's announcements – when we'll tell you how our Mustang minutes compare to the Southport Cougars. Remember, keep filling out your reading log and bring it to HOMEROOM every day. We will collect the next section of your log in a few days, so keep reading! If you've lost your log, stop by the LMC to pick up a new copy. Help us beat Southport!

Sample Wednesday/Friday:

The mighty Perry Mustangs and the Southport Cougars have counted their minutes! So, how are we doing? The Mighty Mustangs have logged _____ minutes and the Southport Cougars have logged _____ minutes. Keep filling out those Reading Logs & help us stampede past the Southport Cougars and leave them in our dust! We will collect the next section of your log _____, so keep reading! If you've lost your log, stop by the LMC to pick up a new copy. Help us beat Southport!

Use building-wide announcements as an opportunity to promote and remind.

Did you turn in your Reading Log yesterday? We put all the turned in Reading Logs in a drawing and today's winners are:

1. _____

2. _____

3. _____

4. _____

Sample on days when new reading log is passed out:

Do you have your PMMS versus SMS Reading Log? Hopefully you do, because it's time to turn in the final section of your blue Reading Log. Get out your reading log and turn it in to your HOMEROOM teacher. Keep an eye on the thermometer in the cafeteria and listen to tomorrow's announcements when we'll tell you how our Mustang minutes compare to the Southport Cougars'. Remember, keep filling out your reading log and bring it to HOMEROOM every day. We will collect the next section of your log in a few days, so keep reading! Help us destroy Southport!

Today's participating Reading Log winners are:

1. _____

2. _____

3. _____

4. _____

Sample to motivate students:

Oh, no! The mighty Mustangs have fallen behind! The Southport Cougars just passed the Perry Mustangs' reading minutes. For the first time this month, Southport has taken the lead. The Mustangs have logged _____ minutes and the Southport Cougars have logged _____ minutes. Keep filling out those Reading Logs & help us regain our lead against Southport! WE CAN'T LET THEM WIN! We will collect the next section of your log tomorrow, so keep reading! If you've lost your log, stop by the LMC to pick up a new copy. Help us beat Southport!

Today's Reading Log winners are:

1. _____

2. _____

3. _____

4. _____

Use building-wide announcements as an opportunity to promote and remind. (*Cont.*)

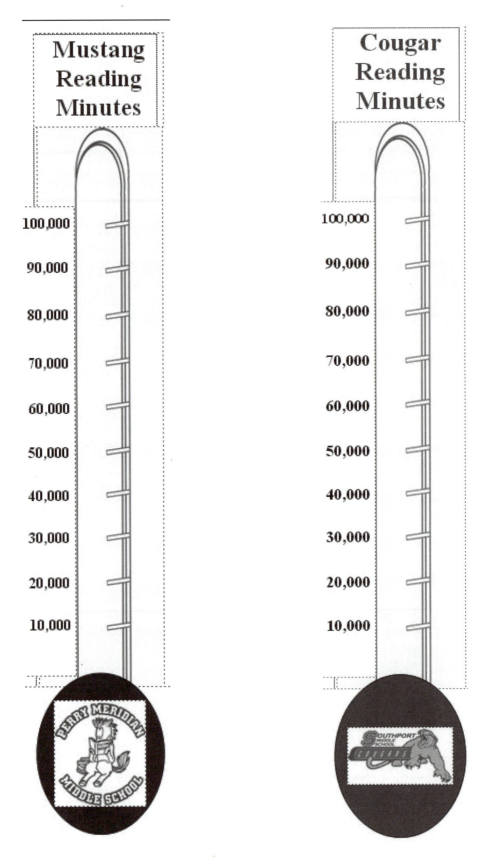

Develop ways to display the school's progress.

From *Social Readers: Promoting Reading in the 21st Century* by Leslie B. Preddy.
Santa Barbara, CA: Libraries Unlimited. Copyright © 2010.

Perry Township Middle School Read-Off

Reading Madness Month 2008

Log Due Date	PMMS REAL Reading Minutes	Reading Minutes		total
		PMMS	**SMS**	
Tuesday, 2-5-08	13,710	**12,202**	**10,720**	22,922
Thursday, 2-7-08	14,015	**12,473**	**9,190**	21,663
Tuesday, 2-12-08	14,230	**12,667**	**12,570**	25,237
Thursday, 2-14-08	11,370	**10,119**	**8,605**	18,724
Tuesday, 2-19-08	8,425	**7,498**	**14,905**	22,403
Thursday, 2-21-08	9,605	**8,548**	**7,570**	16,118
Tuesday, 2-26-08	19,020	**16,928**	**18,740**	35,668
Friday, 2-29-08	28,185	**25,085**	**22,130**	22,130
TOTAL	118,560	**105,520**	**104,430**	184,865

Pop.:1188   Pop.: 1053

PMMS Reading Minutes re-calculated by x.89 due to increased population

Use a spreadsheet to keep an ongoing tally of reading minutes. A school could also keep track of the number of reading logs turned in and students drawn for reader's reward. Note that the schools' populations are also listed on the spreadsheet.

From *Social Readers: Promoting Reading in the 21st Century* by Leslie B. Preddy.
Santa Barbara, CA: Libraries Unlimited. Copyright © 2010.

READ Ribbon Week

During READ Ribbon Week, students pledge to read on a regular basis. Students agree that reading is important, should be included in a well-rounded lifestyle, and make a promise to themselves to find time regularly to read for personal interest and pleasure. READ Ribbon Week is a social event that involves everyone. The whole school community, including parents and staff, is encouraged to commit to reading and celebrate their commitment with a public banner of signed READ ribbons running throughout the school.

Cost: $

READ Ribbon Week should be possible with materials most school already have in stock, such as colored paper and tape.

Planning Time: One and a Half Months

It may require more time than one month to plan ahead and schedule the event onto the school's calendar, but beyond scheduling, the event takes one month or less to prepare and one week to run.

Planning Involvement: One or More People

This event does not require a lot of people to prepare, but if the school has a literacy committee, use it to develop the guidelines or instructions. Teacher teamwork is required to make any schoolwide event successful, and classroom support will be needed to work with students. Student or parent volunteers could be used to help hang signed READ Ribbons around the school.

Suggested Supplies

- Craft supplies: colored paper, tape

- Create: READ ribbon template and publicity and promotional materials

Instructions

During READ Ribbon week students are voluntarily making a conscious commitment to regularly dedicate time to pleasure reading. Once the student makes that commitment, she signs a READ Ribbon to seal her commitment. Student or parent volunteers then tape or staple the ribbons along the designated walls of the school. Choose a high-traffic, public wall, like the main entry or cafeteria, to showcase the line of ribbons.

Consider how and when students will sign the commitment ribbon. Will it be during lunch or recess? Will it be during homeroom? Deciding when the ribbons will be signed will adjust how the event is promoted and run. For example, if it is done during homeroom, homeroom teachers are very involved in its success. If it is promoted during lunch, student, teacher, or parent volunteers will be needed to run a signing table or to move among the cafeteria tables to sign up groups of students.

Preplanning

- Meet with administration to set a date (week), decide on a location to display signed ribbons, and discuss guidelines and instructions.

- Meet with the literacy committee to discuss the event and create a plan.

- Set the date on your school calendar and e-mail staff members to gain their support for the upcoming event.

One Month Before

- Create ribbons with a word processing or desktop publishing program. Make copies and cut the estimated number of ribbons needed.

- Finalize school procedures. Share procedures with every teacher by e-mail and briefly during a staff meeting.

- Solicit for volunteers as needed to help during READ Ribbon Week. Create volunteer instructions.

One to Seven Days Before

- Promote the event during student announcements and through the student newsletter. Include a copy of the ribbon in the student newsletter for family members to sign and return.

- Call or e-mail volunteers to remind them of their commitment and share the instructions so they are prepared for what is expected of them.

- Create a sign and leave extra copies of the READ ribbon to display in the main office where visitors are greeted, making them aware and encouraging visitors to participate.

Week of the Event

- Distribute ribbons as outlined in procedures. Make more copies of ribbons as needed.

- Collect signed ribbons every day, count them, and temporarily adhere them in a row along the wall.

- Create a daily announcement sharing the number of ribbons received that day and the total number collected by the school thus far.

After the Event

- Dismantle the office display.

- Get feedback from volunteers and teachers to make future improvements.

- Send thank you notes to any volunteers.

- Thank families for participating and share the results in the student newsletter.

- After a few weeks, remove the banner of ribbons from the school walls.

READ
Ribbon Week

_____
Sign Here

I Make a Reading Difference!

READ
Ribbon Week

_____
Sign Here

I Make a Reading Difference!

READ
Ribbon Week

_____
Sign Here

I Make a Reading Difference!

Design a ribbon for READ Ribbon Week, fitting three to four per sheet.

Reader's Café

Students often enjoy hanging out before school. They also love the coffeehouse and juice-bar experience. Blend the opportunity this provides with the library media center and reading. Schedule and promote special early hours for the library media center, inviting students to attend and discuss books they are currently reading. Provide decaffeinated hot and cold breakfast beverages and small, nonsticky breakfast foods to round out the café experience.

Planning Time: One Month

Initially, it will take time to organize this event, but after initial setup, the ongoing maintenance is simple, with little time required. To start, begin working up to a year in advance to gain permission and startup funding.

Planning Involvement: One or More People

It only takes one person to create and run the Reader's Café, but more people might be required to volunteer and run the actual events.

Suggested Supplies

- Create: publicity and promotional materials, schedule

- Food: breakfast foods, coffee cups and coffee condiments, decaffeinated cappuccino/coffee/teas, instant cocoas, hot water, snacks

- Optional: cappuccino or coffee machine or coffee takeout

- Technology: microwave and small refrigerator

Instructions

For the Reader's Café, the library media center opens early a certain day or days of the week, welcoming students with breakfast beverages and a space to chat, read, or do homework. The best solution for everyone is to have the Reader's Café open a particular day or days of the week. This could be every Friday that school is in session. With the Reader's Café, the hope is that students will find the library media center a warm and welcoming environment to grow accustomed to and utilize more.

Running the café requires startup money or donations. First, decide whether to buy actual cappuccino and coffee machines, to use instant packets and a microwave, or get take-away from a local store. Also provide breakfast snacks. Donations or sponsors might be willing to contribute condiments and beverages. E-mailing staff or posting a request in the student newsletter to parents may unearth a microwave, coffee makers, and other contributions. If it is permissible, charge a small fee or request donations for drinks and snacks, just enough to break even and buy more for the next event. If all this is not possible, the Reader's Café could be opened with a "bring your own beverage and breakfast" policy.

Approval from administration will also be needed to open the library media center and school facility early for students. During the meeting, discuss reasonable hours and days of operation as well as anticipated startup date, startup budget, and potential funding sources, including any needed school funds and potential grants and donations. Agree on terms for recouping ongoing coffeehouse expenses.

Most library media centers will need volunteers to work the early hours and run the Reader's Café. This could be parents, staff members, or library personnel. For each café date, be sure to have a "substitute" on call to run the café for unexpended absences or illnesses.

Possible Reader's Café enhancements include hosting special events, like poetry readings, book clubs, study sessions, and homework help groups.

Preplanning

- Meet with administration to gain permission for the event concept.

- Apply for grants and seek donations and Reader's Café sponsors.

- Seek volunteers to help during the Reader's Café or to substitute host in the event of the school librarians' absence.

- Meet with students to find out which food and drinks are popular and school appropriate. Purchase needed equipment and supplies.

One Month Before

- Create and post publicity and promotional materials.

- Create and distribute bookmarks advertising and explaining the Reader's Café.

- Place notices in the student newsletter.

- If needed, create a price list sign or donation jar.

One to Seven Days Before

- Run promotions during student announcements.

Day of the Event

- If necessary, pick up beverages from a local store.

- Set up the Reader's Café.

- Work the "coffee shop" and host.

- Survey students for future improvements.

After the Event

- Clean up and store extra supplies for the next café event.

- Send thank you notes to any volunteers and donors.

- Order replacement supplies or locate donations for the next café.

Used Book Drive

Perry Meridian Middle School's first Used Book Drive was inspired by the sudden loss of classroom teacher Cyndi Ewick, whose love of teaching, books, and reading was legendary. We wanted to do something to honor her. With the direction of a fellow educator and the student leadership group, our first Used Book Drive was created to honor Cyndi's passion for motivating readers. Initially, we collected only books for a certain age group but have expanded to promoting donations of all books, prereader through adult.

Before beginning a Used Book Drive, consider the purpose. There may be multiple simultaneous purposes: to enrich the classroom bookshelves, to expand a classroom bookshelf lending library, to add to a staff lending library, to supplement the library media center collection, and to donate to a local charity, hospital or family shelter. Recently we have promoted our book drive to supplement the school library and expand the classroom bookshelf lending library, but the majority of books collected are donated to a local nonprofit agency chosen annually by the student leadership group.

Cost: $

Hosting a Used Book Drive costs nothing but time and supplies already on hand. The only cost that might be incurred is if a competition or reader's rewards for participating students or classes are added to enrich the event.

Planning Time: Two Months

Once this event is placed on the calendar, it takes only two months to collect materials, arrange a donation partnership, and host the event.

Planning Involvement: Two Adults, Student Volunteers

The Used Book Drive can be run with one activity planner for administrative issues and one person to organize the student volunteers. The student volunteers can be a preexisting student group, such as the student council.

Suggested Supplies

- Create: basic guidelines, project timeline, publicity and promotional materials

- Optional: reader's reward prizes

- Student contribution: gently used books

- Miscellaneous: used empty paper bags or shipping boxes for each classroom and public areas

Instructions

Consider how long an effective Used Book Drive would last, usually one or two weeks. One week is suitable if the school is easy to motivate and the community close-knit. If the school is larger or takes some time to build momentum, two weeks might be more effective.

Collections can increase with some creativity. Promote special opportunities to donate during community activities, parent programs, and sport events. Reader's reward prize drawings for donations could be incorporated or a reader's reward earned for every ten (or whatever number is agreed on) books donated.

Hospitals, shelters, and other organizations may be interested in partnering with the school to receive the school's book donations for their guests. When contacting the preferred partner, explain the purpose and scope of the project and what the school is looking for in a partnership.

Preplanning

- Meet with administration to receive permission to host the event, set a date, decide whether to reward participating students, and develop a list of potential organizations to accept the donated books.

- Meet with the student organization sponsor to discuss the event and how the students can help with this service project. Work closely together to collaborate on the event and develop the guidelines and project timeline.

Two Months Before

- Begin collecting boxes. Collect enough for every classroom plus a few extra for public areas, like the main office, cafeteria, and library media center.

- Use the list of potential organizations to contact local agencies until a community partner to accept the book donations is found.

- Inform staff of the upcoming event.

Four to Six Weeks Before

- The student organization decorates or makes signs for the collection boxes.

- The student organization creates posters and signs to decorate the building.

One to Three Weeks Before

- Create and post promotional notices for the student newsletter and announcements.

- The student organization hangs signs throughout the building.

- Share the final plan with the staff, offering ideas on how to help promote it and make it a success.

One to Seven Days Before

- Student volunteers distribute boxes to classrooms and public areas.

- Promote the event during student announcements.

During the Event

- Follow agreed-on guidelines to cosponsor and monitor daily.

- Promote and give away reader's rewards as appropriate.

After the Event

- Student volunteers collect donation boxes, count the number of books donated, and deliver them to the library media center.

- School librarian reviews donations, accepting a few for the library media center, some for class-room bookshelves or the SSR Lending Library and boxing up the rest for community donation. Look carefully for books belonging to other institutions and return them to their rightful owners.

- Arrange for the student group to deliver donations to the prearranged community organization.

- Take photographs and write a press release.

- Meet with student volunteers to discuss what they liked and what they thought could be improved next time.

- Survey staff to improve ease of participation in the future.

- Send thank you to families through the student newsletter, letting them know how many items were donated and how much their efforts were appreciated.

Used Book Drive

February 9-20

Send in your used children's, young adult, and adult novels and non-fiction! Turn in your family's gently used books to Homeroom February 9-20. A portion of the books will remain at the school for the library media center and classroom bookshelves. A majority of the books collected will be donated to Riley Children's Hospital and the Indianapolis Ronald McDonald House.

Post announcements before and during the Used Book Drive in the student newsletter to get families involved.

PMMS 3rd Annual Used Book Drive

WHERE: Homeroom
START: Tuesday, February 19
END: Friday, February 29

Please tell your students to bring any gently used children's, young adult, and adult books. The books will be collected during Homeroom February 19–29. The books will be donated to our library media center, classroom bookshelves, SSR Lending Library, and the family shelter downtown.

1. Boxes are ordered and will hopefully be handed out early next week by the Student Council. If you have crates and the boxes have not come in, please use those for the time being.
2. When students turn in books, have them sign a book ticket. Turn in tickets, and names will be drawn daily during *Mustang News.*
3. Extra book tickets will be available in the library media center (e-mail Leslie, and she will send some down).
4. Student library workers or Student Council will be around to collect book tickets a couple times each week.
5. Please try to keep count of the number of books donated in your class because the class to collect the most books wins a free, new book for each student from the Reader's Reward cart.
6. Student Council will be around each Friday to collect books. If you have a lot of books and want them out before Friday, let Miss M or Ms. H know.

If any of you have questions, please let me know! Thank you in advance. This is always a great success, and I really appreciate the work teachers do in order to make this successful.

Thank you,
The Literacy Committee

Creating and informing staff members of a few simple guidelines will help keep the Used Book Drive running smoothly. If desired, include a little competition to add some fun to the event.

From *Social Readers: Promoting Reading in the 21st Century* by Leslie B. Preddy.
Santa Barbara, CA: Libraries Unlimited. Copyright © 2010.

Games

Introducing patrons to reading materials through games can add flavor and interest to book selections and discussions. Games can make what might otherwise feel tedious into socially engaging entertainment. Through games, patrons become active in the selection process, which naturally generates more commitment and interest in the process. Through games, students may share what they are reading with others, enticing them to read something, which empowers both parties. Interactive activities make it fun to try new books and sample genres never before considered.

Games can be invented, bought, or adapted and converted from an old game into a new one with a reading focus. Included is just a sampling of game ideas, transformed from childhood memories into reading promotion and motivation tools. These are just a few ideas for promoting reading with students, but don't stop here. Create others. Keep your eyes open for ideas, and think back to childhood activities and how to convert those to reading-related themes.

Book Hot Potato

The majority of people's primary selection criteria are title, familiar author, or cover art, but depending too much on these factors can be disappointing. A person may miss a lot of great reading material judging by a book's cover alone. With the Book Hot Potato game, every person in the group spends a few minutes with a book, and then when time is called, they pass the book on to the next person and spend a few minutes with the next one. Through this activity, students move beyond the cover and read the first few pages, sampling the author's writing style, the allure of the content, and the readers' interest in reading further.

Cost: $

There is no direct cost because participants will use materials already present in the library collection.

Planning Time: One Week

It should just take one week to survey reading interests, research reading levels, pull together a book collection, and run Book Hot Potato.

Planning Involvement: Two People

This will require the efforts of the library media specialist, as the expert of the library collection, and the classroom teacher, as a student authority.

Suggested Supplies

• Books: book collection pulled from library media center

• Create: survey of student interests

• Technology: class reading level report (if available), library media center circulation system

• Miscellaneous: sticky notes or scrap paper, extra pencils

Instructions

Often it is difficult and overwhelming for students who are inexperienced with the library media center or who have had unsuccessful past experiences there to enter and find something to read. The vastness of hundreds of books to choose from may seem insurmountable and overwhelming. The student has so much to choose from, it's difficult to focus, and no choice is made. For this reason, consider sharing in the classroom and use remote circulation with paper and pencil or through whatever electronic tools the school's library automation system has available. For struggling or apathetic readers, the comfort of the classroom may be the place to start before moving on to the library media center.

Book Hot Potato narrows down the choices by pulling together a sample, smaller collection for the students to review. In advance, pull together a collection twice the size of the class based on a curricular topic, student survey, or select reading list, such as the state student choice nominees. If trying to help students make book choices for pleasure reading, it may be best to start with a survey. If students are making book choices for assigned reading or personal reading related to curriculum, pull a collection based on the curricular topic.

Include instructional time prior to the event to survey students' interests. Decide whether to use a student survey, when to pass out the survey, and whether to do a written survey or have a verbal discussion. If using a survey, co-create the survey questions and create a written or online survey for students to complete. Surveying students can be done with an online survey tool, paper and pencil, or by coteaching a discussion in the classroom. Which will work best for the students depends on the personality of the classroom teacher and the classroom culture.

Preplanning

- Meet with the classroom teacher to schedule Book Hot Potato into the instructional day, including an advance date for the survey.

One to Seven Days Before

- Survey students' personal interests.

- Based on survey results, pull together a sampling of books approximately double the size of the class. Option: include duplicate copies of titles that may be especially popular.

- If going to the classroom, collect materials necessary for remote checkout.

Game Play

- Before the students arrive, place one book and one sticky note at each seat.

- Once students arrive, explain the book sampling, which is like a food tasting or watching the previews at the theatre. They will try out different books for just a few minutes before passing the book to another.

- As a group, discuss and go through the exercise of basic book selection. Have students use the book at their desks to look at cover art, read the title, and wonder what it might mean. Help students continue by reading the author's name and figuring out whether they have read other books by the author and skimming the back cover or inside front flap for the publisher's summary or tease of the book.

- Discuss how to play Book Hot Potato. Students open the book to the first chapter and read for a few minutes, until time is called. Once time is called, if she liked what she read, write the title and author on the sticky note. When told, pass the book to the next person and take a new book from the person behind her, repeating the process until time is up.

- Have everyone open to the first chapter, read the chapter title if there is one, then call time to read. Everyone reads quietly until time is called. Both educators should circulate around the room.

- After a few minutes, call "time's up," have students write on sticky note if desired, pass the book forward, and take the new book passed to them. Repeat the basic book selection and silent reading until time is up.

- If students have in their possession the book they want to keep, they do nothing. If there is another book that interested them, see if it's still available. If they didn't sample all the books, they may go to the cart to preview more as time allows.

- Allow enough time for checkout. Allow other students to help peers. Stage one educator at the cart helping students struggling to choose a book. The other educator should work circulation and check out books to students.

- Once students are checked out, each returns to his or her seat and continues reading until time is called.

After the Game

- Educators review what worked and didn't work, making notes for future adjustments.

- Return any unused books to the library media center shelves.

- If necessary, download or hand enter student checkouts into the library automation system.

Book Hot Potato
Student Survey Questions to Consider

- What games do you like to play?
- What do you like to do in your free time?
- What are your hobbies and interests?
- What sports do you like to watch or play?
- What TV shows and movies do you like to watch?
- What is your favorite subject in school?
- What do you like to do with family and friends?
- What is the name of your favorite book? Who wrote it?
- What authors have you read before and liked?
- What book genre have you read before and enjoyed?

Adapted from: Preddy, Leslie. *SSR with Intervention: A School Library Action Research Project.* Westport, CT: Libraries Unlimited, 2007.

When surveying students, questions to consider should relate to past reading experiences and personal interests.

Fiction Board Games

Discussing books can be enjoyable for students and more like a game. Students want to be able to read whatever they want and yet need to be able to talk intelligently about the books they read. Students need to be able to share what they are reading, while they are reading it, and students need an outlet for discussing what they have just finished reading. Students should hear about what others were reading and be inspired to read it as well. Consider creating fiction board games. Throughout all the games, the rules are the same, and articulating details about the book and sharing reading is the focus.

Cost: $$

There are startup costs to creating the game boards, including supplies that the school may not keep on hand, but with some creativity, those costs can be diminished. For example, instead of buying perforated business card sheets for the color printer, use card stock printed without color and cut to size. Request donations from staff and parents for used dice and game pawns.

Planning Time: One Month

Each game board will take approximately one month to create and publish; fitting some time into the activity planner's schedule every day to design the game boards on the computer. Comprehension game cards will also be created on the computer, but once those are created, the same file will be used to print cards for every game board created. Give extra time to create the comprehension game cards if custom developing discussion prompts instead of adapting or using preexisting prompts. Game play takes twenty-five to forty-five minutes.

Planning Involvement: One or More People

Game boards can be created by one person, but if there are more people to share the work developing game boards on the computer, a wider variety of game boards can be created in a shorter period of time.

Suggested Supplies

- Create: comprehension game cards (using business-card printer sheets), game boards (using desktop publishing programs and color printer or poster printer machine)

- Equipment and supplies: business card printer sheets or card stock

- Student contribution: library or personal copy of a book

- Technology: color printer or poster printer machine, lamination machine

Miscellaneous: One game die per game board, six game pawns per game board, copy of *SSR with Intervention* or other source of generic reading prompts

Instructions

Fiction board games are a way for students to read what they want, share what they've read, and get recommended reads from fellow students. For the games to be free-choice reading, game cards for playing need to be created with generic reading comprehension questions. Questions should be generic enough to be answered with any book, as long as it is material with a plot. Material with a plot could be fiction, biography, narrative nonfiction, short stories, graphic novels, and so on. These questions could be created by meeting as a group of educators to collect and brainstorm questions or by searching online and text resources. It is easy to adapt writing prompts created for a reading program for game play, which are available in the book *SSR with Intervention* (L. B. Preddy, Libraries Unlimited, 2007). Using this book, more than 250 comprehension game cards can be created for each kit, which gives a wide enough range of questions to keep the game fresh for many student plays. Examples of game questions are the following:

- Describe why you would not want to live in the setting.

- Who is the most interesting character in the book and why?

- What lessons did this book teach you about life?

- What surprised you in this story? Explain why.

- Why do you think the author chose this title?

- What words did the author use to help create a picture in your mind?

- What is your favorite part of the book? Why?

- After reading, I wondered …

Kids like variety, so although each game created has the same basic rules, each game kit can include six different game boards and more than 250 comprehension game cards to divide among the six game boards. Having multiple game boards allows for a variety of games and five to six students per game. A kit of six game boards can accommodate parties, events, and clubs as well as most class sizes. As games are created, arrange with a class or a library club to test game boards and offer feedback to improve as the game boards are being completed.

Use a desktop publishing program to create game boards. When first setting up the file, consider how the game will be published. If using a poster printer to create a game board, the file may use a simple 8½ × 11 design. If using a color printer, the file may need to be custom sized to a larger size, like a nine-sheet poster, which can be printed, then cut and taped together.

Game pawns, or game pieces, and dice may be purchased inexpensively, made, or donated. For donations, e-mail staff or place a notice in the student newsletter requesting donations of used and unwanted game pieces and dice. If the game pieces or dice are collected through donation, write thank you notes to the contributors. Game pieces could also be created by cutting shapes out of colored card stock or construction paper using craft punches or scissors. The local dollar store is also a good place to pick up little trinkets, erasers, or other small objects to use for game pieces.

Preplanning

- Preview game boards and think of enjoyable games from your childhood. Use these memories for inspiration to create original game boards on the computer.

- Collect game pawns or pieces.

- Develop game rules.

One Month Before

- With a word processing program, use the labels template to layout the page for printing comprehension game cards on business card printer sheets. Fill in one question per card, usually about ten per printer sheet.

- If desired, create a separate file, using the same template to fill each label or space with a logo for the back side of the comprehension game cards.

- Print the comprehension game cards. If the logo is desired, run the back side of the game cards through the printer to print the logo on the reverse side. Cut out individual cards.

- With paper and pencil, draft each game board layout.

- Using a computer's desktop publishing program, such as Microsoft Publisher, create game boards. Include space on the game board to include rules and guidelines.

- Publish by printing with a poster machine or color printer.

- Laminate cards and posters for durability.

Game Play

- Students bring the book they are currently reading or have just finished to the activity.

- Divide students into groups of five or six.

- Assign each group a game board and game pieces, and divide the comprehension game cards among groups.

- Review with the students the general rules, then give each student a chance to share the book with his or her group.

- Following the brief sharing time, students read instructions for their game board and begin play.

- Circulate among students as they play the game.

After the Game

- Have students use scraps of paper or sticky notes to write down what they liked and didn't like about the game. Consider possible revisions based on student feedback.

- Collect game kits and store game boards, comprehension game cards, and game pieces until next use.

Rules of the Game:

1. Draw a READ card and answer the question correctly and completely. If the other players agree that you answered thoroughly, roll the dice and move your game piece.
2. If you land on a yellow square, follow the instructions.
3. If you land on an occupied square, you must go back 6 spaces.
4. If you catch another player talking about something not related to his or her book, you move ahead 2 spaces.
5. The first player to reach the end **wins.**

The instructions for playing each game should have core similarities. Customize to each individual game as needed.

Before you begin:

1. Discuss with your group the title, author, and material you read.
2. Show everyone your book.
3. Each player rolls the dice. The player with the highest number goes first.
4. Each player must roll a **3 or less** to **start** the game.
5. Read *Rules of the Game,* then begin playing.

Create general rules to kick off every game.

From *Social Readers: Promoting Reading in the 21st Century* by Leslie B. Preddy. Santa Barbara, CA: Libraries Unlimited. Copyright © 2010.

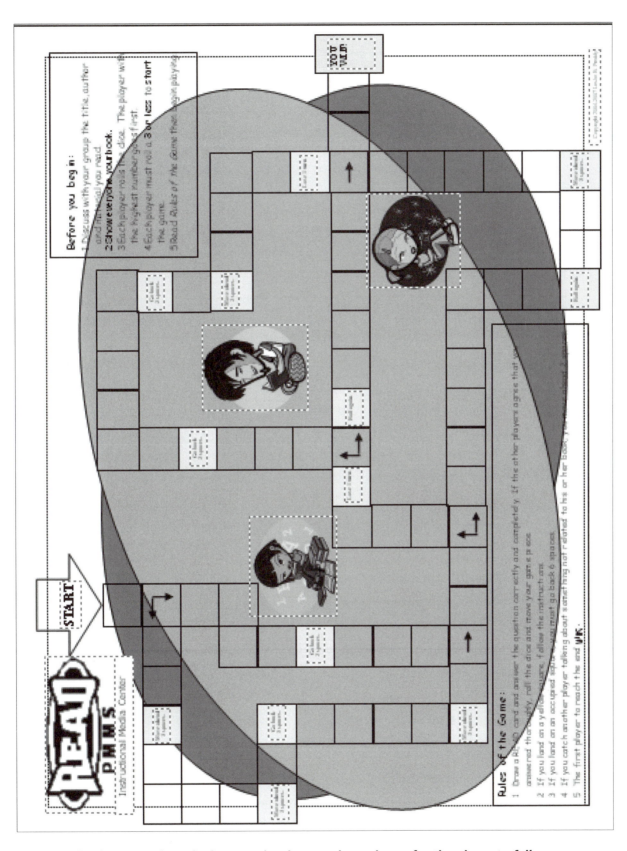

Design game boards that are simple to make and easy for the player to follow.

Library Graffiti

Kids love to pass notes. They love to doodle. They scribble on anything available: notebooks, text-books, agendas, tables. Combine their desire to write notes to each other and doodle on the library tables into something constructive. Offer opportunities to create library graffiti. The completed graffiti can then be placed on display in the library. People love seeing their own writing on the wall and what others wrote.

Cost: $

This simple game can be made possible with supplies already available in most schools.

Planning Time: One Day

One thing that's great about Library Graffiti is the simple setup and the lack of preparation required.

Planning Involvement: One Person

One person can throw this game together quickly.

Suggested Supplies

- Craft supplies: butcher block paper, newsprint paper or strips of bulletin board paper cut to table length, and markers, crayons, colored pencils, or window paint pens
- Create: basic guidelines

Instructions

Library Graffiti is a simple way to throw together a fun activity. It doesn't require much time, money, or preplanning to set up or participate. Set up one station for every six to eight students, so there are enough students in each group for productive book sharing while decorating without so many in a group to be distracting.

Create student guidelines such as the following to include on each table for the book being described to the group and artistically represented in the graffiti.

- Include title, author, and call number.
- Take turns telling the others in your group what was best about the book.
- Draw a key symbol from the story or something to attract others to read the story.
- Only use school-appropriate language and no gang symbols.
- Include a quote, the book's genre, or key words to represent your book.
- Sign with your first name only.

One Day Before

- Create and print guideline sheets.
- Locate butcher paper, newsprint, or bulletin board paper and markers, crayons, colored pencils, or window paint pens for each graffiti station.

Game Play

- Lay paper out on each table (unless using library windows and window paint).
- Place a box of markers, crayons, or colored pencils on top of the paper.

- Optional: write a design in the center of the paper, including words such as "Read This" or "I'm reading…." Include the basic guidelines sheet on each table.

- Once students arrive, divide them into groups of six to eight per station.

- Review the guidelines with students, then circulate among groups during play, encouraging or getting involved as needed.

- Supervise play, discussions, and artwork.

After the Game

- Hang graffiti throughout the school, office, or library media center.

- Store extra supplies for future use.

Memory Game

Remember playing the Memory Game as a child or watching reruns of *Concentration* on the Game Show Network, which was based on the children's memory game? My daughter loves to play the memory game. She even has more than one game, although they are essentially the same, just different pictures: movie theme, traditional, princess, cultures. This phenomenon and interest works for books and book-related themes. Memory Games on many book themes are possible, like a particular genre or promoting the state's current student choice nominees, for example. Students play the game together, then often request the books and genres spotlighted in the game.

The Memory Game is a game of cards. There are five to twenty-five pairs of cards in a deck. In the game, cards are shuffled then laid out facedown. Players alternate turning over two cards per turn. If the player does not make a match, the cards are turned facedown again, and the next player gets a try. Players try to remember what has been turned over and where those cards are so they can make a match. If a player makes a match, the player takes those cards. The player with the most pairs at the end of the game wins.

Cost: $$

Most schools do not have perforated business card printer sheets for the computer printer, so these will need to be budgeted. Cost can be reduced by using card stock instead of business sheets, then taking the time to cut out the individual cards after printing.

Planning Time: Two to Four Weeks

Fitting some time each day into the concept, development, and publishing of each Memory Game will take about two to four weeks, depending on the size of the game and the amount of time able to set aside each week. Game play takes 10 to 20 minutes.

Planning Involvement: One or More People

It requires only one person to create a game, but if more people want to be involved, more games can be created in less time.

Suggested Supplies

- Create: game cards

- Equipment and supplies: business card printer sheets and color printer or photocopier, scanned images of book covers, digital photos, clip art

Instructions

Think about creating a Memory Game of genres, books of a certain genre, books by an author coming to visit, books on the state's student choice book award nominee list, or books by a certain author, new books, concepts from a particular book or series, or any other set of interests. Use the game as a socially engaging way to introduce books and book-related themes. The possibilities are endless. By adapting this game to a reading theme, students have fun, practice memory skills, and are exposed to books and to possible reading material. Memory Games can be used for enrichment in the classroom, entertainment in the library media center, or an activity for a book club event.

Include an image and related text on each card pair. The images could include book covers, clip art, or digital photos taken by staff or students. The text under or above the image is the book title, author's name, call number, genre, or other headings based on the game's reading theme.

Preplanning

- Create a list of possible Memory Game themes.

- Informally survey teachers and students to find out which themes they would prefer created first.

Two to Four Weeks Before

- Decide how many card sets are appropriate for the students' grade level: five to twenty-five pairs.

- Based on the game's theme, create a list of card pairs.

- With a word processing program, use the labels template to lay out the page for printing the game cards on business card sheets.

- Create two identical cards for each card topic, approximately five sets per printed sheet. Include the same graphic and text for the pair. Repeat until all card pairs on the list are created.

- If desired, create a separate file using the business card template to print an identical logo on the back side of each game card. The logo should be identical on every card.

- Print the game cards. If the logo is desired, run the back side of the game cards through the printer to print the logo on the reverse side. Make enough game sets for your student group, considering two to six players per set.

- Laminate individual cards, if desired, for repeated use.

Game Play

- Divide students into groups of two to six. Give each group a Memory Game card set.

- Have students lay the facedown cards in rows, and remind students how to play the game.

- Circulate among groups while students play the game.

- Allow students time to check out books related to the Memory Game theme.

After the Game

- Make note of how long it took students to complete a game and how many card pairs were used. Adjust how many card sets should be in a game based on the student play experience and how much time is available for playing the game in the future.

- Collect Memory Games and store for future use.

Chapter 2

Active Participation

A key component to engaging a new generation of readers is active participation. Students need to be involved. They need to feel that they matter. This can be achieved by helping others make reading choices. Offer the school population activities intended to get reading on their minds. Imagine a variety of unique ways to actively involve students in recommending reading to others. Engage students in developing bookmarks, sharing reading experiences, and social networking. This chapter provides ideas to encourage students to share their love of reading with friends and peers by showcasing their artistic talents: reading, writing, and creativity.

Informed and Involved

Homemade bookmarks are inexpensive and simple to make, usually requiring nothing more than colored card stock and a photocopier. Prepackaged, mass-produced bookmarks can be purchased, and there is a time and place for that, but not everything needs to be factory-produced. Involve students in contests and content area connections to create interesting bookmarks that engage both the creator and user. Custom bookmarks—made at the school, for the school—can be created to be shared with staff, students, and families.

Every bookmark concept suggested in this section has some similarities in cost, planning time, planning involvement, and supplies. Consider the selected size of the bookmark and how many will fit on a page. Design a bookmark template accordingly, with multiple copies distributed evenly across the page.

Cost: $

Bookmarks cost next to nothing to create, other than the cost of card stock or colored paper, which the school may already have on hand. If card stock or colored paper is not desired, there is no expense. When purchasing colored paper or card stock, consider the number of bookmarks needed and how many will fit on a page—usually two to five bookmarks, depending on the size and layout.

Additional cost is optional. Rewards for participating or winning with the gift of a free book to add to the students' home bookshelf can add to costs. Rewarding participation with a book, students receive a prize that continues to encourage reading.

Planning Time: One Month

One month is usually plenty of time to develop a bookmark, even if creating the task requires taking the time to read a particular book.

Planning Involvement: One or More People

Each bookmark project can be done with just one person managing it, but consider partnering with groups, clubs, classes, departments, or teams.

Suggested Supplies

- Create: basic guidelines, bookmark

- Equipment and supplies: colored card stock or paper, scissors or a straight-edge cutting tool

- Optional: colored pencils or crayons, reader's reward prizes

- Technology: word processing or desktop publishing program (e.g., Microsoft Publisher or Microsoft Word)

Anticipation Bookmark

The anticipation bookmark is an adaptation of the anticipation guide, which was developed by Readence, Bean, and Baldwin (2004). Anticipation guides contain a set of true or false statements, often related to moral or ethical values, relating self to text or world to text. The reader responds to the statement before reading the book and then revisits the statement after reading to see whether the reading changed the reader's opinion or knowledge. Prior to reading, students respond to yes/no or agree/disagree statements about the topic or novel. Students use their experiences and background knowledge to make predictions and ask questions. After reading the text, they revisit the statements and revise opinions, meaning, and misconceptions on the basis of what was read. It is a way for students to build a purpose for reading and become immersed in the story and understand it on a personal level before even opening the book.

Instructions

Anticipation bookmarks may be used as a preparatory and post-reading activity. They usually include five to seven thought-provoking statements to respond to before reading. Students make guesses about the content of what they will read based on the anticipation statements. Upon completing the reading, the students use their bookmarks again as a post-reading strategy. This idea can be implemented in a class, a club, or with individual students as an enrichment to a preexisting project. Combine with author visit books, award books, classroom reads, series, or reading lists. Get students and staff members involved in creating the anticipation statements for additional buy-in and ownership.

A way to incorporate anticipation bookmarks into a schoolwide project is to use them with the state student choice award program's annual nominees. Create an anticipation bookmark for each of the novels on the list, then display each bookmark next to its matching title. Students are then able to pick up the book and its companion bookmark together.

Preplanning

- Create a list of book ideas for anticipation bookmarks. If you've never done this before or want to enrich an existing program, begin with titles clearly connected to preexisting projects, like an author visit, schoolwide read, or other event.

- If the concept is partnered with another project, meet with group leaders to discuss adding anticipation bookmarks and how to incorporate them into the existing project.

- Create an anticipation bookmark template using a word processing or desktop publishing program. Include the author and title, and leave space on the template for five to seven anticipation statements.

One Month Before

- Read the selected book. While reading, make note of concepts that arise related to morals, ethics, history, or facts. Notes for possible anticipation statements may be written on a scrap-paper bookmark or on sticky notes flagged on the page that inspired the statement.

- Upon completion of the book, select the most ideal five to seven anticipation statements. Add them to the template.

One to Seven Days Before

- Copy the desired number of bookmarks from the completed template onto colored card stock.

- Cut into individual bookmarks.

Day of the Project

- Distribute bookmarks as planned.

- If students have never completed an anticipation bookmark before, model or explain how to complete it.

After the Project

- Collect unused bookmarks and recycle.

- Consult staff for ideas for future anticipation bookmark projects.

	BEFORE		Title of Book By Author's Name	AFTER		
	Agree	Disagree		Agree	Disagree	
Place Book Cover or Graphic to Represent Book Here						Instructional Media Center

	BEFORE		Title of Book By Author's Name	AFTER		
	Agree	Disagree		Agree	Disagree	
Place Book Cover or Graphic to Represent Book Here						Instructional Media Center

	BEFORE		Title of Book By Author's Name	AFTER		
	Agree	Disagree		Agree	Disagree	
Place Book Cover or Graphic to Represent Book Here						Instructional Media Center

	BEFORE		Title of Book By Author's Name	AFTER		
	Agree	Disagree		Agree	Disagree	
Place Book Cover or Graphic to Represent Book Here						Instructional Media Center

Design a reusable template with a simple, easy-to-recognize layout that can then be used for all anticipation bookmarks.

From *Social Readers: Promoting Reading in the 21st Century* by Leslie B. Preddy.
Santa Barbara, CA: Libraries Unlimited. Copyright © 2010.

Abduction! by Peg Kehret

Agree or Disagree?

- People go to many extremes to get what they want.
- People act irrationally in a time of panic.
- Schools do everything they can to keep students safe.
- Little siblings are always getting in the way.
- Kids should spend more time with their siblings.
- Tragedy experienced by some families is unfair.
- The U.S. has a good plan to help find missing children.
- Kindergarteners are not smart enough to keep themselves out of danger.
- Guilt can ruin one's daily activities.
- Gut feelings predict when something bad is going to happen.

The Winter People by Joseph Bruchac

Agree or Disagree?

- When in danger, women, children and elderly should be protected.
- A fictional story can still teach us about the past.
- When someone experiences great grief and anger, revenge is the best way to resolve the situation.
- Nature can be both helpful and harmful to humans.
- A person cannot survive in the wild on their own.
- One should do anything to protect their family, even if it means putting their own lives in danger.
- Native Americans were savage beasts who killed people and took their scalps for the prize.
- Stories from the past can leave out one side of the situation, giving someone a different picture of what really happened.
- A boy at the age of 14 is old enough to take care of his family.
- The experiences of the past help one make better decisions in the future.

High Heat by Carl Deuker

Agree or Disagree?

- You have to be mentally tough to be a good athlete.
- Sometimes it is hard to face the truth.
- Even the best players make mistakes.
- If people make one mistake with the law, their future is ruined.
- All teenagers are embarrassed by their families.
- You can be disappointed in your family and still love them.
- Expensive things don't make people better.
- Baseball is a game that can cause a lot of pressure on an individual player.
- In baseball, some positions are more important than others.

The Sea of Trolls by Nancy Farmer

Agree or Disagree?

- Nightmares are worse than anything that could happen in real life.
- Happiness cannot exist without evil.
- Magical powers would make life more difficult.
- Even creatures of pure evil can show goodness.
- There is life after death.
- It is a negative trait to show fear.
- People act without thinking, often surprising themselves.
- Children cannot be heroes.
- Live every day with family and friends like it may be the last time you see them.
- People are always in a rush and don't slow down enough to recognize nature and their surroundings.

Anticipation statements are created in a true–false or agree–disagree format for pre- and post-reading reflection and response.

From *Social Readers: Promoting Reading in the 21st Century* by Leslie B. Preddy.
Santa Barbara, CA: Libraries Unlimited. Copyright © 2010.

79

| BEFORE | | Outbreak: Plagues That Changed History | AFTER | |
Agree	Disagree	By Bryn Barnard	Agree	Disagree
		I am a pretty healthy person.		
		I don't worry about diseases or sickness.		
		Mosquitoes bites itch, but mosquitoes cannot transmit disease.		
		Antibiotics have saved everyone's lives.		
		As long as scientists have money for research, almost any disease can be cured.		
		You must wash hands for at least 2 minutes to kill germs.		
		The bubonic plague and black plague were things that happened a long time ago and could never happen again.		

| BEFORE | | House of Tailors | AFTER | |
Agree	Disagree	By Patricia Reilly Giff	Agree	Disagree
		"Sometimes in life there are no choices".		
		Having no choice is easier "than having too many choices."		
		Never risk your life for another.		
		Home is where your loved ones are, not a place.		
		"A dream is nothing unless you can make it happen."		
		If you have a talent, do something with it.		
		Some mistakes are unforgivable.		

| BEFORE | | Code Orange | AFTER | |
Agree	Disagree	By Caroline B. Cooney	Agree	Disagree
		It's always okay to put off homework until the last minute.		
		Ancient diseases don't matter to us today.		
		It is important to follow your curiosity instincts.		
		Being a loyal American is not necessary in the modern world.		
		Nobody can read your personal email unless you send it to them.		
		Parents should know everything about your life.		
		It's okay to post personal information on the Internet.		

| BEFORE | | This Side of Paradise | AFTER | |
Agree	Disagree	By Steven Layne	Agree	Disagree
		"When you're constantly surrounded by beauty, you cease to appreciate it rather quickly."		
		Things aren't always what they seem.		
		Family can always be trusted.		
		There is a price for perfection.		
		Everyone should strive to be perfect.		
		Some people go too far in their actions on their quest for perfection.		
		There are always consequences for your actions.		

From *Social Readers: Promoting Reading in the 21st Century* by Leslie B. Preddy. Santa Barbara, CA: Libraries Unlimited. Copyright © 2010.

Bookmark Design Contest

Students have many talents, which can be expressed through reading, writing, and artwork. With a bookmark design contest, students are able to showcase talents and spread their love of reading to others. Through this contest, the school hosts a competition for students to create a bookmark, with the winners' creations published to distribute throughout the school. Student bookmark designs are turned in by the due date, reviewed, and narrowed down to the top ten or twenty. The semifinalists are posted for public display, and all staff members are invited to vote for their favorites. The top four to eight are copied onto card stock, cut, and shared with everyone through the library media center.

Instructions

When developing the bookmark design entry form, consider procedures, rules, and the size and shape of the bookmark. Take a normal-size sheet of paper, fold it until the ideally sized bookmark is created —often two to five equally sized bookmarks on one sheet. Once you've chosen the right size, measure the length and width, subtracting some from each side for margins and cutting space between bookmarks. An ideal size for four bookmarks per landscaped sheet is approximately two and a half inches wide by eight inches long. Using this measurement, create a long, blank box on a corner of the entry form, which students will fill with artwork. With four bookmarks pasted per copy page, the school could have four to eight winners published per contest.

Place the contest on the calendar during a time when there is no other schoolwide writing or drawing event. Choose a date toward the beginning to middle of the semester to start the contest so there is plenty of time to run it, announce winners, print copies, and share bookmarks. If the winning bookmarks are teamed to be distributed in conjunction with a themed week or event in the school, start the contest approximately three weeks prior to that date.

Students need time from when the contest is announced to create their entries before the due date. When establishing the project timeline, give students one to two weeks to turn in completed bookmark entry forms and two to five days for display and voting for the semifinalists.

Display semifinalists for judging. Cover or cut students' names from entry copies of the semifinalist bookmarks so they can be displayed anonymously. Use a sticker or marker to number entries for voting. Involve everyone by inviting staff to vote for the finalists.

Preplanning

- Review the school and library media center calendar. If the contest is a collaborative effort, meet to decide dates, rules, and theme.

- Set a contest start date on the calendar for one to two school weeks before completed entries are due.

One Month Before

- Use a word processing or desktop publishing program to create an entry form. Include contest rules, deadline, specified space for student artwork, and other important information.

- Develop a simple judging form that allows for semifinalist "judges" to vote for multiple bookmarks.

- If this is a collaborative project, meet with collaborators to review the entry form and finalize plans.

One to Seven Days Before

• Make copies of the entry form. If using colored paper, choose a pale color that won't interfere with reproducing student artwork.

• Create and post a contest announcement in the student newsletter and on the school Web site. If the newsletter is large or has the space, include the full entry form.

• E-mail staff or share the details of the upcoming project at a meeting.

During the Contest

• Promote the contest on student announcements.

• Distribute entry forms through the library media center, office, and classrooms.

• Collect completed entry forms as they are returned.

• Once the deadline has arrived, review entries. Select the top ten if there will be four winners and the top twenty if there will be eight winners.

• Make copies of semifinalist entries, hiding names. Store originals in a safe place.

• Display copies in a public place, such as the library, cafeteria, or office bulletin board.

• Announce that judging is open and distribute judging slips. Allow two to five days for judging.

• When judging is closed, tally votes and announce winners. Post a congratulation notice in the student newsletter and congratulate the winners on student announcements.

After the Contest

• Trim each winning bookmark from the original entry form. Glue or tape bookmarks an equal distance apart on a blank sheet of paper for copying. Label under each bookmark "Created by" with the student's name and grade or class.

• On the back of each bookmark, include a book list, reading advice, or a book-rating form to fill out.

• Copy the desired number of bookmarks onto card stock. Cut into individual bookmarks.

• Distribute as planned. Make more copies as needed until the distribution time period has ended.

• Give each winner copies of his or her final bookmark to share with family. Distribute reader's reward prizes, if offered.

• If semifinalist entries will be on display after voting, mark the winners with a sticker or ribbon cutout. Keep the display up for one to two weeks after voting ends.

• File away all bookmark entries for possible future reference.

First Name_____

Last Name_____

Team_____ Grade _____

BOOKMARK
Design Contest

CONTEST RULES

Bookmark design should:
- be clear and bold enough to be easily copied
- fill the space inside the lines, without going outside the lines or touching the lines and may include text or original artwork or both.
- be drawn with one color using either a marker, black pen, or dark pencil.
- be appropriate for school.

Bookmark design cannot include trademarked or copyrighted characters — examples of unacceptable characters are Looney Tunes, Nickelodeon characters, Yu-Gi-Oh!, Pokemon, Dragon Ball Z, Manga, Disney, graphic novel and comic book characters, etc.

Submission Deadline:
- Each student may turn in up to 3 bookmark designs.
- Bookmark designs must be turned in to the library media center by Wednesday, **January 31.**

Winners:
- The winning designs will be chosen and announced one week after the deadline.
- The artists chosen will win a free book to add to their home bookshelf.

Bookmark designs will become property of the contest & will not be returned.
Ideas from multiple designs may be combined to use on one bookmark.
The library media center will alter designs as necessary for printing.
Winning artists may be asked to re-draw bookmarks as necessary for printing.

Questions? See the library media specialist if you have any questions.

Create a bookmark entry form that includes participation rules, procedures for winners, and precisely measured drawing space.

From *Social Readers: Promoting Reading in the 21st Century* by Leslie B. Preddy.
Santa Barbara, CA: Libraries Unlimited. Copyright © 2010.

BOOKMARK
Design Contest

All students are invited to enter a drawing contest sponsored by the Library Media Center and Perry Township Education Foundation (PTEF). Winning designs will be printed on bookmarks distributed through the LMC. Contest forms are available at the LMC circulation desk. Bookmark designs must be turned in by March 17. Multiple winners will be announced toward the end of March. Good luck to all!

Publicize the contest in the student newsletter and on student announcements. Conclude the contest by publicly congratulating the winners.

Fall Semester
Bookmark Design Contest
Vote Card

PLEASE VOTE FOR Five (5)

• Bookmark 1	• Bookmark 6	• Bookmark 11	• Bookmark 16
• Bookmark 2	• Bookmark 7	• Bookmark 12	• Bookmark 17
• Bookmark 3	• Bookmark 8	• Bookmark 13	• Bookmark 18
• Bookmark 4	• Bookmark 9	• Bookmark 14	• Bookmark 19
• Bookmark 5	• Bookmark 10	• Bookmark 15	• Bookmark 20

Please turn your vote in to the circulation desk.
Votes will be accepted October 15-17.

Winners will be announced next week. Four to eight designs will win & will be printed and distributed this semester through the LMC.

Add depth to the project by displaying a selection of the bookmark entries for all to see and vote on.

Content Area Connections

Some homemade bookmarks have school and content area connections. They have a direct link to students and staff and provide the much needed real-world applications this generation requires. A double-sided content area bookmark is artistic on one side and informative on the other, including, for example, a list of related library media center resources developed by students for students or teachers. Using a content area connection allows the library media center to connect to other schoolwide events and share resources related to the topic. Content area connections could be related to presidential elections, drug prevention week, national poetry week, a science fair, music solo and ensemble competitions, and more. Including students or clubs in the design of bookmarks or with resource list development adds a warm, positive dimension to the activity. Involving others in a library media center project shows that the library is committed to patron interests and makes a connection that may cause other staff members to reciprocate and gain a better respect and understanding for the library media center's efforts.

Instructions

Before beginning the year, review the school calendar, as well as school-sponsored clubs and activities. Create a list of bookmark themes and contact names for prospective partnerships. Content area connection bookmarks can range from student contests and creations to staff-generated materials to a combination of student and staff creations.

Use a computer publishing program to create the template for the number of bookmarks to be cut from one page. For example, if the page orientation is portrait, two oversized bookmarks can fit on each sheet, which may be ideal for themes that require a lot of content space for the resource list side of the bookmark. A landscape template fits three to five bookmarks per sheet. For variety, each page may have a different front design or back content for each bookmark. The more variety, the more fun students have creating and collecting them.

If you are using a copier to make bookmarks but wish they were more colorful, involve your students. They can add flashes of color to each bookmark with colored pencils or crayons.

Preplanning

- Meet with potential collaborators to discuss possibilities. Agree to content theme, type of bookmark, and level of student and staff involvement.

- Review the school and library media center calendar. Set the start date based on when a theme fits according to school or national calendars. For example, if working with the Nature Club for an Earth Day theme, the bookmark should be ready to share during the week of Earth Day.

One Month Before

- For the front of the bookmark, students and staff collaborate to create graphic designs related to the chosen theme either on the computer or by hand.

- Work together to create a recommended reading list, advice, an interactive tool like a checklist or rating form, or other content for the backs of the bookmarks—all based on the activity theme.

- Meet with the collaborating group to finalize plans and designs.

One to Seven Days Before

- Print the final bookmark designs, and photocopy the desired quantity onto card stock.

- Cut to individual size.

- If the student group desires, add color to the bookmarks with pencils or crayons.

During the Project

- Distribute bookmarks as planned.

- Make more copies as needed until distribution time period has ended.

After the Project

- Recycle any leftover bookmarks, or place them in main office for parents and visitors.

- Send a thank you note to collaborating staff and student groups.

First Name_____

Last Name_____

Team_____ **Grade** _____

Drug Free Week
Bookmark Design Contest

CONTEST RULES

Bookmark design should:
- represent the theme, "**Don't be Tricked, Drugs are No Treat**".
- be clear and bold enough to be easily copied.
- fill the space inside the lines, without going outside the lines or touching the lines and may include text or original artwork or both,
- be drawn with one color using either a black marker, black pen, or dark pencil.
- be appropriate for school.

Bookmark design cannot include trademarked or copyrighted characters — examples of unacceptable characters are Looney Tunes, Nickelodeon, Yu-Gi-Oh!, Pokemon, Dragon Ball Z, Manga, Disney, name brand logos, sports logos, graphic novel and comic book characters, etc.

Submission Deadline:
- Each student may turn in up to 3 bookmark designs.
- Bookmark designs must be turned in to the library media center by Friday, **October 17.**

Winners:
- The winning designs will be announced and bookmarks distributed through PE class and the library media center during "Drug Free Week".
- Prizes will be awarded to winning artists.

Bookmark designs will become property of the contest & will not be returned.
Ideas from multiple designs may be combined to use on one bookmark.
The library media center will alter designs as necessary for printing.
Winning artists may be asked to re-draw as necessary for printing.

Questions? See Mrs. Preddy in the LMC or Mrs. Brooking in the gym if you have any questions.

Connecting bookmarks to schoolwide projects could include cosponsoring a bookmark design contest with a club or other student organization.

From *Social Readers: Promoting Reading in the 21st Century* by Leslie B. Preddy. Santa Barbara, CA: Libraries Unlimited. Copyright © 2010.

Bookmarks are ideal for promoting content area themes.

READ & VOTE

Title: _____

MY VOTE:

◊ Excellent—I might even read this one again!

◊ Great—I could recommend this to others.

◊ Good—I liked it, but it took me awhile to get into it.

◊ Poor—A very disappointing read.

Title: _____

MY VOTE:

◊ Excellent—I might even read this one again!

◊ Great—I could recommend this to others.

◊ Good—I liked it, but it took me awhile to get into it.

◊ Poor—A very disappointing read.

Title: _____

MY VOTE:

◊ Excellent—I might even read this one again!

◊ Great—I could recommend this to others.

◊ Good—I liked it, but it took me awhile to get into it.

◊ Poor—A very disappointing read.

READ

P M M S

Instructional Media Center

Create double-sided bookmarks with one side decorative and the other side a book list or other interactive feature to engage students in reading.

Free Book Evaluation

Have students ever mentioned to you that they read an enjoyable book, but so many characters, setting shifts, complicated transitions, personal thoughts, or questions formed that they had a hard time keeping track of it all? Students often need a simple way to take notes about what they are reading and feeling and to track the questions that develop as they read and interact with the book. It requires a simple tool for students to use that is intuitive and easy to carry around with the book. The obvious answer comes in the form of a bookmark. While students read, they often use a bookmark to keep their place. Turn this place marker into a tool that's readily available for students to take notes on and refer to as they read.

Instructions

The book evaluation bookmark encourages students to thoughtfully process what they are reading until they learn to do this intuitively. It's a flexible tool to use with schoolwide reading projects, such as an author visit or the state's student choice reading list books. This could be combined with other bookmark ideas by placing the evaluation form on one side with another design, like the anticipation bookmark for a particular book, on the other side. For schoolwide projects, completed bookmarks turned in with a teacher's signature could go into a monthly drawing for a free book to add to a student's home bookshelf, which achieves two important goals with one project.

One Month Before

- Use a word processing or desktop publishing program to design a landscape or portrait sheet with two to five evaluation bookmarks per page.

- If desired, create a design for the other side of the bookmark.

One to Seven Days Before

- Print and copy onto card stock or colored paper.

- Share the project with language arts teachers.

- Cut bookmarks to size.

During the Project

- Display and distribute bookmarks as desired.

- If rewarding students for completing a book evaluation bookmark, hold a drawing regularly.

After the Project

- If the material isn't dated, store extras for future use.

- E-mail language arts teachers, thanking them for helping and participating.

My Name:

_____

Language Arts Teacher:

_____

My Thought and Opinions
as I Read This Book:

_____
_____
_____
_____
_____
_____
_____
_____
_____
_____
_____
_____
_____
_____
_____
_____
_____
_____
_____
_____
_____
_____
_____
_____
_____
_____
_____
_____
_____

Book Rating

1   2   3   4   5

*Get this bookmark signed by your
Language Arts teacher, then turn it in
to the Library Media Center for a
chance to win a FREE book!*

**With a simple design, students will have space for personal reflection
and reading notes.**

From *Social Readers: Promoting Reading in the 21st Century* by Leslie B. Preddy.
Santa Barbara, CA: Libraries Unlimited. Copyright © 2010.

Sharing

Students thirst for opportunities to share what they know and to give their opinions. It behooves promoters of literacy and reading to grasp this and blend it into reading promotion that spotlights this interest and talent. A wide range of sharing opportunities include, but are not limited to, artists and authors contests, booktalks, cool picks, library lounge lizards, new books book club, picture-book writing project, and read-alouds.

Artists and Authors Contest

Promoting reading encompasses so much more than just the act of reading. A well-rounded reading promotion plan for youth includes opportunities to actively participate in the publishing process through writing text and graphics. Through the Artists and Authors Contest, students can express themselves in many forms: short story, essay, poetry, music compositions, lyrics, two-dimensional artwork, or a combination thereof. All that is needed is an entry form with rules, a few weeks to accept entries, a review process for accepting winners, and space in the library media center for sharing an anthology.

Cost: $

Costs are limited to the book production. This could be as simple as a binder and plastic sleeves. Prizes are an option, which, if desired, should be added to the budget.

Planning Time: One Month

Once the contest is on the calendar, it should only take one month to complete: one week to plan, two weeks to host, and one week to select entries and create the final book.

Planning Involvement: One or More People

Although the planning requires only one person, the contest is enhanced if a committee of people meet, making final selections.

Suggested Supplies

- Create: entry form, publicity and promotion materials, and timeline
- Optional: reader's reward prizes
- Miscellaneous: binder with page covers or book binding system

Instructions

Before beginning, consider entry rules and guidelines. Students will need to know what is acceptable and what is not, as well as due dates and protocol. Try to think of concerns that might arise, such as how to handle sampling of copyrighted materials. As always, though, much may not be thought of until after the project is already in motion and problems occur. Prepare to make immediate changes for future incarnations of the project; evaluate the project at its completion.

If possible, host the project once a semester and set it for the same approximate dates every year as family and students begin to plan for and expect it.

Preplanning

- Set the project on school calendar.

- Place a committee selection meeting date on the calendar for the day after entries are due.

- Invite staff to participate in the selection committee. If needed, seek out particular staff with expertise in different artistic areas, such as art, poetry, music, and narrative writing.

One Week Before

- Create and post promotion for the student newsletter.

- Design an entry form and make copies.

- Share the project entry form and timeline with staff.

During the Project

- Write and turn in promotions for student announcements.

- Set entry form copies out in prominent public places throughout school.

- Prepare front and back cover for final "book" anthology.

- Collect and organize student entries as received.

After the Project

- Meet as a committee the day after entry deadline to select finalists.

- Announce winners in the student newsletter and on announcements.

- Send congratulations to all participants for their efforts.

- Optional: Give winners a certificate or reader's reward.

- Insert winning works into a final book and display as planned.

- Send a thank you to committee members.

First and Last Name_____

Team_____ **Grade** _____ **Date** _____

Do you draw or sketch?
Do you write poetry, music compositions or song lyrics?
Do you write short stories or essays?
If you answered yes to one of these questions, then we are looking for you!
All work must be original (nothing taken from something already published or created by somebody else). Winning entries will be 'published' by the school. The original student artwork or writing will be part of a 'book' added to the school library media center collection to be shared by everyone.
Hurry-get your entry turned into the library media center soon!

Writers & Artists
Contest
CONTEST RULES

All entries should:
- be signed and dated by the artist/author.
- be school appropriate in language, design, or theme.
- include this application form with each entry.

Writer entries should:
- be original works of poetry, song, essay, or short story written by you.
- be typed or hand printed clearly.

Artwork entries should:
- be original artwork created by you.
- be 8 1/2 x 11 or smaller, or if larger is able to be shrunk to fit in an 8 1/2 x 11 book.
Artwork cannot include trademarked or copyrighted materials — examples of unacceptable characters are Looney Tunes, Nickelodeon characters, Yu-Gi-Oh!, Pokemon, Dragon Ball Z, Manga, Disney, graphic novel character, comic book characters, etc.

Submission Deadline: Entries are due no later than Wednesday, **December 1.**

Winners:
- The winning entries will be chosen and announced one week after the deadline.
- Winners will win a free book to take home and keep.

Entries will become property of the contest & will not be returned.
Winning authors may be asked to re-type or print their entry if necessary.
Winning artists may be asked to re-draw if necessary.
Questions? See Mrs. Preddy in the library media center if you have any questions.

A one-page contest entry form that includes the contest rules should be simple and brief but include all the important information including deadlines and what is acceptable.

From *Social Readers: Promoting Reading in the 21st Century* by Leslie B. Preddy.
Santa Barbara, CA: Libraries Unlimited. Copyright © 2010.

Wanted!

P M M S
Instructional Media Center

Artists, Poets, Authors!

Do you draw or sketch? Do you write poetry, music compositions or song lyrics? Do you write short stories or essays? If you answered yes to any of these questions, then we are looking for you! All work must be original (nothing taken from something already published or created by somebody else). Winning entries will be 'published' by PMMS and the original, Perry Meridian Middle School student work will be part of a 'book' added to the school library media center collection to be shared by everyone. Hurry-get your entry turned in to the Library Media Center soon!

Deadline for entries: December 1

Questions? Please contact the
Library Media Specialist. *Thank You*

Promote the Artist and Authors Contest to parents through the student newsletter.

From *Social Readers: Promoting Reading in the 21st Century* by Leslie B. Preddy. Santa Barbara, CA: Libraries Unlimited. Copyright © 2010.

Thank you for participating in the Perry Meridian Middle School Artists & Authors Contest. There were so many wonderful entries the committee had a difficult job selecting finalists. Unfortunately, your entry was not selected. Please continue writing, drawing, and revising your work because we know you are capable of the time and talent needed to succeed. We hope to see your participation and entries in the next Perry Meridian Middle School Artists & Authors Contest!

After reviewing entries for age-acceptable quality and adherence to the contest rules, there will be some students to acknowledge for their efforts, even though the entries didn't make the final cut.

Booktalking Classrooms

Booktalks have a rich history in libraries and classrooms. An informal booktalk or book commercial is an ideal way for students to share reading with each other, as well as for teachers to share with students, but faculty members need help and training to get started. Booktalks provide an opportunity to share a book or other reading that a person is passionate about; booktalks may even allow students to stretch their wings while trying something new: speaking to a group of peers. Through a verbal "tease" to promote a particular read (a book or other reading format), students can tantalize their peers with just a taste of the mood, theme, characters, setting, or plot. The booktalker "talks" the audience into wanting to read his or her recommendation without giving away too much—especially the ending! The booktalk discussed here is for casual sharing opportunities. For a detailed, lessoned booktalk, see Chapter 3.

Cost: $

This project costs nothing but time.

Planning Time: Minimal

Encouraging informal booktalks requires little planning time, except modeling for students, encouragement, and allowing students time to booktalk when they are ready and willing. Some time will be required to create training materials.

Planning Involvement: The School Community

It takes a school to raise a reader. This is most effective if the school is working toward a culture and climate of readers, which allows students the confidence and freedom to stand in front of peers and share.

Suggested Supplies

• Create: training materials

- Books: reading material from home, classroom, or library media center
- Student contribution: library or personal copy of a book or other reading material

Instructions

Students will not be able just to jump right into the idea of book advertising or booktalking. In the classroom, teachers must begin by modeling for students, as frequently as possible, informal booktalking on a reading that really mattered to him or her. Modeling once a week imprints the habit of reading. Booktalk materials that may or may not be content related. For booktalks to be successful, consider the following:

- Include only age-appropriate materials.
- Conclude each modeling experience by reminding students that they can booktalk too, and ask if anyone would like to come up and share something about what they are reading.
- The booktalk can be from any reading format, but it's often easy to start with fiction and narrative nonfiction.
- Include why you picked up this particular reading.
- Share what you thought the material was going to be about versus what it turned out to be about.
- Tell students why you wanted to share it with them.
- After modeling the first few times, you may need to speak directly to a particular student to encourage him or her to booktalk, too.

Plan for when the class will be receptive to booktalks. For example, during the five-minute warm-up at the beginning of class, a segue or transition at a particular time of day, or as a wrap-up or exit activity at the conclusion of the class period or time segment.

Preplanning

- The activity planner prepares and presents staff training on effective classroom booktalks, including modeling sample booktalks to faculty.
- The classroom teacher reads student-appropriate books, articles, and Internet material.
- The classroom teacher selects items to booktalk, making a list of important points to share.
- Select a time during the day or period to do booktalks.

During the Booktalk

- The classroom teacher models giving booktalks approximately once a week.
- Encourage students to present informal booktalks to class, too.
- Optional: the classroom teacher recommends students to booktalk on the student announcements.

After the Booktalk

- The classroom teacher writes a thank you or positive praise note to students who booktalk.

Booktalking in the Classroom

What to include:

- What is the title, author, format, and genre?
- Where did you find it?
- Why did you pick up the reading?
- What spoke to you? Why did it matter?
- How did it connect to prior knowledge or experiences?
- How did it change you?

Teacher training includes a few helpful hints, reminders, and modeling.

Cool Picks Project

We educators are always looking for new ways to involve students in the book recommendation business, so consider sponsoring a book review project. The reason the book picks are "cool" is because fellow students are making the recommendations. The project is as simple as inviting students to fill out a review form and then displaying completed recommendation forms along with an image of the book so that fellow students can read reviews and easily locate the recommended book in the library media center. Many times, the recommended books will fly off the shelves!

Cost: $

With the use of a color printer, most, if not all, of the supplies needed for this project are usually already in stock in the school, including colored paper and images of book covers.

Planning Time: One Month and More

Time varies, depending on how long recommendations will be accepted and displayed. It will take one week to prepare, two or more weeks to accept completed forms, plus time to display forms as they are collected and shared. The Cool Picks Project is flexible and can run for a month, grading period, or semester.

Planning Involvement: One Person

This simple, schoolwide project requires only one person to run effectively.

Suggested Supplies

- Create: publicity and promotional materials and the recommendation form

- Display: display promotional materials on a wall, window, or bulletin board

- Optional: flatbed scanner, laminator, reader's reward, still digital camera

- Paper: colored paper

- Technology: color printer

- Miscellaneous: color copies of book covers

Instructions

Through this project, students recommend books to other students. Create a recommendation form that is easy for an audience to read as part of a bulletin board, display wall, or window. Students fill in the recommendation form, ensuring that the intended audience has enough information to make an informed reading decision quickly. This could include, but is not limited to, age recommendation, rating scales, finish-the-sentence blanks, and author, title, and call number for the book. Consider the following:

- Will books that are not in the library media center collection be accepted?

- Does the library media center have money to buy a copy of a book not in the collection to prepare for student interest after a form is displayed?

- Instead of purchasing a book, is this an opportunity to teach the concept of interlibrary loan?

- Will there be praise or a reader's reward for students whose work appears on the display?

When choosing a wall, bulletin board, or window for the project, choose an area that receives a lot of traffic. Create a heading and simple project announcements in bright colors so they will stand out around all the book recommendations. For example, "Cool Picks Projects—Recommended for You, by You."

Print book recommendation forms on a variety of colored papers, if available, because the accepted forms will be part of the display. Displayed book reviews may need to be laminated first to limit vandalism or accidental tearing. Include an image of the book cover with the book recommendation form so viewers interested in reading a recommendation can easily recognize the book on the shelf. The cover can be the actual book jacket or a printout of a digital picture or scanned image of the cover.

Decide in advance how long recommendation forms will be accepted and displayed. It could be a revolving display that goes on all semester or be more static for a much briefer period.

Preplanning

- Create a recommendation form in a design and layout appropriate for display.

- Review the recommendation form with classroom teachers or students. Make changes based on their advice.

One Week Before

- Make color copies of the recommendation form.

- Create and post an announcement in the student newsletter.

- Create promotions for student announcements.

• Create a display wall in preparation for completed recommendation forms and to advertise the project.

• Share the Cool Picks Project purpose and recommendation form with staff through e-mail or during a staff meeting.

During the Project

• Prepare the display and post the entries as they are turned in.

• Have promotions run on student announcements.

• Display blank recommendation forms in public areas for distribution.

• Review recommendation forms as they are turned in, selecting appropriately completed forms for the display wall.

• Pair approved recommendation forms with book cover copies for the display wall.

• Decorate the display wall with completed forms as they are turned in and approved.

After the Project

• Take down display wall and recycle or save any extra copies of the recommendation form.

• Store reusable materials from the display for future use.

• Review and make changes to the electronic copy of the recommendation form in preparation for future use.

I am recommending

Title_____

Author _____

IMC Call # _____

READ

P M M S

Library Media Center

Book Rating - I score this book Good — Better — The Best 1 2 3 4 5	**Reading Difficulty** Easy—Medium—Challenge 1 2 3 4 5

Genre (circle one)

Adventure   African American   Historical Fiction   Horror/Suspense   Humor

Fantasy   Graphic Novel   Holiday   Multi-Cultural   Mystery

Romance   Science Fiction   Sports Fiction   Biography   Non-Fiction

or Other: _____

I like this book because _____
_____
_____
_____ .

I think others would like reading this book because _____
_____
_____
_____ .

My favorite part of this book was _____
_____
_____
_____ .

This story reminds me of _____
_____
_____
_____ .

Name _____   Grade _____

Language Arts Teacher: _____

Include enough details on the recommendation form to entice a future reader. Make it trouble-free for the applicant to complete and easy for the audience to read when on display.

From *Social Readers: Promoting Reading in the 21st Century* by Leslie B. Preddy.
Santa Barbara, CA: Libraries Unlimited. Copyright © 2010.

Cool Picks Project

PMMS
Library Media Center

Read a Great Book Lately?

The library media center wants to know what great books you've been reading! If you've read a book that you think other students would like to read, stop by the library and fill out a book recommendation form. Completed forms can be turned in throughout this semester. Students who return a completed form which is accepted for display will be awarded a *free* book!

Promote the project to students through announcements and newsletter advertisements.

Don't Know What to Read?
Try a book recommended by a student!

Have You Read A Great Book Lately?
Let us know by completing a book recommendation form! If your recommendation makes it to this display, you win a *free* book!

Add to the display area basic signs on bright paper to draw viewers and quickly explain what is happening on the display.

Library Lounge Lizards

Students are always looking for a place to hang out and talk. Offer up opportunities through a Library Lounge Lizards Club. With this club, things are kept casual, with no scheduled activities during the meetings. These students are just looking for a place to hang out, a chance to talk about what they're reading, and an opportunity to express some opinions while they relax and unwind.

Cost: $

The cost incurred is usually minimal or nonexistent if using a music player you already have in the media center. Snacks and drinks are optional, or students could be encouraged to bring their own. Purchasing special furniture is an optional, one-time cost that would increase expenses dramatically.

Planning Time: Varied and Ongoing

It does not require much to set up Library Lounge Lizards, but it does require ongoing, scheduled dates and staff supervision.

Planning Involvement: One or More People

This program can be run with one person in charge, but it is good to include others to take turns as host or to host when the program coordinator is absent.

Suggested Supplies

- Optional: drinks, snacks, specialty furniture

- Student contribution: library or personal copy of book

- Miscellaneous: specially arranged "hangout" area in the library media center or other public location.

- Technology: music player

Instructions

When choosing a location, choose a place that is easily transformed into something that does not look like a school space. Seating should not be school desks or other uncomfortable seats. Consider inviting some students into the decision-making process for where it should be and how the area should be arranged and look. Location could be permanent or any temporary space that is easy to set up and dismantle. Seating could be cushions, pillows, rug squares, bean bags, or storable seating appealing to the intended participants. Students like the coffeehouse and bookstore feel, therefore consider inviting them to bring in their own beverage and possibly even snack food, unless you will be providing it for them. Depending on the student population, it might be possible to establish a snack rotation, asking students to bring snacks to share. If it is in agreement with school district policies, you can also bring snacks and sell them with the purpose of using the money to buy more snacks for future meetings and reader's rewards or library books.

Decide when to host the Library Lounge Lizards. Time of day could be before or after school or during lunch or recess. Create a schedule, which has a pattern to it so that students can remember. It could be certain days (or a day) of every week or certain days of every month.

Preplanning

- Create an outline plan for the project, including purpose, schedule, budget, and audience.

- Meet with administration for project approval and discussion of plan outline.

- Consulting with students and staff, create a permanent or temporary space and design for the lounge.

- If purchasing special seating or decorations, locate funding and seek startup grants.

One to Seven Days Before

- Create and display posters, signs, or banners.

- Advertise on student announcements.

- Publish advertisements and calendar dates for Library Lounge Lizards in the student newsletter.

- Purchase or make snacks if needed.

Day of the Event

- Air a reminder advertisement on student announcements, either the day of or the day before the event.

- Arrange and decorate the location for the lounge-style readers' hangout.

- Circulate among students to talk about what they're reading. If discussions are going well, leave them to it without interceding. Keep it casual.

After the Event

- Ask students for advice to make improvements for future dates.

- Clean up the lounge area.

- Store any extra supplies for the next event.

Picture-Book Project

One way to help students better understand the importance of reading and sharing reading experiences is a picture-book writing project. The project includes writing the story, creating companion artwork, "publishing" the work, and, of key importance, reading the book aloud to younger students. Prepare students and take them on a field trip to a local elementary school or down the hall to the primary grade classes to read their books to younger students. This makes what was once an educational exercise into an experience with real purpose and meaning. Older students are treated like superstars by the primary students, and teachers fight over the chance the fit their class into the student authors' tour schedule.

Cost: $

This project is managed with student-purchased materials and classroom supplies already on hand. Students may prefer to purchase their own notebook or blank book if they do not want to use the papers provided by the school. Unless the partnering elementary schools are within walking distance (or intermediate students are writing and reading to primary students in the same building), a bus and field trip will need to be scheduled and included in the budget, as required by the school.

Planning Time: One Month

With a one month plan, take one week to create the lesson plans and schedule collaboratively with the partnering school, two weeks for classroom instruction and book creation, and one final week to develop oral interpretation of literature skills and read to primary classrooms.

Planning Involvement: Three People

This project requires a classroom teacher and school librarian working together collaboratively to plan and teach, plus a contact person to organize and coordinate the story time in the primary school and classes.

Suggested Supplies

- Craft supplies: blank books (could be homemade with printer paper and construction paper covers), colored pencils, construction paper, crayons, glue, markers, paper, rules, scissors, tape, and other miscellaneous illustration supplies

- Create: field trip permission form if needed, lesson plans, project timeline, student handouts, storyboard, or graphic organizer tool

- Student contribution: any special art supplies desired, "book" created during the unit

Instructions

The classroom teacher and school librarian work together collaboratively to plan and teach the picture-book project. If feasible, include the art teacher. The classroom teacher is the expert on her individual students' writing abilities and expectations and the content area standards. The school librarian is the expert on standards of picture-book publication, illustration styles, and oral interpretation (read-aloud) of the picture-book format. The art teacher is the expert on art mediums and how to represent text with illustrations.

There are two parts to this unit. Part one is the writing and production of the picture book, which entails understanding the audience, story line, character development, setting, theme, word choice, learning how to use a book's two-page spread effectively, and developing illustrations to enrich and enhance the story. Illustrations could be hand drawn, photographs, magazine collages, computer drawn, or made through other artistic means ideal for illustrating the written story. Part two is presenting the final books to younger students, but first learning how to read aloud to a group: how to hold the book so the audience can see, how to pause and point out details in the illustrations, how to model questioning and answering while reading, modeling how to bring prior knowledge or experiences to the story, how to project the reader's voice, and how to use pacing, inflection, and intonation.

Apply what is known about picture-book publication to make the lesson authentic. All information may not be incorporated, but integrate what is deemed important to make it a real-world experience, meet standards, and reinforce skills.

- The standard picture book is thirty-two pages, so student books should be thirty-two pages or less.

- There is a tease about the book on the inside front flap or back cover.

- There is an About the Author and Illustrator section on the back flap, back cover, or a page after the story.

- There is a title page, copyright page, and dedication page. Sometimes a description of the art style and how the art was created is included.

Meet with administration for preliminary approval of the field trip and permission to contact lower grades or feeder elementary schools for a partnership. Be prepared to defend the reason for the field trip, if needed, with standards met through the storytelling experience. For example, Grade 8 Indiana Academic Standard 8.7 refers to "Listening and Speaking: Skills, Strategies, and Applications."

When contacting the primary grades or potential elementary partnership, communicate the need for a contact to handle the responsibility of local arrangements. The contact will need to approve the date and opportunity with the school and find teachers willing to have classes participate in the project and prepare a schedule of which classroom will be read to and when. Divide the older kids into groups of three to five, so multiple classroom readings occurs simultaneously. Have more than one older group rotate into each classroom, if time allows and the younger students' attention span is sufficient.

Preplanning

- Meet with administration for preliminary approval.
- Work with collaborating teacher(s) to prepare lesson plans and a timeline.
- Develop training materials and student organization tools.
- Make contact through an administrator or the school librarian with primary grades or feeder elementary schools until a partnership is found and date agreed.

Three to Four Weeks Before

- Complete the bus and field trip request, if needed.
- Coteach picture-book styles and the writing process, from outline to final revision.
- Create and distribute a field trip permission slip and send home, if needed.

Two Weeks Before

- Coteach how to write and illustrate a picture-book effectively.
- Students create a storyboard or graphic organizer to design the book layout.
- Peer review the work during production.
- Students complete the picture-book production.

One Week Before

- Coteach how to interpret picture books orally for the intended audience. Students practice and evaluate and advise each other.
- Confirm arrangements with your contact in the primary grades or at the partnering elementary school.
- Follow-up with home contacts for missing field trip forms as necessary.
- If needed, confirm the bus.
- Create field trip schedule and assign students to reading groups.

Day of the Event

- Coordinate and supervise field trip.
- Take pictures with digital still camera.

After the Event

- Have students write thank you notes to primary classroom teachers.
- Cowrite an article and turn it in with digital pictures to the local newspaper, district Web site, student newsletter, and yearbook committee.
- Write thank you notes to the primary grades coordinator.
- Ask for feedback from all involved and make any necessary changes to the project.

Things for students to consider during story development:

- Remember what it's like to be a little kid.
- What were your fears as a child?
- What was fun when you were 5, 6, 7, and 8 years old?
- How did your parents and friends play with you?

Important traits of a picture book:

- Story should have a beginning, middle, and satisfying end.
- Word choice and sentences should be simple, brief, straightforward, and age appropriate for the intended reader.
- Illustrations matter as much as the text.
- Illustrations should follow and enrich the text, retelling the story in pictures.
- Text font should be large, and pictures should fill the page.

Student goals:

- Show kids the fun found in reading and listening to books.
- Help kids develop an imagination.
- Help kids develop language skills.
- Help kids learn good grammar.

Things to avoid:

- Stories and pictures that are too scary or mature.
- Long words and overly long sentences.
- Alphabet and counting books that do not lend themselves well to this project.

Suggested story themes for first-time picture book writers:

- Everyday Experiences
- Family Stories
- Friendship Tales
- Imaginary
- Learning Experiences
- Nature
- Predictable
- Rhyming

Basic suggestions to consider when developing lesson plans.

From *Social Readers: Promoting Reading in the 21st Century* by Leslie B. Preddy.
Santa Barbara, CA: Libraries Unlimited. Copyright © 2010.

Picture Book Creation Guidelines

Audience: primary students (kindergarten, first grade, or second grade)

Book Style: tiny, tall, pop-up, lift-the-flap, particular shape, accordion, interactive (objects to touch), or what best suits the story

Illustrations: student artwork, traced images, clip art, magazine clippings, photographs, created using craft tools, or any other art medium. Illustrations must be colorful and used to enhance the written text.

Text: age appropriate for primary students, printed from a computer or legibly by hand (no cursive).

Length: book cover, 30 two-page spreads, back cover

Book Grading:
- ✓ Story Originality and Age Appropriateness
- ✓ Illustration Creativity and Connection to Text
- ✓ Overall Appearance, including Neatness
- ✓ Appropriate Vocabulary: Word and Sentence Choice
- ✓ Length

Picture-book design guidelines should be simple yet allow for student creativity and originality.

From *Social Readers: Promoting Reading in the 21st Century* by Leslie B. Preddy. Santa Barbara, CA: Libraries Unlimited. Copyright © 2010.

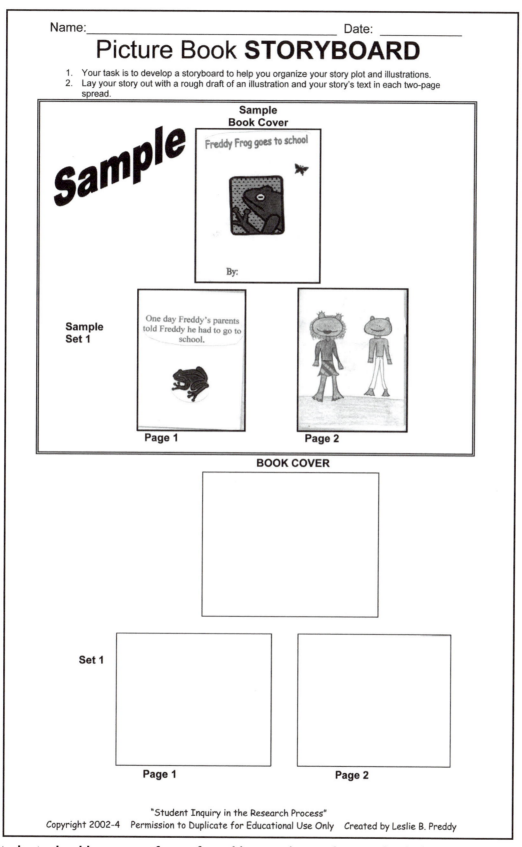

Name:_____ Date: _____

Picture Book STORYBOARD

1. Your task is to develop a storyboard to help you organize your story plot and illustrations.
2. Lay your story out with a rough draft of an illustration and your story's text in each two-page spread.

Sample

Sample Book Cover

Freddy Frog goes to school

By:

Sample Set 1

One day Freddy's parents told Freddy he had to go to school.

Page 1

Page 2

BOOK COVER

Set 1

Page 1

Page 2

Students should use some form of graphic organizer to lay out the design for each page.

From *Social Readers: Promoting Reading in the 21st Century* by Leslie B. Preddy.
Santa Barbara, CA: Libraries Unlimited. Copyright © 2010.

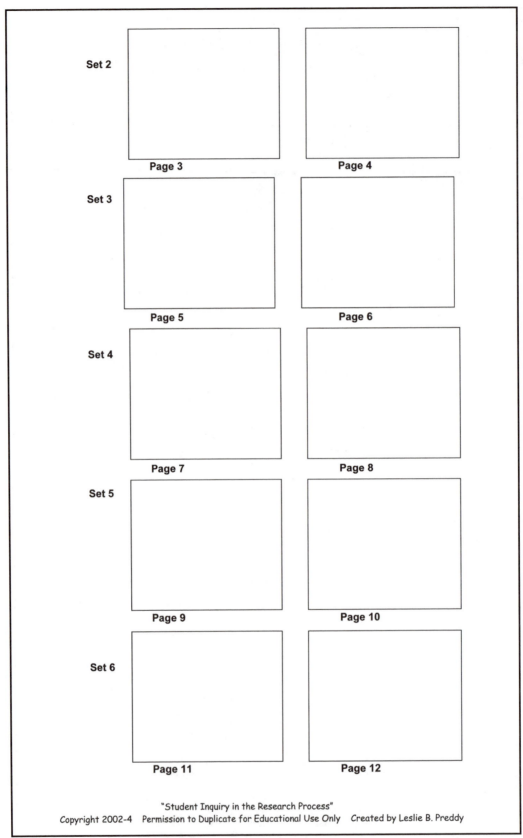

Set 2   Page 3   Page 4

Set 3   Page 5   Page 6

Set 4   Page 7   Page 8

Set 5   Page 9   Page 10

Set 6   Page 11   Page 12

Students should use some form of graphic organizer to lay out the design for each page. (*Cont.*)

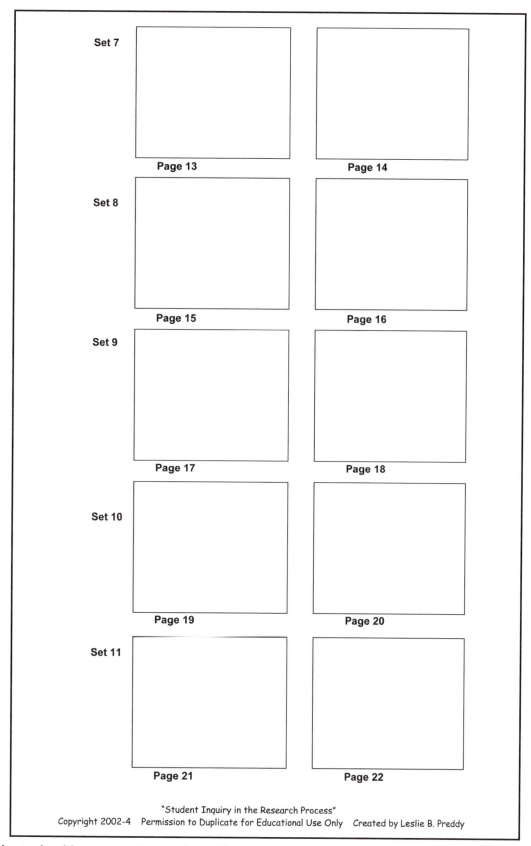

Set 7

Page 13

Page 14

Set 8

Page 15

Page 16

Set 9

Page 17

Page 18

Set 10

Page 19

Page 20

Set 11

Page 21

Page 22

"Student Inquiry in the Research Process"

Copyright 2002-4   Permission to Duplicate for Educational Use Only   Created by Leslie B. Preddy

Students should use some form of graphic organizer to lay out the design for each page. (*Cont.*)

Set 12

Page 23	Page 24

Set 13

Page 25	Page 26

Set 14

Page 27	Page 28

Set 15

Page 29	Page 30

END PAGE

"Student Inquiry in the Research Process"
Copyright 2002-4   Permission to Duplicate for Educational Use Only   Created by Leslie B. Preddy

Students should use some form of graphic organizer to lay out the design for each page. (*Cont.*)

From *Social Readers: Promoting Reading in the 21st Century* by Leslie B. Preddy.
Santa Barbara, CA: Libraries Unlimited. Copyright © 2010.

Read-Aloud Feedback

Author: _____   Book Title:_____

Pace	❑ too slow	❑ too fast	❑ just right
Volume	❑ too soft	❑ too loud	❑ just right
Expression	❑ too little	❑ too much	❑ just right
Eye contact	❑ too little	❑ too much	❑ just enough

What I enjoyed most about this picture book was …..

To make the reading even better, I would suggest that ……

After students learn and practice the traits of effective reading aloud, have them try their oral interpretation skills and gain feedback from peers before going to the primary grades to read.

From *Social Readers: Promoting Reading in the 21st Century* by Leslie B. Preddy.
Santa Barbara, CA: Libraries Unlimited. Copyright © 2010.

Read-Aloud Classrooms

Adults spend time reading aloud to students. Students spend instructional time reading aloud as required and directed in the classroom. But what cannot be forgotten are moments for students to read aloud material inspiring enough to share. Creating an environment where students cannot help but share a passage of text is enviable and a goal worth striving to reach. Faculty members need training, and students need moments to share personal readings.

Cost: $

This costs nothing but time.

Planning Time: Minimal

When encouraging spontaneous read-alouds, there is no true planning time, except staff training. Read-Aloud Classrooms help classroom teachers learn to model for students and encourage and allow them time to read aloud whenever students are ready and willing.

Planning Involvement: The School Community

It takes a school to raise a reader. As in booktalks, read-alouds are most effective if the school is working toward a culture and climate of readers, which allows students the confidence and freedom to stand in front of peers and share.

Suggested Supplies

- Books: reading materials from home, classroom, or the library media center

- Student contribution: library or personal copy of a book, an article, or Internet material

Instructions

With a little prodding, most students will help by choosing to read aloud to the class voluntarily. Although they are naturally social creatures, students will need to feel safe. Reading aloud starts with teachers modeling once or more a week. Classroom teachers "spontaneously" read aloud a piece of something they read the night before in a newspaper, magazine, book, or other medium. This may or may not be content related but should, of course, be age appropriate for students. Here are some hints for success when modeling:

- Explain why you are reading the piece aloud.

- Discuss how the material fit or didn't fit into what you thought you already knew.

- Discuss how the material moved or changed you, or why it mattered enough to share it.

- Conclude each modeling experience by reminding students that they can share, too.

- Ask if anyone would like to come in the next day and read a piece of something they are reading.

- After modeling the first few times, you may need to speak directly to a particular student to encourage him or her to do it.

It is also important to choose the most receptive class time to read aloud. This could be during warm-up, cool-down, or transition time in the established classroom routine.

Preplanning

- The activity planner prepares and presents staff training on effective reading aloud. Include modeling a read-aloud to faculty.

- As the classroom teachers read material in their spare time, they should keep their minds open to read-aloud possibilities they may encounter.

- The classroom teacher selects read-aloud passages, making note of important points to share.

- The classroom teacher selects a time in the day or period to share through read-alouds.

- All school read-alouds by a staff member could be a regular feature incorporated into student announcements.

During the Read-Aloud Project

- The classroom teacher frequently models reading aloud.

- Students are encouraged to read aloud to the class as well.

After the Read-Aloud Project

- Offer a thank you or positive praise note for students who read aloud to their peers.

Chapter 3
Control and Choice

Today's youth require creative instructional interventions and opportunities that allow them to share and interact with each other. Sharing is important to this generation. Your students need variety, creativity, options, and frequent opportunities to share what they have read with others; always requiring a traditional written or oral book report will no longer do. Innovative reading projects should do more than just teach students to report on what they are reading; instead, teach students to express creatively to others what they have read—and perhaps encourage their friends to pick up a book. In this chapter, you'll find alternatives to the traditional book report, training hints for helping your students make informed reading choices, and ways to involve everyone in the social and shared reading process.

Book Promotion Book Report

Traditional book reports are obsolete and often destroy reading motivation among today's generation of students. How often do people in everyday life finish a pleasure reading experience by writing about it in an essay or report? Not very often. In contrast, if a person shares a reading experience with others, it is through more entertaining visual, verbal, or written avenues. Social reading, or chances to share literary experiences, has a greater impact on the younger generation. Give students opportunities with applications to the real world by creating products intended to contribute to the good of the reading community through sharing, distribution, communication, and public display. Each book promotion described in this section may be used individually or combined to offer multiple options, allowing for student choice in book selection and the final product created.

BOOK RECOMMENDATION BASICS BEFORE YOU BEGIN

KNOW YOUR AUDIENCE:
Your audience for this book review is other students your age and grade.

READ THE BOOK!
You can't have enthusiasm for a book you haven't read!

LIKE THE BOOK!
Your audience will read, or not read, the book based on what you say about it. This is your time to make a personal recommendation!

DON'T TELL THE ENDING!
Don't spoil the book for your audience. Your goal is to get people to read the book themselves.

WHAT TO LOOK FOR:
- What did you like about the book?
- Make notes about the basics of the genre, plot, characters, and setting.
- Write down quotes you liked as you read.
- Record thoughts, ideas, opinions, and insights as they occur while reading the book.
- Find the hook. Somewhere in the book will be a plot, scene, circumstance, or event that "caught" you and made you want to read more. Share that with your audience.

KNOW THE GRADING RUBRIC!

Basic points for students and staff to consider when recommending books to others.

From *Social Readers: Promoting Reading in the 21st Century* by Leslie B. Preddy.
Santa Barbara, CA: Libraries Unlimited. Copyright © 2010.

Incorporating book promotions, as alternatives to book reports, into the school and library media center collection, décor, or distribution is vital for the creator, the audience, and fellow students to feel the full impact of such projects. Share students' creations with their peers. Make copies of bookmarks, brochures, newsletters, and booklets and set them out for distribution in the school office and library media center. Display posters, scrapbooks, and read-alikes in high-traffic areas throughout the school. Add student book reviews and booktalks as guest speaker events on student announcements.

No matter the assignment, instruction is needed to guide students toward effective reading strategies. Instruction can be self-directed through training brochures available and readily accessible in the library media center, through classroom training, or through club projects. Offer classroom teachers training on teaching alternatives; promote opportunities to teach collaboratively and publicize where student training materials are located in the library media center. Book reports can be converted into opportunities to share and promote reading if educators work with students to consider a few basic thoughts while reading:

- Keep a reader's notebook or use a bookmark or sticky notes to write personal thoughts and ideas. The more one records while the book is still fresh in the memory, the better.

- What is appealing about the book? Find the hook! Somewhere in the book will be a plot, scene, circumstance, or event that lures the reader in, and can be shared with the audience.

- Make brief notes about genre, plot basics, characters' physical and personality traits, and setting time and place.

- Write down passages or quotes that are especially interesting or meaningful.

Many book report alternatives lend themselves to incorporating technology. Technology is not necessary for any of the products suggested in this section, but see Chapter 4 for technology-rich book-promotion ideas. Consider the instructional skills and standards the project meets, as well as the availability of technology, when deciding whether to incorporate word processing, desktop publishing, the Internet, image scanning, or other enrichments.

The are a few similarities in time and supplies to all book-promotion book reports described in this section.

Cost: $

Adapt needed supplies to what is already available and cost-effective for the school and library media center.

Estimated Unit Time: Four Weeks

Each book report alternative takes approximately four weeks to complete, from book selection to final product completion, although unit time should be adjusted according to the particular needs and abilities of the students. After initial book selection, basic training on making note of important details while reading and a brief overview of the final product to be created are important. From there, students may or may not, depending on the nature of the group, need in-class silent reading time for the first weeks. In the final weeks, again depending on the nature of the group, students may need in-class work time and supplies to create the final product. Have students draft their concept onto a graphic organizer, then hold a peer or teacher conference to discuss plans and make revisions based on the peer or teacher's advice before working on the final product. When the final products are complete, sharing occurs naturally within the class and beyond into the school.

Suggested Supplies

- Create: guidelines and expectations, lesson plans, rubric, storyboard or graphic organizer

- Paper: lined notebook

- Writing and drawing instruments: pen, pencil

Book Fair

True learning occurs by doing and teaching. Through a book fair, each student prepares a display and presentation for fellow students touring the fair. Guests stop by each booth, and the student persuades them to read the book he or she recommends. Students work individually to read a book and create an attractive display, or booth, to draw in fellow students and prospective readers. Each booth includes an eye-catching poster, informational brochure, and persuasive presentation.

Suggested Supplies

- Create: "I Want to Read" bookmarks for students touring the book fair

- Craft supplies: glue, poster or other display board, rulers, scissors

- Paper: construction paper, colored paper, printer paper

- Technology (optional): computer, scanner, printer

- Writing and drawing instruments: colored pencils, crayons, markers

Instructions

After reading, students will need time during and after class to complete their book-fair space, as well as to draft and practice their script and presentation. Divide the class in half, allowing an opportunity for half the students to set up their book-fair booth and practice while the other half pretend to be the visiting audience, repeating until all students have had the chance to practice their presentation.

The book fair will require a large space. Reserve a public location where the students can set up the fair and show off while still leaving plenty of room for visitors. Ideally, set up booths on top of counters or tables. The library media center, LGI (large group instruction) room, or cafeteria are prime locations.

After reserving the book-fair space, arrange with other classes for peer groups to tour the exhibit. Rotate one class through the fair at a time. Create a simple "I Want to Read" bookmark for visiting students. Give the bookmark a heading and guidance for writing down titles and authors of books they hear about and later want to read.

Student booths should be set up with space between exhibits. This ensures that distractions are limited and increases on-task talking, sharing, and presenting their knowledge of the book.

Building Your BOOK FAIR BOOTH:

The class is hosting a book fair. The book fair will allow you to share information about the book you've chosen to read. You will be setting up your own "booth" in our library media center. Students and teachers will visit your booth, see your poster, hear your presentation and read a brochure about your book. The booth must include a poster, brochure and presentation.

☐ ## Poster
The poster is an advertisement of the book. It should attract people to the booth. It should display the title and author of the book. It must have a large, colorful picture of a major event or theme in the story.

☐ ## Brochure
The brochure gives more detailed information about your book. This is where you will discuss the conflict, the climax, and other major elements of the story. The brochure will be folded into thirds.
Front Flap
- Title, author, heading, and the picture of the front cover of the book

Inside the brochure each flap should include colored illustrations and one to two paragraphs, writing very small or using a computer. Illustrations should be hand-drawn.
- First Flap: summary
- Second Flap: conflict
- Third Flap: resolution
- Fourth Flap: characters

☐ ## Presentation
Students and teachers will tour the Book Fair. You must persuade them to stop by the booth and encourage them to read the book. You will need to answer questions that anyone may have. Be prepared to answer questions about the plot, characters, conflict, setting, etc.

Don't give away any surprises or important details that should be left for the reader!

Suggested book-fair booth guidelines and expectations.

From *Social Readers: Promoting Reading in the 21st Century* by Leslie B. Preddy.
Santa Barbara, CA: Libraries Unlimited. Copyright © 2010.

BOOK FAIR RUBRIC

Name: _____

Teacher: _____

Period: _____ Date: _____

Book Title: _____

Poster

Neatness	0	1	2	3	4	5
Title	0		2			
Author	0		2			
Illustration	0	1	2	3	4	5
Colorful	0	1	2	3	4	5

Total points____/19

Brochure

Neatness	0	1	2	3	4	5
Cover	0	1	2	3	4	5
Characters						
paragraphs	0	1	2	3	4	5
illustrations	0	1	2			
Setting						
paragraphs	0	1	2	3	4	5
illustration	0	1	2			
Conflict						
paragraphs	0	1	2	3	4	5
illustrations	0	1	2			
Summary						
paragraphs	0	1	2	3	4	5
illustrations	0	1	2			
Resolution						
paragraphs	0	1	2	3	4	5
illustrations	0	1	2			
Effort	0	1	2	3	4	5

Total_____/50

Presentation

Knowledge of Book	0	1	2	3	4	5
Engaging Audience	0	1	2	3	4	5
Answers questions	0	1	2	3	4	5

Total_____/15

Sample book-fair booth grading rubric.

Book Jacket

A book jacket usually includes appealing cover artwork, back cover information, a booktalk on the inside front flap, and often an About the Author section on the inside back flap. In this activity, students create a book jacket of their own design for hardback or paperback books. The completed jacket is then placed on the intended book in the library media center or classroom bookshelf so that it is shared with fellow students.

Suggested Supplies

- Books: collection pulled from the library media center

- Paper: Newsprint, paper tablecloth rolls, or other long paper cut to book-cover size

- Writing and drawing instruments: colored pencils, crayons, markers, ruler

- Miscellaneous: filament tape, laminator, or book jacket covers

Instructions

Before students begin the project, pull together a collection of books from the library media center. Share the books, going through the components of the book jacket and giving students a thorough understanding through examples of what they will create.

Books come in different shapes and sizes. Before a student begins drafting a layout and design, the book should be measured to ensure proper fit. If the book already has a jacket, measure it. If the book does not have a jacket, create one that is the height of the book, with enough width to wrap around the book and have the extra paper necessary for the flaps to fold over and hug the cover. For example, a 1-inch-thick paperback with a cover height of 8 inches and a width of 5.5 inches needs a book jacket that is 8 by 20 inches. Imagine a 1-inch-thick hardback with a cover height of 10 inches and a width of 8 inches; it needs a book jacket that is 10 by 27 inches.

Once the student has finished the new book jacket, prepare it for circulation and extensive use by other students. Add a call number to the spine. Cover the homemade book jacket with an official library book jacket cover, or laminate it with a hot or cold laminate. Attach it to the book using filament tape. Once completed, set it on special display in the library media center or classroom, showing it off to other students until it is borrowed.

Building Your BOOK JACKET:

☐ ## Front Cover
The cover art is intended to attract the attention of a potential reader. The cover art should make a person want to pick up the book and find out more about it. It should be interesting, appealing, colorful, convey a message about the book, and include the author and title.

Spine and Back Cover
☐
- Spine: Include the title of the book and the author's last name on the spine. The text should be written sideways (see teacher's example) with the title larger than the author.
- Back Cover: Be creative about what is included on the back cover. The back cover could include a list of awards the book has received, quotes from readers who liked the book, genre, and/or an attention getting quote from inside the book.

Inside Front Flap
☐
Write a brief booktalk to persuade a potential reader into reading the book. A booktalk is a 'tease' used to promote the book. A booktalk 'talks' someone into reading the book to find out what happens and how it ends. It can be written in first or third person. DON'T GIVE AWAY THE "SECRETS" OR THE   ENDING OF YOUR BOOK!

Inside Back Flap
☐
Write a brief biography about the author. Include information for two or more of the following categories:
- Author's personal life (childhood, education, adulthood)
- Career highlights
- Personal connections to the book or special reason for writing the book
- Awards the author has received throughout his or her career
- An accurate, hand-drawn sketch of the author's face

Don't give away any surprises or important details that should be left for the reader!

Suggested book jacket guidelines and expectations.

From *Social Readers: Promoting Reading in the 21st Century* by Leslie B. Preddy.
Santa Barbara, CA: Libraries Unlimited. Copyright © 2010.

BOOK JACKET RUBRIC

Name: _____

Teacher: _____

Period: _____ Date: _____

Book Title: _____

The front cover is colorful, attracts a reader's interest and follows the guideline requirements.

5   4   3   2   1

The spine is attractive, meets the guideline requirements and can easily be read when placed on the intended book. The back cover is attractive and follows the guideline requirements.

5   4   3   2   1

The inside front flap is legible, appropriate length, follows the guidelines, and helps a potential reader become more interested in reading the book without giving away too much of the story or ending.

5   4   3   2   1

The inside back flap is legible, information is accurate and up-to-date, and includes at least two of the options listed in the guidelines.

5   4   3   2   1

The overall look of the book jacket is creative, neat and fits well on the intended book. The layout is carefully planned. Spelling, grammar, punctuation, paragraphing, and capitalization are correct.

5   4   3   2   1

FINAL GRADE:

Sample book jacket grading rubric.

From *Social Readers: Promoting Reading in the 21st Century* by Leslie B. Preddy. Santa Barbara, CA: Libraries Unlimited. Copyright © 2010.

Book Review

A book review is written to help others figure out whether they would be interested in reading the book, too. For this purpose, it is a summary of the book, without giving too much away, but also includes the constructive thoughts, ideas, opinions, and criticisms of the book reviewer, which is then shared with a potential reader. Students place the book review on display in the library, adhere it to the inside front of the book, or guest talk on student announcements.

Suggested Supplies

• Optional: labels for bookplates

Instructions

Students may need to see professional examples before beginning to write their own book reviews. When introducing the assignment, provide samples that show an ideal review so students know your expectations. These professional reviews can be found on Web sites and in newspapers and magazines. Be sure that the books being reviewed in the examples are age and school appropriate. It may be that different reviews do different things better, so one professional review might be used to point out an ideal for a particular expectation, such as incorporating a quote, whereas another review offers an example of how to conclude a review.

For this writing experience to have real-world effect, students need to be able to share book reviews. Allow time for self and peer editing before sharing the finished review. Once the book review is completed, students share by putting the review on display in the library, adhering it inside the front of the book, or presenting it orally to other students as a guest speaker on student announcements.

See Chapter 4 for more details on writing and posting completed book reviews online for more global distribution.

Building Your BOOK REVIEW:

Type or Print Clearly

☐ ### The Beginning
This is the entry into the book for your audience. It leads them to the book and introduces the novel. Be sure to include the following:
- Title and Author
- Main Theme
- Genre
- A quote from the book
- What about the writing style was good and improved the reading, or made it bad and difficult to read?

☐ ### The Summary
Write a summary of the book in a well-developed paragraph that includes:
1. using correct paragraph form.
2. details about plot, main characters, setting, and major events.
   Don't tell the ending or give away too much about the story!

☐ ### The Author
Include a brief biography about the author. Use the information you have learned about the author to make connections between the author's life experiences and the book or what happened in the author's life to make the author decide to write the book.

☐ ### The Close
Wrap up your book review with your opinion about the book. How do you feel about this book and why? A good review will help the potential reader decide whether to read or not read the book.

Don't give away any surprises or important details that should be left for the reader!

Suggested book review guidelines and expectations.

From *Social Readers: Promoting Reading in the 21st Century* by Leslie B. Preddy. Santa Barbara, CA: Libraries Unlimited. Copyright © 2010.

BOOK REVIEW RUBRIC

Name: _____

Teacher: _____

Period: _____ Date: _____

Book Title: _____

The beginning grabs the audience's attention and follows the guideline requirements.

5   4   3   2   1

A well-written summary of appropriate length, follows the guideline requirements, and engages the reader.

5   4   3   2   1

The author biography makes an effort to connect what is known about the author with the book and meets the guideline requirements.

5   4   3   2   1

The close effectively evaluates the book for interest, information, and writing quality.

5   4   3   2   1

Book review was an appropriate length. Spelling, grammar, punctuation, paragraphing, and capitalization are correct.

5   4   3   2   1

FINAL GRADE:

Sample book review grading rubric.

From *Social Readers: Promoting Reading in the 21st Century* by Leslie B. Preddy. Santa Barbara, CA: Libraries Unlimited. Copyright © 2010.

Bookmark

As described in Chapter 2, an anticipation bookmark includes moral or value statements that are completed before and after reading, first as an anticipatory activity to prepare the reader for what is to come and then to see whether the reader's opinions changed after reading. Anticipation bookmarks require the student to think carefully about the ethical and moral implications in the story and create bookmarks that will be distributed to and used by other students.

Suggested Supplies

- Paper: printer paper folded into bookmark size and shape

- Optional: colored paper or card stock

Instructions

Before students begin reading, have them experience using anticipation statements before and after a brief reading. Using a different short reading, brainstorm a variety of anticipation statements for the new reading. Model turning the brainstormed list into a final and revised selection.

Before students begin, decide how many final bookmarks will be printed on a page. Make the decision based on how many bookmarks can fit on each sheet and how much workspace students should need and use. Bookmarks could be half a portrait sheet, which will create two bookmarks per copy, or one-third to one-fourth of a landscape sheet, which will create three or four bookmarks per copy, respectively. The smaller the bookmark, the smaller the workspace available for student creativity. Give students a blank strip of paper to use as a bookmark to place ideas for anticipation statements as they read.

Once students complete their bookmarks, arrange them so that multiple copies are made on the copier using colored paper or card stock, then cut into individual bookmarks. Share bookmarks with students by distributing them at the library media center checkout desk and in the school office, as well as by placing a copy of the bookmarks inside the respective titles on media center and classroom bookshelves.

Building Your BOOKMARK:

☐ **Layout & Design**
- Fold a regular sheet of printer paper into 1/3, then cut and use only 1/3 of the paper.
- Print and draw legibly.

The FRONT

☐ **Heading and Artwork**
Use creativity and include the author, title, and art work to represent the book.

☐ **Anticipation Statements**
Prior to reading, the reader responds to the anticipation statements using personal experiences and background knowledge to make predictions. After reading the book, the reader revisits the statements and revises opinions, meaning and misconceptions based on what they read.
- Write 4-6 anticipation statements related to the book.
- Each sentence should be a statement that can be answered true/false or agree/disagree. For example, "A person should always lie when the truth would be hurtful."
- Statements should relate to moral or ethical issues related to the book.

The BACK

☐ **Summary & Quote**
Use the back of the bookmark to write a summary of the book in a well-developed paragraph that includes:
1. using correct paragraph form.
2. details about plot, main characters, setting, and major events.
3. book quotes that catch a reader's interest.
4. artwork and decoration.

Don't give away any surprises or important details that should be left for the reader!

Suggested bookmark guidelines and expectations.

ANTICIPATION BOOKMARK RUBRIC

Name: _____

Teacher: _____

Period: _____ Date: _____

Book Title: _____

The anticipation bookmark is colorful, attracts a reader's interest and is created following the layout and design guidelines.

5   4   3   2   1

The bookmark front includes heading and artwork that meets the guideline requirements.

5   4   3   2   1

The bookmark front include 4-6 anticipation statements that meet the guideline requirements and help a potential reader become more interested in reading the book.

5   4   3   2   1

The bookmark back includes artwork, summary, and quotes that meet the guideline requirements and help a potential reader become more interested in reading the book.

5   4   3   2   1

The overall look of the anticipation bookmark is creative and neat. The layout is carefully planned. Spelling, grammar, punctuation, paragraphing, and capitalization are correct.

5   4   3   2   1

FINAL GRADE:

Sample bookmark grading rubric.

Booktalk

A booktalk is a "tease" used to promote the book. A booktalk "talks" the audience into wanting to read the book by sharing tantalizing tidbits without giving away too much about the story or the ending. Booktalking is a social activity. When students share booktalks, they are actively involved. Students first write their booktalks and then orally present them using a prop. See Chapter 4 for information on taking booktalks a step further by digitally recording them and posting them on the school or school library Web site to share with an even wider audience.

Suggested Supplies

- Student contribution: prop created or brought in by the student

Instructions

Booktalks, especially those integrating a prop integral to the story, should be modeled to give students an idea of how to incorporate the prop into the script requirements. For example, work a bell on a red ribbon into a sample booktalk while wearing a bathrobe and slippers for Chris Van Allsburg's *The Polar Express*.

After reading, students write a script for a booktalk, incorporating the book and a prop that represents an object or theme integral to the story's plot, characters, or setting. Students may need you to model examples before they fully grasp the concept. Allow time for draft, revision, and peer-pairing for oral practice. Once students are practiced and ready, they take turns sharing with peers in their class, being guests, presenting to other classes or primary grades, or guest booktalking on student announcements.

Building Your BOOKTALK:

PLEASE WRITE YOUR BOOKTALK IN THIRD PERSON.

☐ **The Beginning & Lead-In**
This is the beginning that introduces the audience to the novel. The lead-in is the background you need to give the audience before you lead up to the hook. You need to give just enough information for the hook to make sense.

☐ **The Hook**
This is the critical scene that will entice the audience into the book. They will want to find out how a conflict is resolved or meet more interesting characters.

☐ **The Close**
If your hook is strong enough, you may not need much more and a full closure will be unnecessary. At the very least, give some final thoughts on the book to end the booktalk, and remind your audience why you loved the book. REMEMBER, DON'T GIVE AWAY THE SECRETS OR THE ENDING OF YOUR BOOK!

☐ **Prop**
Include an item to use as a prop during your booktalk. The prop should directly relate to the book's theme, setting, moral, action, or a character. The prop could be something you wear, hold or display. It can be something found around the house, made with simple school or other supplies you already have, or borrowed. The prop must be incorporated into the booktalk so that your audience understands the connection between the prop and the story.

PAY CLOSE ATTENTION TO YOUR INTRODUCTION AND CONCLUSION—The first sentence captures your audience and the last sentence leads them to the book. Using just the right wording in those two key places can make your booktalk special.

LENGTH—Your booktalk (when read aloud) should be approximately one minute. This will be approximately one page (front and back) written or one page (front only) typed.

Don't give away any surprises or important details that should be left for the reader!

Suggested booktalk guidelines and expectations.

From *Social Readers: Promoting Reading in the 21st Century* by Leslie B. Preddy. Santa Barbara, CA: Libraries Unlimited. Copyright © 2010.

BOOKTALK RUBRIC

Name: _____

Teacher: _____

Period: _____ Date: _____

Book Title: _____

You included a beginning that introduces your audience to your book and captures their attention. You included the background of the characters, setting, and plot that you need to give the audience before you lead up to the hook.

5   4   3   2   1

You included a hook, the critical scene that will lure the audience into the book and leave them wanting more, that really grabs the audience.

5   4   3   2   1

You included a closing that gives some final thoughts on the book to end the booktalk and reminds your audience why you loved the book.

5   4   3   2   1

Booktalk was an appropriate length and written in third person. Spelling, grammar, punctuation, paragraphing and capitalization are correct.

5   4   3   2   1

The prop was incorporated into the booktalk in a way the audience would notice. The prop relates to the book's theme, setting, moral, action, or a character.

5   4   3   2   1

FINAL GRADE:

Sample booktalk grading rubric.

From *Social Readers: Promoting Reading in the 21st Century* by Leslie B. Preddy. Santa Barbara, CA: Libraries Unlimited. Copyright © 2010.

Brochure

In this project, students create bi-fold brochures by hand or with a computer to promote the strengths of the book and persuade prospective readers into reading it. Placing the brochure prominently on display gives the student who created it a feeling of pride and achievement, plus it has the added benefit of using peer promotion to motivate other students to read the book. Promoting books through the display and distribution of student-created informative and entertaining brochures takes advantage of students' need to be socially prominent (the peer creator) and read what is socially acceptable (the prospective peer readers).

Suggested Supplies

• Paper: folded printer paper; colored paper may also be used

Instructions

When teaching students the elements of an effective brochure, examples may include professional samples created for other purposes beyond the library or homemade samples created by the educator.

For the brochure to be socially effective and have an impact on students' need to network with peers, completed brochures need to be copied for display and distribution. Make copies of the brochures, possibly on colored paper to draw attention to them, and display them in a prominent location. The location could be a designated display, the circulation desk, a special display with the book and brochures spotlighted together, or available at the bookshelf where the books by that author are located.

Building Your BROCHURE:

☐ ## Layout & Design
- Fold a sheet of printer paper in half, like a book.
- Print and draw legibly.
- Use correct grammar and punctuation.

☐ ## The FRONT
Heading and Artwork
Use creativity and include the author, title, and custom artwork to represent the book.

The INSIDE
☐ ### Left Side
On the left side of the booklet include the following:
- List the "Top Five Reasons to Read This Book". Be original and relate your reasons to the book's content, how the book relates to the world today, and how readers might relate to the book.
- A colorful illustration to represent the setting. Include a detailed paragraph caption to describe the setting.

☐ ### Right Side
The right side of the booklet is for the story characters. Draw a colorful illustration for each of at least 3 characters. Include with each illustration a paragraph caption for each illustration.
- Illustrations should be hand-drawn.
- For each character description include physical traits, personality traits and how the character is connected to other characters.

☐ ## The BACK
Summary
Use the back of the brochure to write a summary of the book in a well-developed paragraph that includes:
1. using correct paragraph form.
2. details about plot, main characters, setting, and major events.
3. book quotes that catch a reader's interest.
4. artwork and decoration.

Don't give away any surprises or important details that should be left for the reader!

Suggested brochure guidelines and expectations.

From *Social Readers: Promoting Reading in the 21st Century* by Leslie B. Preddy. Santa Barbara, CA: Libraries Unlimited. Copyright © 2010.

BROCHURE RUBRIC

Name: _____

Teacher: _____

Period: _____ Date: _____

Book Title: _____

The overall look of the brochure is attractive, creative and neat. The layout is carefully planned. Spelling, grammar, punctuation, paragraphing, and capitalization are correct.

5   4   3   2   1

The 'Top Five Reasons to Read This Book' list is entertaining, connects to the book, and meets the guideline requirements. The setting artwork and caption are well-written to attract potential readers to the book and meets the guideline requirements.

5   4   3   2   1

There are at least three characters illustrations and captions. The artwork and captions are well-written to attract potential readers to the book and meets the guideline requirements.

5   4   3   2   1

The characters artwork and article is well-written to attract potential readers to the book and meets the guideline requirements.

5   4   3   2   1

The book summary and artwork is well-written to attract potential readers to the book and meets the guideline requirements.

5   4   3   2   1

FINAL GRADE:

Sample brochure grading rubric.

From *Social Readers: Promoting Reading in the 21st Century* by Leslie B. Preddy.
Santa Barbara, CA: Libraries Unlimited. Copyright © 2010.

Comic Strip

Through a comic strip, a book is introduced and promoted to others using integrated text and graphics to convey the novel's key message. To feed students' need to share and communicate with peers, the completed comic strips may be temporarily framed and displayed, reduced and copied onto double-sided bookmarks, or incorporated into the student newsletter or newspaper.

Suggested Supplies

• Optional: card stock, colored paper, or clear plastic display frames

• Paper: printer paper folded in half, then into thirds, then reopened to make six equal boxes

• Writing and drawing instruments: colored pencils, colored pens, pencil chalk

Instructions

Students are familiar with cartoon comic strips and graphic novels, but they may need some help understanding the elements of incorporating text and images to convey a message in a limited amount of space. They may need to become familiar with text bubbles, thought bubbles, narration, or captions.

Students divide a sheet of paper into six equal sections, each representing a "frame" of a comic strip. With the paper in landscape orientation, each section will equal one frame of the story that students will communicate through illustrations, captions and text bubbles.

Share comic strips with other students through a display or by publishing them. If comic strips are going to be displayed, place the final strip into a clear plastic frame, then display it and the book in a special location, or place the frame near the shelf where the book can be found. To make bookmarks out of the comic strips using a photocopier, student instructions may include using only black ink with shadowing techniques for the artwork for most effective copying. To prepare the student comic strip for copying, make a copy of the original work. To make bookmarks, cut the strip so that the first three frames will be on the front and the last three frames are on the back. This will allow for two oversized bookmarks cut out of one sheet of card stock or colored paper.

Building Your COMIC STRIP

1. Please write your comic strip in third person and use correct grammar and punctuation.
2. Fold the paper into thirds, like a brochure, then fold again in half. Open paper up and number boxes 1-6.

☐ Use colored artwork to illustrate the action. Create text bubbles for the words, just as seen in graphic novels and newspaper comic strips.

☐ Characters and Setting
  • Introduce the characters appearance through the drawing and personality traits through the action in the text bubbles.
  • Pictures should match where the story took place. Be sure to include the time and place of the setting.

☐ Box 1: Introduce the Book
  Make this resemble the book cover. Include the title, author, and include a colored picture. Be sure to give yourself credit as the comic strip artist and author.

☐ Boxes 2-5: The Hook
  Use the center four boxes to re-enact a critical event from the book, which will entice the audience into reading the book.
  • Give a hint toward the conflict the characters will encounter.
  • Incorporate a quote from the book into a text bubble.
  • Pictures should show the action represented in the text bubbles.

☐ Box 6: The Close
  Wrap it up. Give some final thoughts on the book and tell the audience the genre and why you loved it or why they should read it.

Don't give away any surprises or important details that should be left for the reader!

Suggested comic strip guidelines and expectations.

COMIC STRIP RUBRIC

Name: _____

Teacher: _____

Period: _____ Date: _____

Book Title: _____

The overall look of the newsletter is attractive, creative and neat. The layout is carefully planned. Spelling, grammar, punctuation, paragraphing, and capitalization are correct.

5   4   3   2   1

The comic strip includes accurate representations of the main characters and setting (time and place) and includes the information listed in the guidelines.

5   4   3   2   1

The first box resembles the book cover and meets the guideline requirements.

5   4   3   2   1

Boxes 2-5 depict an important scene from the book in an interesting and captivating manner. The artwork and text bubbles are well-written to attract potential readers to the book. Each box meets the guideline requirements.

5   4   3   2   1

The closing box wraps up the comic strip well, includes the genre, incorporates an informed opinion, and meets the guideline requirements.

5   4   3   2   1

FINAL GRADE:

Sample comic strip grading rubric.

From *Social Readers: Promoting Reading in the 21st Century* by Leslie B. Preddy. Santa Barbara, CA: Libraries Unlimited. Copyright © 2010.

Newsletter

A booktalk newsletter is written by one student or a group of students to promote a particular book to fellow students. The newsletter may be created by hand or with a computer. The sharing necessary for today's social students may occur by contributing the book newsletter to the school's student newsletter, framing and displaying it in the library media center, or making copies to distribute through the library media center and school office.

Suggested Supplies

- Paper: printer and colored paper

- Optional: clear plastic display frames

- Writing and drawing instruments: colored pencils, colored pens

Instructions

Newsletters are fairly common and easy for students to understand. Classroom introduction may be limited to maintain students' freedom of creativity, but the instructor may prefer to show some examples from businesses that incorporate layout design or certain elements.

Decide in advance how students may create the newsletter. Newsletters may be handwritten and hand drawn or created using a computer's word processing or desktop publishing program, depending on the skills and standards being met. Handmade projects, instead of using a desktop publishing program, allow students to focus on personal and artistic creativity.

Place completed newsletters for display in clear plastic display frames in the designated location with the book on the shelf or special display area. Newsletters copied to distribute to fellow students need to be placed in a visible location, such as the shelf next to the book, a special display area, a circulation desk, or the school office.

Building Your One Page NEWSLETTER

☐ **Newsletter Name**
Design a title, or heading, for your newsletter. It should relate to the book in some way: theme, setting, genre, characters, etc.

☐ **Review**
Write a review of the book in a well-developed paragraph that includes:
1. using correct paragraph form.
2. details about the major events and how they effect the story.
   Don't tell the ending or give away too much about the story!
3. clearly printed or type.
4. artwork that relates to the article and book.

☐ **Characters**
Write an article about your favorite characters that you love or love to hate.
1. Describe who the character is, what he or she did, personality traits, and other interesting things you could add.
2. Create a headline that relates to the article.
3. Include artwork that relates to the article.

☐ **Setting**
Write a brief article capturing the setting.
1. Describe the setting, how it plays a role in the story, how it related to other places, and other interesting things you could add.
2. Create a headline that relates to the article.
3. Include artwork that relates to the article.

Don't give away any surprises or important details that should be left for the reader!

Suggested newsletter guidelines and expectations.

From *Social Readers: Promoting Reading in the 21st Century* by Leslie B. Preddy. Santa Barbara, CA: Libraries Unlimited. Copyright © 2010.

NEWSLETTER RUBRIC

Name: _____

Teacher: _____

Period: _____ Date: _____

Book Title: _____

The newsletter name sets the right mood for the novel, attracts a reader's interest and included the information listed guidelines.

5　4　3　2　1

The book review and artwork is well-written to attract potential readers to the book and meets the guideline requirements.

5　4　3　2　1

The characters artwork and article is well-written to attract potential readers to the book and meets the guideline requirements.

5　4　3　2　1

The setting artwork and article is well-written to attract potential
readers to the book and meets the guideline requirements.

5　4　3　2　1

The overall look of the newsletter is attractive, creative and neat. The layout is carefully planned. Spelling, grammar, punctuation, paragraphing, and capitalization are correct.

5　4　3　2　1

FINAL GRADE:

Sample newsletter grading rubric.

From *Social Readers: Promoting Reading in the 21st Century* by Leslie B. Preddy.
Santa Barbara, CA: Libraries Unlimited. Copyright © 2010.

Poster

A student-made poster is displayed to advertise a book to peers through informative and entertaining visuals and text. The poster is created for the sole intention of promoting reading material to fellow students while persuading them that the book is interesting and a must-read experience.

The poster includes pictures, memorabilia, artifacts, and text to enlighten the audience and encourage others to read the book.

Suggested Supplies

- Craft supplies: glue, poster/foam board or tri-fold display board, rulers, scissors, and other miscellaneous supplies

- Paper: construction paper, colored paper, printer paper

- Writing and drawing instruments: colored pencils, colored pens, crayons, markers

Instructions

The beauty of this old pastime—creating a poster—is its ease of public display for sharing. Altering the requirements changes the whole look and feel of the final product for the intended audience, so be flexible and open to trying new combinations and expectations based on individual and class personality and talents.

Posters can and should be displayed everywhere throughout the building, choosing prominent and high-visibility areas or designated display locations. Enhance the experience by pulling the book advertised on a poster and temporarily displaying them together in a designated space, periodically exchanging the book and poster on display.

Building Your POSTER:

☐ **Title and Heading**

The title and author of the book should appear in large print.

☐ **Book Summary**

Write a diary entry from the main character's point of view that gives a summary of the book.
- Write using correct paragraph form.
- Include these details: main characters, setting, and major events. Don't tell the ending!
- Type or write clearly on a separate sheet of paper before gluing onto the poster.

☐ **Photographs, Artifacts, Memorabilia**

Include artwork, which could be in the form of a photograph, artifact or memorabilia. Be creative! Photographs, artifacts and memorabilia can be drawn by hand or found in magazines, newspapers, or around the house. A piece of artwork should illustrate one of the following:
1. The main character in a scene from the book.
2. The character's family or friends.
3. The main problem in your story.
4. The setting of the story.
5. One picture of your choice related to the story.

☐ **Captions**

Write a caption for each photograph, artifact, or memorabilia included.
- Use paragraph form.
- Use the caption to help explain the image and its meaning to the plot, characters, setting, or theme.
- Type or write clearly on a separate sheet before gluing it onto the poster board.

Don't give away any surprises or important details that should be left for the reader!

Suggested poster guidelines and expectations.

POSTER RUBRIC

Name: _____

Teacher: _____

Period: _____ Date: _____

Book Title: _____

The title and author are included in a colorful and clear manner.

5   4   3   2   1

The book summary is written in first person and contains the requirements listed in the guidelines.

5   4   3   2   1

The artwork meets the guideline requirements and is attractive, neat and colorful.

5   4   3   2   1

The captions help explain the artwork, are written in paragraph form, and meet the guideline requirements.

5   4   3   2   1

The overall look of the poster board is creative and neat. The layout is carefully planned. Spelling, grammar, punctuation, paragraphing, and capitalization are correct.

5   4   3   2   1

FINAL GRADE:

Sample poster grading rubric.

From *Social Readers: Promoting Reading in the 21st Century* by Leslie B. Preddy. Santa Barbara, CA: Libraries Unlimited. Copyright © 2010.

Scrapbook

Think of a scrapbook as a type of storytelling in the form of a keepsake album. It includes artifacts, memorabilia, diary or journal entries, and photographs. This scrapbook project uses student creativity with text and graphics to draw fellow students' interest. After previewing the scrapbook, other students are encouraged to read the book.

Suggested Supplies

• Craft supplies: glue, old magazines for collage, rulers, scissors, and other miscellaneous supplies

• Optional: blank books, still digital camera, student-created artifacts and memorabilia

• Paper: construction paper, colored paper, printer paper

• Writing and drawing instruments: colored pencils, colored pens, crayons, markers

Instructions

Scrapbooks are more and more common today, even with the modern digital scrapbook, but some students may not have much exposure to scrapbooks, so some real-world examples would be helpful to ensure all students have common background knowledge. Sample pages could be borrowed and copied from scrapbooking friends and staff, found online or photographed from 4-H projects on display at the county or state fair. Some books are even written in scrapbook style and could be examples, such as Jennifer Holm's *Middle School Is Worse than Meatloaf.* Look for samples that include the key elements of headings, pictures, journaling, memorabilia, and artifacts. Brainstorm as a class a list of made-up artifacts and memorabilia that might be incorporated into a scrapbook. The list might begin with ticket stub, lock of hair, note, program book, ribbon, certificate, name badge, leaf, flower, autograph, keepsake, postcard, note, money, receipts, and much more.

Scrapbooks may take on many sizes and be made out of a variety of materials. Blank books may be purchased online or through local teacher or office supply stores. Using supplies already found in the classroom also makes successful scrapbooks. Large scrapbooks can be created by sandwiching printer paper between two sheets of construction-paper for covers. Make a smaller size by placing printer paper on top of one sheet of construction paper, then folding it in half to make smaller books with the construction paper as the cover and the printer paper for the inside pages.

Sharing and showing off book promotion scrapbooks can be as far-reaching as it is easy. Have students brainstorm places to set out their scrapbooks for public consumption. Lay completed scrapbooks out on tables in casual seating areas in the library media center, office, and other public spaces throughout the school.

Building Your SCRAPBOOK:

☐ **Scrapbook Cover**
1. The scrapbook cover should include the main character's name, the title of the book, the author's name, and your name. Be creative!
2. Illustrate the cover by drawing it yourself, taking pictures yourself, or finding pictures or images.

☐ **Book Summary**
Write a diary entry from the main character's point of view that gives a summary of the book.
1. Write using correct paragraph form.
2. Include these details: main characters, setting, and major events. Don't tell the ending!
3. Type or write clearly on a separate sheet of paper before gluing into the scrapbook.
4. Include a date that reflects the "date" the character wrote it.

☐ **Photographs, Artifacts, Memorabilia**
Five images, which could be in the form of a photograph, artifact, or memorabilia should be included. "Photos", artifacts and memorabilia can be drawn by hand or found. Include captions describing each image. Items should illustrate each of the following:
1. The main character in a scene from the book.
2. The character's family or friends.
3. The main problem in your story.
4. The setting of the story.
5. One picture of your choice related to the story.

☐ **Diary Entry: Journaling**
Write a diary entry from the main character's point of view that reflects the main character's feelings about themselves or reflects how they've changed throughout the story.
1. Use paragraph form.
2. Type or write clearly on a separate sheet before gluing into the scrapbook.

Don't give away any surprises or important details that should be left for the reader!

Suggested scrapbook guidelines and expectations.

From *Social Readers: Promoting Reading in the 21st Century* by Leslie B. Preddy. Santa Barbara, CA: Libraries Unlimited. Copyright © 2010.

SCRAPBOOK RUBRIC

Name: _____

Teacher: _____

Period: _____ Date: _____

Book Title: _____

The scrapbook cover is colorful, attracts a reader's interest and includes the information listed in the guidelines.

5   4   3   2   1

The book summary is written in first person and contains each of the four items listed.

5   4   3   2   1

The photographs, artifacts and memorabilia illustrate the five required categories, and a caption is included to describe each picture.

5   4   3   2   1

The diary entry reflects how the main character feels about themselves or how they feel they have changed throughout the story and follows the guidelines listed.

5   4   3   2   1

The overall look of the scrapbook is creative and neat. The layout is carefully planned. Spelling, grammar, punctuation, paragraphing, and capitalization are correct.

5   4   3   2   1

FINAL GRADE:

Sample scrapbook grading rubric.

From *Social Readers: Promoting Reading in the 21st Century* by Leslie B. Preddy.
Santa Barbara, CA: Libraries Unlimited. Copyright © 2010.

Making Informed Decisions

For today's generation of social students, making personal reading choices may be challenging. Often, they need to be taught how to make decisions for themselves instead of taking the easy road of being told what to do and read. They do not like being told what to read, yet they are also often at a loss about how to find reading materials that would be personally appealing and interesting. Students today need help learning how to make personal reading choices and come up with ideas to narrow down the great variety of available materials to a small, more manageable sampling before they are able to read socially and share their reading knowledge and experience with peers. A sample of ideas to reach students and teach them to become independent readers capable of attaining the level of social readership necessary for lifetime success includes training on basic personal selection strategies and meeting the reading needs of all students.

Book Choice—Personal Selection

Before our students' generation can take on the sharing traits necessary to become social readers, they need help with the basics. Too often, they have learned the path of least resistance and passive learning. Through this life-coasting, they've lost the ability to figure out for themselves what to read for personal pleasure. Without the ability to find what is worthy of their reading time, they are unable to go to the next level and talk, share, or recommend reading. The simple skills necessary for basic book selection are lost to many students today; therefore, they need help, practice, and retraining.

Cost: $

There is no cost for this activity if you use books you have in the library media center collection and card stock or colored paper that are regularly purchased by the school or library media center.

Estimated Unit Time: One Session

Basic book selection training requires only one instructional session but may need follow-up opportunities for reinforcement, depending on the nature of the group.

Suggested Supplies

- Copies of bookmark on card stock or colored paper
- Selection of books from the library media center collection

Instructions

Before student training and practice, preplanning includes creating an informative bookmark and collecting a sampling of books.

Allow the bookmark to guide instruction: list basic book selection strategies, beginning with what first draws a student to the book and finishing with how to dig in and sample it. The bookmarks are take-home, step-by-step guides to help novice readers remember what was practiced as a group, and it's handy for them to keep their place in the book they select to read.

For practice and instruction, select a variety of library books to pile at each table before students arrive. The book selection may be random or selected for a specific purpose, theme, genre, or interest. These are not necessarily the books students will check out but the books they will use while they get hands-on practice. (Of course, some students may decide to check out the book they sample.) The lead instructor will also need a book when modeling.

Once students arrive and settle in at the table, pass out the bookmarks and go through each step, one at a time. Interact with students to get ideas and input by talking, modeling, and giving students time to practice with a sample book before going on to the next self-selection skill. Once all skills have been completed, have students trade books and go through it again. After students appear to have confidence and experience, allow them to take their bookmark to the shelves and perform self-selection as they pick out a book to check out using the strategies they have just practiced.

Book Choice
The Right Book for You

When selecting a book...

☐ look at the book cover artwork. Is it interesting?

☐ find the author's name. Have you heard of this author? What else has the author written?

☐ skim the chapter titles or table of contents.

☐ read the first few sentences or pages.

☐ read the book summary on the inside flap of the book jacket. If it is a paperback, is the summary on the back of the book? (Warning: Make sure you are not reading an advertisement for a different book!)

Get reading ideas from...

☐ another student or friend.

☐ a teacher.

☐ a library media specialist.

☐ a public librarian.

☐ family.

☐ recommended reading lists.

☐ a book review or book talk.

☐ searching the library catalog.

☐ an award list.

READ

P M M S

Library Media Center

Creating a bookmark keepsake for students to follow during instruction and keep afterward as a reminder is helpful to emerging readers and nonreaders.

From *Social Readers: Promoting Reading in the 21st Century* by Leslie B. Preddy. Santa Barbara, CA: Libraries Unlimited. Copyright © 2010.

READING MATTERS

Ways to Help Yourself Become a Successful Reader

- Make regular visits to the library and book sales.
- Have reading material with you wherever you go.
- Build a home library of favorite books & magazines.
- Read at least 15 minutes every day.
- Participate as a family in reading and reading discussions: sharing thoughts and opinions about the reading and how it relates to your life.

READ

PMMS

Instructional Media Center

READING MATTERS BECAUSE YOU MATTER!

Multicultural Authors

- Joseph Bruchac
- Elisa Carbone
- Christopher Paul Curtis
- Sharon Draper
- Nikki Grimes
- Virginia Hamilton
- Dorothy Hoobler
- Beverly Jenkins
- Francisco Jimenez
- Angela Johnson
- Cynthia Kadohata
- Julius Lester
- Patricia McKissack
- Walter Dean Myers
- An Na
- Linda Sue Park
- Shelley Pearsall
- Pam Munoz Ryan
- Gary Soto
- Jacqueline Woodson
- Lisa Yee
- Laurence Yep

Stop by your neighborhood branch public library or school library and try books by these suggested authors.

Create a take-home keepsake, like a bookmark, as a reminder to students and parents.

From *Social Readers: Promoting Reading in the 21st Century* by Leslie B. Preddy. Santa Barbara, CA: Libraries Unlimited. Copyright © 2010.

Multicultural Reading Matters

Minority students have deeper difficulties finding their reading voice: that internal influence that helps them locate and become immersed in a story that speaks to them on a personal level. The reading voice is necessary to become a lifelong social reader. All students need books with characters and plots they can relate to, and minority students may have a more difficult time finding resources that speak to them and their experiences. They need help finding positive experiences with books that speak to their specific background and culture. With guidance and help taking this first step toward locating authors that write for a specific audience, minority students can take the next steps toward socializing and sharing reading experiences with others. After the Reading Matters activity, minority students make better choices for themselves, read more, and bring friends in to pass on reading experiences to them, too.

Cost: $

There is no cost if using books already existing in the library media center collection and card stock or colored paper already purchased by the school or library media center.

Estimated Unit Time: One Session

Reading Matters takes one instructional session, plus a spotlight display shelving area in the library media center. Training may occur in a club or group setting. This may also be an opportunity to build cultural awareness in all students by working with a heterogenous class.

Suggested Supplies

- Copies of bookmark on card stock or colored paper
- Selection of culturally diverse books from the library media center collection
- Decorated spotlight display shelving area

Instructions

Before student training and practice, preplanning includes creating an informative bookmark and collecting a sampling of library books.

Create the bookmark to guide instruction. On one side, list suggestions and advice for how to become or continue to be a reader. On the other side, list age-appropriate multicultural authors recommended for the particular school's ethnic and racial population. Be sure multiple copies of the author's book may be found in the library media center collection. If not, seek grant money to expand the diversity of the fiction and narrative nonfiction collection.

In preparation for instruction, pull a collection of books by the authors listed on the bookmark. Place a variety on each table. After students arrive, begin instruction by passing out the bookmark and hosting an open discussion about diversity and culture in literature. Cover the points listed on the bookmark. Conclude by sharing the list of recommended authors on the reverse side of the bookmark. Give students time to peruse the sample of books, and allow time for every child to check out a book from the tables or among the books still on the shelves.

Decorate a special, permanent display or shelving area of the library media center for new multicultural books. Include copies of the bookmark in the display. As new books with multicultural themes are added to the library media center collection, place them in the display. Also include books written by authors from diverse backgrounds. Direct students to the display until they know to go themselves. They will begin drawing their friends there, too.

Family Connection

Whenever possible, include family in the Reading Matters Campaign. Choose a day when parents will already be in the building, like registration day, back-to-school night or parent-teacher conference days. Include an invitation to visit the library media center in the newsletter, announcement or postcard going out to families from the school. Prepare treats, copies of the bookmark, and, if possible, books to give away to help attendees set up a home library. Set up a display and give a brief presentation to share with families how they can encourage reading habits. Share the bookmark with caregivers. If possible, allow families to choose a giveaway book for home.

READING MATTERS

Dear Student and Parent:

Reading is key to success in life. Whether reading for personal interest or school, let us help you develop or add to your home bookshelf. Please stop by the library media center Reading Matters booth during the Student Led Conferences held Tuesday, October 16 or Wednesday, October 17 to receive additional information. Also, present this postcard to receive your free book to keep and add to your home bookshelf and to enter our drawing for a complimentary prize.
We look forward to seeing you!

Read during free time!

R E A D

P M M S
Library Media Center

Send home postcards to make a critical connection with families and caregivers.

From *Social Readers: Promoting Reading in the 21st Century* by Leslie B. Preddy.
Santa Barbara, CA: Libraries Unlimited. Copyright © 2010.

Involving Everyone

Social reading takes on many forms, but all come back to one basic trait: sharing. Thinking of ways students can verbally, visually, and physically share reading experiences is integral to meeting students where they are and developing them into the readers they are destined to become. Students want control and choice in their lives but often do not know where to start when it comes to reading. They need guidance and assistance through reading lists, peer recommendations, conversations, and time to build the reading habit.

Give One, Take One

As students become more social in their reading habits, a desire to share and trade reading materials becomes natural to them. It is important to encourage this desire. Give students a variety of opportunities to meet their need to pass on and collect reading advice. A simple Give One, Take One display allows students to bring in a book they enjoyed and want to share. In exchange for the book left, the student picks out a book already existing in the display. Students share what they've read with other students and also choose something to read that another student left behind.

Cost: $$

The Give One, Take One project may begin through donations or the purchase of paperback books. Because this is a sharing opportunity, start with gently used books. Once the startup collection is established, the occasional supplemental used book purchase may be needed. If no shelving is available, a display or book rack will be necessary.

Estimated Unit Time: Ongoing

Although this project is ongoing, it takes just a few days to set up and occasional spare moments to maintain.

Planning Involvement: One Person

This project can be managed by one person or by a student club willing to take on the organization, maintenance, and promotion.

Suggested Supplies

- Books: gently used books

- Create: publicity and promotional materials, signage

- Display: designated book display and shelving

- Student contribution: gently used books

Instructions

Locate a small grant or collect book donations. You can also buy gently used popular fiction and narrative nonfiction. Gently used paperbacks can be purchased from used bookstores or secondhand thrift stores, such as Goodwill or the Salvation Army. New paperbacks may be purchased at an educator's discount or a special price arranged through a local bookstore or paperback book distributor. If necessary, purchase an inexpensive tabletop or floor book rack.

Locate a space in the library media center, preferably near an entrance or in a reading area away from the regular library bookshelves to designate for the Give One, Take One display. Keeping it slightly physically distanced from the regular library media center collection will reduce patron confusion. Create a self-explanatory sign for the space, and decorate the book rack or shelving area as desired. Once completed, promote the grand opening through a week-long blitz of advertising in the student newsletter, on student announcements, and through announcements to classes visiting the library media center. Occasionally re-advertise throughout the year.

Set up the Give One, Take One display on the honor system. It should be worry-free and low maintenance. If more books are disappearing that are donated, just be happy the books found a home and put some more gently used books in the rack, or ask students to donate books to fill it back up again. This can also be done at the end or beginning of the school year with unclaimed, unnamed books left in the lost and found over the summer.

GIVE ONE, TAKE ONE

Have you read a great book lately?

Do you love to share?

Do you have a good book at home you're done reading?

If you have a great paperback book that would be appropriate to share and is in good condition, bring it in to the Library Media Center's "Give One, Take One Project" bookshelf.

Bring your gently used book in & exchange it for another book on the "Give One, Take One Project" bookshelf. You know it'll be a great read because it has been donated by your peer.

Placing a sign at the Give One, Take One location will explain the program to students walking by and help sell the program without any other explanation or publicity.

Personal Reading

Our students' generation needs time and practice reading. They need to learn to dedicate time to reading for personal reasons. Many young people need to be reminded to set aside time for reading before they can begin to do it for themselves intuitively. They need practice talking about reading to significant people in their lives. They need to have reading conversations with people they feel safe with, like caregivers, parents, guardians, and adults in the school before they can be confident enough to share reading experiences with peers. Conversations about how reading has an impact on knowledge, feelings, opinion, and other aspects of the self is vital for young people. Through a home reading log, students are reminded to read, enter reading information into the log, and discuss the reading experience with a significant adult at home.

Cost: $

This will cost nothing but paper that's already in stock, unless the school plans to collect reading logs for reader's reward prize drawings. If rewards are an option, discounted but new paperback books or small school supplies will need to be included in your budget.

Estimated Unit Time: Varies

The reading log can be done for a brief period of time, like a kickoff to the first month of school, or it can continue throughout the year or over the summer.

Planning Involvement: Three People

Reading logs require the combined cooperation of the project coordinator, classroom teachers, and a parent or guardian.

Suggested Supplies

- Create: basic guidelines, publicity, and promotional materials; reading logs

- Optional: reader's rewards

- Student contribution: library or personal copy of a book

Instructions

Create a home reading log that includes the desired details. Consider the following details:

- Suggested reading time

- Date

- Title of book

- Pages read

- Actual minutes spent reading

- Encouraging reading conversations between caregiver and child

Distribute reading logs and train students how to use them. If possible, model for students how to hold a conversation about something they've read at home. Post an explanatory announcement in the student newsletter to help families understand the importance and need for participation. Collect completed reading logs and reward or enter returned logs into reader's reward prize drawings, which could be done as frequently as desired: daily, weekly, monthly, or quarterly.

Personal Reading Log

Name: _____   Teacher: _____   Period/Block: _____
(please print first and last name)

Date	Title of Book	Pages Read	Minutes Spent Reading	Guardian Initials

Parent or Guardian: After reading, have a conversation about what your child has been reading, then sign your initials. Ask questions about things such as how your child feels about the book, what he or she is learning from it, and how it relates to your child, the world, and others.

Date	Title of Book	Pages Read	Minutes Spent Reading	Guardian Initials
Example: *May 28*	*Harry Potter & the Deathly Hallows*	*Pgs 22–35*	*16 minutes*	*JCB*
			...more reading on back...	

Leslie B. Preddy   Perry Meridian Middle School   Instructional Media Center

A simple reading log will help students and parents remember the importance of setting aside time to read and encourage conversation about reading.

Personal Reading Log

Parent or Guardian: Before signing each day, have a conversation about what your child has been reading.
Ask questions like how your child feels about it, what your child is learning from it, and how it relates to your child, the world, and others.

Date	Title of Book	Pages Read	Minutes Spent Reading	Guardian Initials
	Happy Reading!			

Leslie B. Preddy   Perry Meridian Middle School   Instructional Media Center

A simple reading log will help students and parents remember the importance of setting aside time to read and encourage conversation about reading. (*Cont.*)

From *Social Readers: Promoting Reading in the 21st Century* by Leslie B. Preddy.
Santa Barbara, CA: Libraries Unlimited. Copyright © 2010.

Read to Vote

Forward-thinking organizations realize that students need more than a recommended reading list to branch out and try new genres and themes. Many state student choice awards require, by nature, active participation. Throughout the year, students read from the nominee list, trying to read the minimum necessary to be eligible to vote. The actively social goal to achieve is the commonality of reading the same books and voting along with other students throughout the school and state. If there is no state program in your area, create a school, district, or regional student choice project.

This project connects students at the local and state level. Done effectively, the state student choice program builds into a unifying reading force within the school. The titles are read and promoted by many students and staff throughout the building. Informal booktalks occur. Conversations happen. A frenzy of recommended reading ensues.

Cost: $$$$

To make this a successful program requires annual funding to purchase multiple copies of the nominated books. Otherwise, it will be challenging to bring this program to a socially invasive level.

Estimated Unit Time: Varies

Begin preparation in the spring for the coming year by ordering books and developing promotional material (this also includes creating the nominee list, if you are creating the list locally). Check the state program's Web site for details on how to register and participate, when the nominee list will be released, and how and when student voting should be performed. Base the school participation calendar on how much time will be allowed for reading and promoting the nominees and when the voting will occur.

Planning Involvement: One Person up to the Entire Faculty

Although this can be accomplished with just an activity planner, it is most effective when all faculty members are on board and willing to support and promote the program annually.

Suggested Supplies

- Books: multiple copies of nominee books (paperback)
- Create: nominee list, program brochure, project timeline, publicity and promotional materials, signage, voting form
- Optional: reader's rewards, spine labels, designated shelving

Instructions

In the preceding year, locate funding to support the purchase of multiple copies of the next year's nominees. This could be funded through donations, grants, fundraisers, PTA support, book fairs, or other ongoing funding sources. Seek purchasing discounts through vendors and local booksellers. In the spring, check the program Web site to confirm registration and participation details. If needed, prepare a procedure to monitor students and keep track of which books they have read. As soon as the nominee list is released, begin ordering copies. Read the books in advance and encourage staff members to read them as well in preparation for promoting the upcoming program. Take note of what was read and write brief booktalks for future use. Encourage staff members to help generate promotional materials.

If creating a reading list because there is no state student choice award, pull together a representative group of educators to select the books for the nominee list. Research other states' student choice awards to learn about different ways that nominees are selected and programs are run, how to establish timelines, and how to organize the voting process. Choose the key aspects that best suit the school's needs and personality. Consider the following:

May an author have more than one title on the list?

Is it important for books to be available in paperback (affordability)?

Should there be a range of genres, themes, genders, and ethnic groups among the list of titles?

How many titles should be on the list?

How many copies of each book should the library purchase?

Should copies of the nominated books be purchased for the classrooms?

How many books from the list should a student read to become eligible to vote?

How long should the program run? Beginning when? Ending when?

What will the voting date be, and how will students vote?

Will there be reader's rewards to celebrate students who are eligible to vote?

Annual promotion is necessary for this program to become a tradition that is expected and looked forward to by students, staff, and families. Prepare an informational brochure, bookmark, or flyer to share with students and staff. Include all information that staff, students, and families need to reduce confusion: the list of nominated books, rules and requirements, purpose, deadlines, and any other important details. Promotion should also include signs or posters for the library media center and for teachers to display throughout the school, book reviews posted by students, and, if at all possible, video booktalks created by students and staff for Web posting and student announcements. Details for the video promotions and book reviews may be found in Chapter 4.

As the opening date of the program approaches, prepare a display and shelving area for the nominees. Consider placing a special spine label on the nominated books to mark them as part of the special voting project. Make copies of the signs or other promotional materials to decorate the shelving area, as well as other public areas in the school. Share information through the student newsletter and student announcements. Distribute the promotional materials to staff members and encourage them to display and promote the nominees up through voting day.

Schedule a time to introduce all classes to the program and books. Share a copy of the informative brochure with all students, encouraging them to mark the books of interest as they listen to brief, teasing booktalks.

As the program progresses, consider ways to keep up the momentum and interest. For example, decorate student lockers or desks as students meet or surpass the goal, air video booktalks during student announcements, and post program updates and book advertisements for families in the student newsletter. Offer many opportunities for students to share ideas and opinions about the nominees through club meetings, group sharing, posting online book reviews, informal booktalks to classes, and other socially engaging ways.

Toward the end of the program year, prepare for voting day. If no procedure is in place and this is the school's first year to participate, brainstorm ideas with fellow teachers on how to promote and manage voting day. Many states provide voting forms and final reporting procedures through a Web site. If voting forms are not provided, create one. If needed, establish a procedure to monitor student progress and keep track of how many students are eligible to vote. If reader's rewards are offered for eligible students, prepare for more than enough prizes.

Wrap up the program year by tabulating votes and announcing the school's winning book from the nominee list in student announcements and the school newsletter, then, when the state posts the state winner, announce the state winner, comparing it to the school's winner.

P M M s
Instructional Media Center

2009-2010 Young Hoosier Book Award Program

Leslie Preddy, Library Media Specialist
lpreddy@msdpt.k12.in.us
Perry Meridian Middle School
Instructional Media Center
202 W. Meridian School Road
Indianapolis, IN 46217
317-789-4171, fax 317-865-2710
http://pmms.msdpt.k12.in.us/imc/index.htm

Official YHBA Wesite:
http://www.ilfonline.org/Programs/yhba.htm
PMMS IMC Website:
http://pmms.msdpt.k12.in.us/imc/index.htm
PMMS Library Collection:
http://destiny.msdpt.k12.in.us/

Remember: People mature at different rates. Not every book is appropriate for every person at every age. When choosing a book, use wisdom—do not read a book that is inappropriate for you or your family. When choosing and reading a book, talk to your parent about your choices and what you are reading.

YHBA Purpose/Goal

The purpose of the Young Hoosier Book Award Program (YHBA) is to stimulate recreational reading among middle/junior high school children and to encourage cooperation between administrators, school library media specialists, and classroom teachers in providing reading experiences for Indiana school children.

The GOAL is to read at least 5 of the 20 books by the deadline so that the student may vote for his/her favorite book of the year. Each vote is counted at the state level, with a book announced as the state winner in May. Nearly 100,000 students (K-8) complete the Indiana program and vote for their favorite book every year. Hundreds of Perry Meridian Middle students participate each year.

Reading something new you think should be a YHBA nominee? Let the library media specialist know and your recommendation will be turned into the state committee!

An effortless way to promote the program and guidelines is to create an easy-to-update annual brochure to share with staff, students, and parents.

PMMS

2009-2010 NOMINEES

All of the Above	by Shelley Pearsall
Bella at Midnight	by Diane Stanley
Confessions From the Principal's Chair	by Anna Myers
The Cryptid Hunters	by Roland Smith
Dark Water Rising	by Marion Hale
Double Identity	by Margaret Peterson Haddix
Firegirl	by Tony Abbott
Giving Up the Ghost	by Sheri Sinykin
Home of the Brave	by Katherine Applegate
Hurt Go Happy	by Ginny Rorby
If a Tree Falls at Lunch Period	by Jennifer Choldenko
Lawn Boy	by Gary Paulsen
Listen!	by Stephanie Tolan
The Mailbox	by Audrey Shafer
Middle School is Worse Than Meatloaf	by Jennifer L. Holm
Night of the Howling Dog	by Graham Salisbury
One-Handed Catch	by Mary Jane Auch
This is Just to Say: Poems of Apology and Forgiveness	by Joyce Sidman
Throwing Stones	by Kristi Collier
The Ultimate Weapon, The Race to Develop the Atomic Bomb	by Edward T. Sullivan

LAST DAY TO TAKE A TEST: April 19, 2010
VOTING DAY: April 22, 2010

EVERY READER COMPLETING THE PROGRAM WINS A READER'S REWARD!

Earn Reader's Rewards throughout the year!

READ ALL 20 BOOKS TO EARN PARTICIPATION IN A READER'S REWARD CELEBRATION!

Any book that you or your family finds objectionable, need not be read. If you are trying to read all twenty titles, see your library media specialist about making arrangements to read an alternate title.

P.M.M.S. RULES

1) Read books off this school year's *Middle Grades* YHBA nominee list. The books may be borrowed from your IMC, public library, purchased from a bookstore, or borrowed from a friend.

2) After reading a YHBA nominee book, take and pass a computer test using the *Scholastic Reading Counts!* program.

3) Read, Read, Read, then Read some more!

4) Read five or more to meet the state rules for voting.

5) Reader's Reward prizes are awarded for those who meet goals throughout the school year. Extra prize opportunities are available for reading ten or more.

Perry Meridian Middle School Instructional Media Center
MISSION STATEMENT

The mission of Perry Meridian Middle School's Instructional Media Center staff is to work collaboratively with teachers and administrators to plan, implement, and evaluate instruction, to promote reading, and to provide resources and services that allow students and teachers to be effective users of information in a variety of formats.

An effortless way to promote the program and guidelines is to create an easy-to-update annual brochure to share with staff, students, and parents. (*Cont.*)

Wondering what to read this summer?

Get a jump on next year— Read a Young Hoosier Book Award Nominee!

P M M S
Instructional Media Center

YHBA Middle Grades Nominees

101 Ways to Bug Your Teacher — by Lee Wardlaw
Black Canary — by Jane Louise Curry
Boys of San Joaquin — by D. James Smith
Captured! A Boy Trapped in the Civil War — by Mary Blair Immel
Code Orange — by Caroline B. Cooney
Dust to Eat: Drought & Depression in the 1930s — by Michael L. Cooper
Each Little Bird That Sings — by Deborah Wiles
Flush — by Carl Hiaasen
For Freedom: The Story of a French Spy — by Kimberly Brubaker Bradley
Heartbeat — by Sharon Creech
House of Tailors — by Patricia Reilly Giff
Lonek's Journey: True Story of a Boy's Escape to Freedom — by Dorit Bader Whiteman
Messenger — by Lois Lowry
Missing Manatee — by Cynthia DeFelice
Old Willis Place: A Ghost Story — by Mary Downing Hahn
Schwa was Here — by Neal Shusterman
So B. It — by Sarah Weeks
Travel Team — by Mike Lupica
Truth About Sparrows — by Marian Hale
The Warriors — by Joseph Bruchac

Remember: Kids are maturing at different rates. Not every book is appropriate for every child at every age. When choosing a book, use wisdom—do not read a book that is inappropriate for you or your family. When choosing and reading a book, talk to your parent about what you're reading. Read together with your parent.

Promote the books as a recommended summer reading list to parents and students a year in advance in the school newsletter and student newspaper.

Heartbeat

"Why do people not listen when you say no?
Why do they think you are too stupid
or too young
to understand?
Why do they think you are too shy
to reply?
Why do they keep badgering you
until you will say yes?"

Read this humorous and sweet novel about a girl, a guy, life, and running.

By Sharon Creech

Place Cover Art Here

During the year, display homemade posters or signs throughout the library media center and in high traffic areas of the building.

Read a Young Hoosier Book Award Book today!

(pick up a brochure in the IMC for program details)

PMMS
Instructional Media Center

YHBA Middle Grades Nominees

<u>Abduction!</u>	by Peg Kehret
<u>An American Plague</u>	by Jim Murphy
<u>Becoming Naomi Leon</u>	by Pam Munoz Ryan
<u>Big Nothing</u>	by Adrian Fogelin
<u>Blue Fingers: A Ninja Tale</u>	by Cheryl Whitesel
<u>Boy Who Saved Baseball</u>	by John H. Ritter
<u>Cabin on Trouble Creek</u>	by Jean Van Leeuwen
<u>Chu Ju's House</u>	by Gloria Whelan
<u>Ghost Girl</u>	by Delia Ray
<u>Here Today</u>	by Ann M. Martin
<u>High Heat</u>	by Carl Deuker
<u>How I Found the Strong</u>	by Margaret McMullan
<u>Lizzie Bright and the Buckminster Boy</u>	by Gary D. Schmidt
<u>Promises to Keep: How Jackie Robinson Changed America</u>	by Sharon Robinson
<u>Red Kayak</u>	by Priscilla Cummings
<u>Sea of Trolls</u>	by Nancy Farmer
<u>Teacher's Funeral: Comedy in 3 Parts</u>	by Richard Peck
<u>Technically, It's Not My Fault</u>	by John Grandits
<u>Winter People</u>	by Joseph Bruchac
<u>Young Man and the Sea</u>	by Rodman Philbrick

Vote Day: April 27   Final Test Day: April 25

Remember: Kids are maturing at different rates. Not every book is appropriate for every child at every age. When choosing a book, use wisdom—do not read a book that is inappropriate for you or your family. When choosing and reading a book, talk to your parent about what you're reading. Read together with your parent.

Remind families of the program, reading list, and voting day with announcements in the student newsletter.

P M M S

Instructional Media Center

Young Hoosier Book Award
State Winner Announced!

Over 76,300 students throughout the state of Indiana voted, and the 2006-2007 YHBA Middle Grades winner is...

Abduction
By Peg Kehret

Your little brother is in kindergarten…

What would happen if you were responsible for watching your little brother after school and he never got off the bus?

Despite police help, days go by and there is no word from Matt or his abductor.
  Where is Matt?
    Is he still alive?

It is important to share the voting results with students and families. If space allows, praise students in the student newsletter as well, and include a congratulatory list of students eligible to vote.

We Like These and Think You Will, Too!

Through "We Like These and Think You Will, Too!," classes, teams, grade levels, PTAs, clubs, sports teams, or other school groups share their selected books with other students by compiling a list of favorite books. This project invites groups to share and develop a display of their favorite reads to share and promote to students.

Cost: $

Using preexisting supplies and equipment, such as a color printer or book jackets you already have on hand, no extra expenses incur.

Estimated Unit Time: Two to Six Weeks

Each student group will need a week or two to compile a list for sharing, then another week or two to take digital photos posing with the books or scan and print book covers or collect the book jackets, or to design their own book artwork. Then students design and decorate the display, which should remain up for a few weeks before replacing it with a new group's display.

Planning Involvement: One Person

This project needs the leadership of an activity planner to coordinate groups and the timeline, but each display also depends on the cooperation of a student or adult group and that group's adult leader.

Suggested Supplies

- Create: invitation, signage
- Display: bulletin board, wall or window display, and digital pictures or scanned, color copy, original, or student-created book covers

Instructions

Decide in advance where to place the revolving display and whether to hang some of the decorations, like the display title, or whether student groups will totally redecorate the space. Personal preference and a desire to establish a pattern for students may help create consistency among the display title and other decorations.

Work with adult leaders to invite student groups to submit favorite read lists. Before working with students, agree how many titles the students will promote based on display space and how involved the students will be in decorating the display area. It is important for the group leader and students to do as much decorating as possible. Along with adult leaders, work with students to initiate and finalize their list. Once the student group has created its final list, work together to photograph or scan and color print book covers onto printer paper; you can also collect actual book jackets or use students' talents to depict each book artistically. The student group then uses the book covers as the focal point of its display. Work together to put up the display. Include the call number for each book cover so other students may easily locate the recommended book. Most important, be sure to display credit to the student group that created the list.

Repeat the process every few weeks to involve as many student groups as possible and to keep the display active and fresh.

Chapter 4
Technology

Incorporating technology into any school activity automatically enhances student interest and engagement. For this social generation, technology makes everything taste better, including classroom instruction and assigned tasks. Although they grew up on technology, students may need help learning how to use the tools more successfully and correctly. Prepare to teach students to use technologies as needed, including the appropriate use of a storyboard for preproduction design. Teach students, but also be open to learning from them. Nothing is more effective for truly knowing something than doing and teaching. Welcome opportunities for students to teach the educators' tools, tips, and tricks.

As schools ensure the safety of students in this interactive Web world, policies are established to protect students. Before posting any student product online, refer to the school district's Web posting, videotaping, and audio taping policies and procedures. A parent permission form may need to be sent home and signed and returned in advance before any public posting may occur. Some schools may also have specific locations where material may be posted. For example, TeacherTube may be acceptable, but YouTube may not; or schools may be limited to posting online only on the school's official Web site.

Because educators should model ethical behavior and often the intent of the final product is to share final book promotion products online, carefully review licensing agreements for any professionally produced audio, video, or images incorporated into the students' final product. If the student project includes material that cannot be legally posted and shared outside of the school, licensing may still allow sharing within the school through televised announcements, in-house information channels, the local password-secured Web site, and other means available to you. Carefully review licensing agreements before production.

Project production can be inexpensive with the use of open source software. Save the final products in a universal format for easy sharing and posting, like avi, pdf, or mp3. The final product can then be uploaded to the library media center's or school's Web site and incorporated into televised student announcements or the student information channel. Through these venues, students share reading promotion products within their school community as well as with the outside world, including showing off the link to their product to extended family and friends.

Gain an understanding for utilizing technology to promote books and reading by previewing professional and educational examples, like the one found at Scholastic's The Stacks site (http://www.scholastic.com/kids/stacks). Share with fellow educators and students the professional examples of author connections, videos, games, blogs, widgets, polls, booktalks, book reviews, and much more.

Book Promotion Book Report

For our students' generation, book reports are taken to the next, real-world level of sharing when the prime purpose of the final product is to promote books and reading by sharing within the school community and global distribution via the Internet and other social technologies. Through these means, students are contributing to the international reading community and sharing with family and friends beyond their specific school and classroom.

Although there are some common, logical supplies for all technology projects, there are also some supplies unique to each project. Common supplies are listed below, and project-specific supplies are listed within that project's entry.

Common Supplies

• Create: guidelines, lesson plans, rubric, storyboard or graphic organizer, training materials for equipment and program

• Student contribution: library or personal copy of a book

• Technology: computer

Music Lyrics

Music is a large part of young people's lives. They listen to music. They critique music. They argue about music. They emote about music. Embrace students' need to express themselves musically by creating an audio book promotion. Students create their own lyrics and sound or copyright-compliant karaoke or mash-ups. Songs can be written to old, classic tunes like "Twinkle, Twinkle, Little Star" or to original scores created by the students. Through a song, students are able to draw interest in the book by connecting other students to it emotionally through song lyrics. Songs can be a cappella or sung with instrumental or copyright-compliant, royalty-free karaoke accompaniment. Share by posting the song on the school or library Web site and online catalog as well as other social opportunities where music is involved, such as the school talent show, sporting event half-time, and other opportunities.

Suggested Supplies

- Possible software programs: sound editing software such as Audacity or other free, open source audio editor

- Student contributions: musical instruments (optional)

- Technology: digital audio recorder, Internet, purchased royalty-free music or free downloads for education

Instructions

Select the program students will use and create or locate training materials. For example, Audacity has its own training wiki (http://audacityteam.org/wiki), which includes tutorials and tips. An example book promotion song to share with students until the school has its own student samples could be the Sammy Keyes mystery series song by author Wendelin Van Draanen. Both song and lyrics are free downloads at http://www.randomhouse.com/kids/vandraanen/sammykeyes. As in the Sammy Keyes song, students would have more lyrical freedom and creativity if creating their own instead of rewriting lyrics from a well-known song. Once students have drafted a written copy of the lyrics, work with them to record the song digitally using an external digital audio recorder or microphone with a USB port for easy download into the sound editing software. Once recorded and downloaded into the editing software, students then edit and revise until finalized and saved into an MP format.

Building Your MUSIC LYRICS

The Music Lyrics can be made as an original score, or to the tune of a childhood classic, like 'Mary Had a Little Lamb', or copyright compliant mash-up. Save in MP format.

☐ **Audio**
- Song lyrics are homemade by you. Sound must include the singing of your lyrics.
- Musical instruments or background music may also be included, but are not required.

The following do not have to be in any certain order, but must be found somewhere in the lyrics/song:

☐ **The Author, Title, Genre**
The author, title and genre must be incorporated into the song lyrics.

☐ **The Characters and Setting**
- Lyrics include introducing the characters and setting to potential readers. This is background information needed for the audience to understand the characters and setting of the book.
- Include details about when and where the story takes place.
- Include details about the major characters' appearance and personality traits.

☐ **The Hook**
- Include in the song critical events to entice the audience into reading the book.
- Give a hint toward the conflict the characters will encounter. Consider including a quote from the book.
- Do not give away too many secrets or the ending.

☐ **The Wrap-Up**
The lyrics should include some personal thoughts and emotions on the book, which tell the audience why a reader would love the book and why they should read it.

Don't give away any surprises or important details that should be left for the reader!

Suggested music lyrics guidelines and expectations.

From *Social Readers: Promoting Reading in the 21st Century* by Leslie B. Preddy. Santa Barbara, CA: Libraries Unlimited. Copyright © 2010.

MUSIC LYRICS RUBRIC

Name: _____

Teacher: _____

Period: _____ Date: _____

Book Title: _____

A written copy of the lyrics is turned in and includes homemade lyrics. The song is creative, follows the listed guidelines, is copyright compliant, and is saved in .mp format.

5   4   3   2   1

The author, title and genre are incorporated into the lyrics and meet the guideline requirements.

5   4   3   2   1

Physical and personality traits of the characters as well as the setting's time and place are incorporated into the lyrics and meet the guideline requirements.

5   4   3   2   1

The lyrics hook the reader by including critical events and the conflict without giving too much of the story away and meet the guideline requirements.

5   4   3   2   1

The lyrics include personal thought and emotions related to the story meet the guideline requirements.

5   4   3   2   1

FINAL GRADE:

Sample music lyrics grading rubric.

From *Social Readers: Promoting Reading in the 21st Century* by Leslie B. Preddy.
Santa Barbara, CA: Libraries Unlimited. Copyright © 2010.

Music Video

A song tells a story and a music video can visually represent the content and emotion of the lyrics. Through a music video, students create lyrics for a song, then envision and record visual images to go along with the audio. The music video is intended to illicit student interest in a book through visual and musical representation. Review the previous music lyrics entry to understand the lyrics for the music video. The video can be created using live action, computer graphics, computer animation, or still image video elements. Within a music video, students can express their feelings, ideas, impressions, and experiences with a book. Air final products on televised announcements and post on school and library Web sites online.

Suggested Supplies

- Possible software programs: sound editing software, such as Audacity or another free open source audio editor, Microsoft PowerPoint, Microsoft Movie Maker (free download), Microsoft Photo Story (free downloads), or preferred comparable program

- Technology: digital still camera, digital video camera, Internet, purchased royalty-free music or free downloads for education, scanner

Instructions

Through video sharing social sites such as YouTube and TeacherTube, as well as digital commercials, students are inundated with ideas and examples for what their music video might look like. Select the production tools students will use to create sound and video. Students may require training for each of the production tools selected and how to insert and edit materials in selected programs. Work with students to understand the elements of a song and build a storyboard or graphic organizer for the visual elements around the song lyrics. Do not allow students to work with the technology for the video until the lyrics are written, the song recorded, and the storyboard for the video approved.

Building Your MUSIC VIDEO

The Music Video can be made with Microsoft PowerPoint, Movie-Maker, PhotoStory, or other computer program capable of saving in .mp or .avi format. The song may be an original score, or to the tune of a childhood classic, like 'Mary Had a Little Lamb', or copyright compliant mash-up.

☐ **Audio**

Song lyrics are homemade by you. Sound must include the singing of your lyrics. Musical instruments or background music may also be included, but is not required.

☐ **Video**

Images are homemade by you. Images can be digital pictures, scanned artwork, digital video, live action, custom animation, or a combination.

The following do not have to be in any certain order, but must be found somewhere in the lyrics/song:

☐ **Author, Title, Genre, Characters, Setting**

- Incorporate the author, title and genre into the lyrics.
- Lyrics include introducing the characters and setting to potential readers. This is background information needed for the audience to understand the characters and setting of the book.
- Include when and where the story takes place.
- Include details about the major characters' appearance and personality traits.

☐ **The Hook**

- Include in the song critical events to entice the audience into reading the book.
- Give a hint toward the conflict the characters will encounter.
- Do not give away too many secrets or the ending.

☐ **The Wrap-Up**

The lyrics should include some personal thoughts and emotions on the book. Help the audience understand why a reader would love the book and should read it.

Don't give away any surprises or important details that should be left for the reader!

Suggested music video guidelines and expectations.

MUSIC VIDEO RUBRIC

Name: _____

Teacher: _____

Period: _____ Date: _____

Book Title: _____

A written copy of the lyrics is turned in, is copyright compliant, and includes homemade lyrics. Lyrics are creative and follow guideline requirements.

5   4   3   2   1

The video is creative, connects to the lyrics, follows the listed guidelines, is copyright compliant, and is saved in .avi or .mp format.

5   4   3   2   1

The author, title, genre, characters, and setting are incorporated into the lyrics and video and meet the guideline requirements.

5   4   3   2   1

The lyrics and video hook the reader by including critical events and the conflict without giving too much of the story away and meet the guideline requirements.

5   4   3   2   1

The lyrics and video include personal thought and emotions related to the story and meet the guideline requirements.

5   4   3   2   1

FINAL GRADE:

Sample music video grading rubric.

Digital "Book Hook"

A digital "book hook" is an alternative to the traditional book report. It is a visual booktalk promoting a book using technology to create and share. The "Book Hook" is a student-produced video with student narration. A student script and graphic organizer are the foundation for developing a video from digital video camera footage, digital still camera shots, or digital images. A book hook is written to entice the viewing audience. It should make the need to read the book for themselves an imperative. Share by posting the final product on the school or library Web site and airing it on the school's closed-circuit information channel and televised announcements.

Suggested Supplies

- Possible software programs: Microsoft PowerPoint, Microsoft Movie Maker (free download), Microsoft Photo Story (free downloads), or preferred comparable program

- Technology: digital still camera, digital video camera, Internet, purchased royalty-free music or free downloads for education, scanner

Instructions

Select the format (still photos, scanned graphics, computer-generated graphics, action/video, background music, etc.) and software program students will use to create the digital book hook. Training and equipment needs will greatly depend on the format, which could be, but is not limited to, a video or a slide or picture show with audio incorporated. Search software Web sites for training videos and resources. The material may help the instructor learn and may be used to train students. Training on the use and insertion or creations from other programs, flatbed scanners, audio files, microphones, digital still cameras, digital video cameras, and other equipment may be needed depending on the technology available in the school, the complexity of the assignment, and the technology experiences desired for students. The book hook will require thorough training on and understanding of the development and use of a graphic organizer and script. Students will need a rough draft in the form of a graphic organizer or storyboard before they can record and create.

Building Your DIGITAL "BOOK HOOK"

The Digital "Book Hook" can be made with Microsoft PowerPoint, MovieMaker, PhotoStory, or other computer program capable of saving in .mp or .avi format.

☐ Images and Audio
- Images are homemade by you. Images can be digital pictures, scanned artwork, digital video, custom animation, or a combination.
- Sound must include your narration or scrip. Sound effects and music may also be included.

☐ SCENE ONE—Introduce the book
The opening scene should be like the opening credits of a movie at the theater. Include the book cover, title, author's name, and your name as writer and director.

☐ SCENE TWO—The Lead-In
- Write a script introducing the characters and setting to potential readers. This is background information needed for the audience to understand the characters and setting of the book.
- Includes graphics that connect to the text.
- Do not give away too many secrets or the ending.

☐ SCENE THREE—The Hook
- Include in the script a critical scene that will entice the audience into reading the book. Give a hint toward the conflict the characters will encounter.
- Include one or both of the following:
  1. quote from the book.
  2. graphic that connects to the text included in the scene.

☐ SCENE FOUR—The Close
Wrap it up. Give some final thoughts on the book and tell the audience the genre and why you loved it or why they should read it.

Don't give away any surprises or important details that should be left for the reader!

Suggested digital "book hook" guidelines and expectations.

DIGITAL "BOOK HOOK" RUBRIC

Name: _____

Teacher: _____

Period: _____ Date: _____

Book Title: _____

The first scene is opening credits, attractive and follows the guideline requirements.

5 4 3 2 1

Scene two attracts a reader's attention, introduces the characters and setting, and follows the guideline requirements.

5 4 3 2 1

The third scene describes a critical event in the book which "hooks" the audience into the book and follows the guideline requirements.

5 4 3 2 1

The fourth scene concludes the book hook with some final thoughts on the book and follows the guideline requirements.

5 4 3 2 1

The overall look of the digital "book hook" is creative and neat. Images are custom made. Sound includes custom made narration and script.

5 4 3 2 1

FINAL GRADE:

Sample digital "book hook" grading rubric.

Read-Alike

A read-alike is a list of books recommended for a person who already enjoyed a particular book or type of book. The list includes similar titles based on writing style, theme, character, genre, setting, or author. The list helps fellow students find other books similar to one they've already enjoyed. Through the development of a read-alike list into signs or posters, students share reading recommendations with fellow students based on personal opinion and similar interests.

Suggested Supplies

- Computer: color printer, online library catalog, word processing or desktop publishing program

- Optional: scanner, clear plastic display frames

Instructions

Read-alikes are a simple concept for students to understand. If a friend of theirs liked this book, what other book might their friend like? Work with students to develop a list of read-alike ideas: other books by the same author, similar genre, common subject, matching theme, similar setting, and much more. Brainstorm with the students ideas for where to start if they are unsure of how to begin developing the list: looking at the book flaps and other page information in the book, online library catalog, online bookstores, book reviews and summaries, and other resources.

In advance, select a computer program available through the school that will allow for text and graphics on the layout, such as Microsoft Word or Microsoft Publisher. Incorporate text (author, title, call number) and images (book cover) into an attractive display. Use the final read-alike signs as a centerpiece for special displays of read-alike signs and matching books. Read-alikes may also be printed and used in a wall or bulletin board display, showing off the read-alike list, covers of the recommended books, and call numbers for where fellow students may locate their peers' recommendations.

Option: The read-alike list a student creates could also be posted online wherever students meet to post and share book reviews. For details on electronic book reviews, see the entry later in this chapter.

Building Your READ ALIKE:

The Read Alike can be created with Microsoft Word, Publisher, or other computer program capable of text and graphics. Artwork may be custom made by you, then scanned into the computer.

☐ ### The Heading
Use creativity and artwork to create a heading for your sign that include the title and "If You Like___, You'll Love…" For example, "If You Like *Percy Jackson*, You'll Love…" Use artwork that helps emphasize your list's theme, which can be based on writing style, theme, character, genre, setting, or author.

☐ ### The List
Research and read related books. Create a list of 8-10 books related to the list's theme. Design into your poster the title, author, and call number of the 8-10 related books you are recommending to people who read and liked the book listed in your heading.

☐ ### Summary
Write and include a two-three sentence summary of each book on your list. Type or write clearly. The summary should be a well-written 'tease' to make others want to read the books on your list.

☐ ### Artwork
Include book cover images or artwork for each book on your list. Artwork should be colorful, unique, and make a specific connection to each book on the list.

Don't give away any surprises or important details that should be left for the reader!

Suggested read-alike guidelines and expectations.

READ ALIKE RUBRIC

Name: _____

Teacher: _____

Period: _____ Date: _____

Book Title: _____

The heading is colorful, attracts a reader's interest and includes the information listed in the guidelines.

5   4   3   2   1

The list is well thought out, includes 8-10 books, fits together in the overall theme and follows the listed guidelines.

5   4   3   2   1

A book summary is included for each book on the list and meets the guideline requirements.

5   4   3   2   1

Artwork for each book on the list attracts attention and meets the guideline requirements.

5   4   3   2   1

The overall look of the project is creative and neat. The layout is carefully planned. Spelling, grammar, punctuation, paragraphing, and capitalization are correct.

5   4   3   2   1

FINAL GRADE:

Sample read-alike grading rubric.

From *Social Readers: Promoting Reading in the 21st Century* by Leslie B. Preddy.
Santa Barbara, CA: Libraries Unlimited. Copyright © 2010.

Events

Events are productions worthy of participation of large groups. Often this means thorough organization and coordination of time, multiple groups, and space. Technology can alleviate much of that burden. What is great about many virtual events is that not everyone has to be at the same place at the same time. This allows freedom and flexibility among participants. Through technology, events can bring groups together under a common interest or goal without time or distance hindering active engagement and participation.

Author Virtual Visit

Students greatly benefit by experiencing an author visit, but cost or distance may be prohibitive. A flexible, convenient, and often more affordable alternative is to host a virtual visit with an author. Through a virtual visit, in the form of a blog or other social networking tool, a personal relationship between author and students is established without the travel expense of a live visit. The author and the students' questions and concerns are addressed with a personal, but electronically virtual, touch.

Cost

Author: $–$$$. Cost ranges from free to moderate, depending on if or how much the author will charge for the experience. Cost varies depending on the author's enthusiasm for the event, fees, and his or her prominence and reputation as an author and speaker. Usually, the more globally famous the author, the greater the fee.

Books: $–$$$$. Supplying the author's books to students ranges from free to moderately expensive, depending on the size of the student population, cost of the book (paperback versus hardback, publisher or vendor discount), and whether students will have their own or share copies of the book. Depending on the community, this cost can be nearly eliminated from the budget if families are able to purchase the book themselves without being overburdened by the expense.

Planning Time: Six Months or Longer

Consider planning with enough time to develop and implement a school plan, locate funding as needed, purchase books, coordinate an author, and test and prepare technology.

Planning Involvement: Committee of Four or More

This project will require leadership from various experts. One person will need to build and supervise the social networking tool, another to coordinate staff involvement, another to work with the author, and an administrator to work out the schedule, finances and other administrative issues that arise.

Suggested Supplies

- Books: enough copies of the selected book for staff and each student, or class sets for students and classes to share; extra copies of all the author's titles for the library media center collection to meet the increased interest and demand.

- Create: instructional and rules sheet, lesson plans, publicity and promotional materials, reminders, timeline or calendar

- Display: decorated spotlight display shelving area

- Technology: computer, Internet, a school-authorized social networking tool that includes a blog or conversation tool, such as pbwiki or Moodle

- Miscellaneous: guest speaker (author)

Instructions

Before contacting an author, be prepared to provide basic information about the school and the virtual event. Establish ground rules or author virtual visit etiquette for the school. Meet with administration in advance to guarantee support for the schoolwide event, technology, instructional concept, and funding.

In advance, consider how much of the author's time will be requested. How much time each day and how many days will the author expect to spend in virtual communication or posting responses? Approximately one hour per day of the author's time is a reasonable expectation. In the beginning, until personal experience can dictate selection, ask the author for an hour a day for two to five days of virtual time. If the days are consecutive and at or near the conclusion of the reading, ask for two to three days from one week. If the preference is a day here and there as students progress through the reading, the author may be willing to agree to more days spread out over three to five weeks. If the school wants more interaction, plan virtual communication experiences between classes or grades for kids to communicate electronically among classes. This could be done before the author event to give teachers and classrooms time to practice communicating via the social networking tool.

Consider how and who will post comments and questions so the author is not overwhelmed with too much correspondence or duplicate questions. For example, each class could discuss among themselves the questions and experiences to include, then decide as a group only a few to post as a class. Will students be permitted to post personal questions, or will all discussion directly relate to the reading? Participating classes could research to make sure they are not asking questions already answered in published biographies or on the author's or publisher's Web pages. Students will also want to reply to the author's posts. Responses to the author's posts could also be agreed on and posted from the group.

Before meeting with administration and as a committee, create some basic participation rules that can be altered later and discussed by the committee. Prepare a collection of potential books or authors for starter ideas but be open to discussion and input from the group.

When developing a committee, if the whole school will participate, ensure all grade levels are represented. If you are working with one grade, include all the teachers for that grade. Meet as a committee to review and revise the basic rules and discuss potential authors and titles.

Share the idea with all building educators, especially those who would eventually be involved in classroom participation, not just committee members. Throughout the process, keep communication global, especially as pieces and parts are finalized and the committee creates classroom resources for sharing. Consider how the school will handle the logistics of the event. Possible questions to consider might include:

If the author charges a fee, how much are we willing or able to pay? (This question should also be discussed with administration before the committee meets.)

Will this be a schoolwide event, grade-level specific, or will just select classes be involved?

Will students read the same book, or will it be a collection of the author's work, choosing from various titles?

Does the school need extra funding for classroom sets? Could parents pay for their child's copy? Is there a way to share copies? Is the title available in paperback? How will extra copies be purchased for the library media center?

When would the virtual visit fit the school's schedule? Be flexible and think about a particular month or months from which the author could select dates that suit him or her.

Because some authors may not be interested or available to participate, who are the top five choices to contact? Search the Web to find the author's homepage with contact information or if the publisher has created a page for the author that includes contact information. The actual contact may be the author, his or her assistant, or a publisher's representative.

Contact an author on the priority list. Contact the author, her assistant, or a publisher's representative by e-mail or phone. Make the e-mail brief but include the school demographics, outline the event expectations, and when the event would occur. Be prepared to wait a few days between the school's initial contact and the author's initial response. Repeat contacting authors, one at a time, until an author and the school agree to terms.

Before purchasing copies of the book, contact the publisher. If the publisher considers this an author visit, the school may be able to receive a deep discount on books. No matter where the books are ordered, be sure to find out the anticipated wait from order to delivery for the needed quantity. Order books so they arrive six to twelve weeks before the first virtual conversation, depending on how much time is needed to distribute the books and the instructional time needed to read the book.

Preplanning

- Meet with administration to review the concept and gain approval to pursue the event and budget.

- Establish basic participation rules to be discussed and revised by the committee. Prepare a collection of potential books or authors.

- Locate a funding source for books and the author's fee, if needed.

- Research and select the online communication environment, if one has not already been preselected by the school district.

- Create the committee and begin meeting and preliminary planning: potential authors and titles, budget, basic participation expectations, and technology issues.

Six Months Before

- Contact one author at a time on the committee's list of potential authors. Repeat this process until an author and the school agree to terms.

- If the author requires a contract, the principal signs it, and both the activity planner and the administrator keep a copy.

- Order books for students and staff.

- Learn and practice the online communication environment.

Three Months Before

- The committee continues meeting to locate, create, and share resources, lessons, and promotion ideas for the selected reading and author.

One to Two Months Before

- Once books have arrived, schedule to distribute sets to participating classrooms, along with event details, rules, reminders, and resources created by the committee.

- Promote the event with special announcements and homemade posters, signs and bookmarks.

- Confirm the online schedule (and time zone) with the author. Make adjustments as needed. Notify participating teachers and classes of any changes.

- Set up the online communication environment and run test sessions with the author.

One to Seven Days Before

- Meet with teachers to train on the use of the online communication environment and review the event timeline and protocol.

- E-mail follow-up reminders with the author's final schedule.

During the Virtual Visit

- Monitor the event while in progress.

- Make adjustments and fix problems as needed.

- Make arrangements for contracted payment, if one applies, to be sent to the author.

After the Virtual Visit

- Gather follow-up feedback from the committee and participants.

- Send thank you notes to the participating author, administration, and other appropriate supporters and funders of the event.

Book around the World

Social networking has taught students to stay connected to the world virtually. Through Book around the World, participants read a designated book, go to a Web site, and post comments about the book; pass the book on to another person to read and participate; then check back periodically and interact virtually to learn where the book has been and what others thought of the read. Participants could physically pass the book to the next person or leave it in an actively public location like a doctor's waiting room, airport, or bus or train station.

Cost: $$$

The key expenses are printer labels and paperback copies to distribute to participants. There are social networking Web sites available free for educators, if one is not already supported by the school or district.

Planning Time: Three Months

Book around the World can be planned and implemented in as little as three months. Consider the need to get approval to begin the project, select a book title or titles, create the Web page, and order, receive, and prepare the books for participation.

Planning Involvement: One Person

This project is surprisingly simple to implement and can be managed by one person to plan, prepare, promote, coordinate, and run. Work with the technology committee to review instructions and social networking etiquette.

Suggested Supplies

- Books: Copies of the selected books for distribution

- Create: labels, publicity and promotional materials, social etiquette guidelines, timeline

- Display: decorated spotlight display shelving area

- Paper: printer label/sticker sheets

- Technology: computer, Internet, a school-authorized social networking tool that includes a blog or conversation tool, such as pbwiki or Moodle

Instructions

Initial planning begins by consulting administration. Before meeting with administration, create a basic plan, budget, and timeline to guide discussion. Finding a funding source is important. Seek support from the PTA, local businesses, or a small grant.

Book selection and quantity is also important. Quantity will depend on budget, affordability of individual titles, and number of participating books desired. First, consider whether the project will be run with multiple copies of one title, many titles by one author, or a variety of books related by a particular theme. Selections should be age-appropriate, available in paperback, and affordable. Consult students and staff for help with selection.

Each book requires two labels, one for the front cover and one for the inside cover. The front cover label is brief and simple—an open invitation encouraging people to look inside the book, to take it, read it, post on the Web site about it, and pass it on. The label on the inside cover is more specific with details about how and where to post after reading, what to do with the book when done, project participation date range, and other details considered important for random participants. Remember to keep it simple. More detailed information about what to post and etiquette can be posted online and easily updated and revised on the Web site.

Each book will be assigned an identifying number. Set up the inviting Web site so each book's assigned number has a separate blog, allowing participants to track the activity and location of their particular book. Include instructions for posting etiquette, what to include, and a sample post. Basics to consider asking participants to include are the date, the individual's location, his or her thoughts and ideas about the book, and a signature of first name or initials only.

Book around the World is an independent project with the participants getting as much out of it as they put in through follow-up and periodic checking of the Web site.

Preplanning

- Decide the specific number of books to be involved. Develop a budget and timeline.

- Meet with administration to review the concept and gain approval to pursue funding.

- Consult students and staff for potential books, authors, and themes.

- Research and select the online communication environment, if one has not already been selected by the school district.

Three Months Before

- Finalize title selection and order books.

- Learn and practice the online communication environment.

- Prepare cover and inside book labels using Microsoft Word or other word processing software with label templates. The outer sticker is an advertisement. The inner label provides details for participating and accessing the Web site.

- Prepare project promotional materials.

One to Two Months Before

- Once books have arrived, assign each book a number and adhere labels.

- Set up the online communication environment. Include etiquette, posting instructions, and a blog entry for each book number.

One to Seven Days Before

- Create project display and promotion area.

- Promote the event with special announcements and homemade posters, signs, and bookmarks.

- Share the event opening with coworkers at a staff meeting.

During the Project

- Introduce the project to classes, clubs, and students.

- Monitor the Web site while in progress.

- Make adjustments and fix problems as needed.

After the Project

- Close active blogs.

- Make adjustments for the next year, if repeating the project.

- Send a thank you to event funders.

Take Me, Read Me, Pass Me On

This book is a
"Book Around the World".

Open to learn more.

Take Me, Read Me, Pass Me On

Take Me, Read Me, Pass Me On

This book is a
"Book Around the World".

Open to learn more.

Take Me, Read Me, Pass Me On

Take Me, Read Me, Pass Me On

This book is a
"Book Around the World".

Open to learn more.

Take Me, Read Me, Pass Me On

Take Me, Read Me, Pass Me On

This book is a
"Book Around the World".

Open to learn more.

Take Me, Read Me, Pass Me On

Take Me, Read Me, Pass Me On

This book is a
"Book Around the World".

Open to learn more.

Take Me, Read Me, Pass Me On

Take Me, Read Me, Pass Me On

This book is a
"Book Around the World".

Open to learn more.

Take Me, Read Me, Pass Me On

Take Me, Read Me, Pass Me On

This book is a
"Book Around the World".

Open to learn more.

Take Me, Read Me, Pass Me On

Take Me, Read Me, Pass Me On

This book is a
"Book Around the World".

Open to learn more.

Take Me, Read Me, Pass Me On

Take Me, Read Me, Pass Me On

This book is a
"Book Around the World".

Open to learn more.

Take Me, Read Me, Pass Me On

Take Me, Read Me, Pass Me On

This book is a
"Book Around the World".

Open to learn more.

Take Me, Read Me, Pass Me On

Create an advertising sticker for the book cover, inviting readers to participate in Book around the World.

Sharing

The socially interactive aspects of today's technology, especially the Internet, are ideal for sharing book interests and experiences. The social creatures of today thrive on the mix of technology, real-world applications, and showcasing reading. Technology strikes a positive nerve in this generation. To persuade and share books through technology intrigues students and draws their attention, whether they are the creator, an active participant, or just a voyeur.

To gain confidence adults may prefer creating book promotions with technology before passing the task to students. Students will naturally be more confident than some adults and ready to try different and creative things to see what works. Being open and receptive to learning from students often advances the quality and creativity of technology-rich adult- or student-produced products.

Booktalk Digital Picture Frames

Instead of verbally booktalking a book, students or staff create an electronic booktalk, or book trailer, using formats compatible with the school's digital picture frames. Depending on the picture frame, this may be still images, video, or Microsoft PowerPoint or other video presentation files, as long as it may be finalized and saved in a format accepted by the digital picture frame. The library media center, lobby, and main office now have digital picture frames full of book promotions, instead of having only static artwork on the walls. These can be created by staff or by students for students.

Cost: $$$

Technology costs change frequently, and digital picture frame costs vary widely, depending on make and model. Expense will also vary depending on the quantity of frames purchased, size of memory, whether the frame runs on a battery or needs to be plugged in, screen size, and other options.

Planning Time: Four Weeks

Planning time varies greatly, depending on how frequently students meet to work on the project and the level of difficulty and complexity of the task.

Planning Involvement: Club, Class, or Student Group

This project requires one adult and as many students as is desired. The students involved could range from those in a club, a specially selected group, or individual classes.

Suggested Supplies

- Books: books from the library media center
- Create: lesson plans or training materials
- Technology: digital picture frame, digital still camera, digital video camera, flatbed scanner, other peripherals as needed, presentation programs compatible with the digital picture frame
- Miscellaneous: sticky notes

Instructions

Before purchasing the digital picture frames, research options. Decide on screen and memory size, file formats accepted, and whether it is powered with battery or electricity. Other personal issues to consider are décor preferences, such as the frame size and color.

What is being created is a wall decoration that should not make distracting noises. Consider it similar to a silent movie or silent book trailer. The book promotion is communicated through images and over-sized text filling the digital picture frame screen. Promotions could be one "slide" or a longer feature with a handful of visual images or slides and transitions.

Before meeting with the student group, decide whether there will be free choice or a theme to the booktalks placed on a digital picture frame. A theme could be based on genre, author, or special event, like Read Across America Day, books to movies, new national award winners, or holiday gift ideas.

If making a larger file and not just one "slide," students could work in teams or pairs to accomplish their goal. Depending on the formats accepted by the digital picture frame, students may want to read and create the promotions as a group effort.

Preplanning

- Research and purchase digital picture frames.

- Practice until the minimum font size needed for display readability is established.

- Practice to gauge a maximum screen word count for full-text and half-text screens.

- Create sample digital booktalks and download to a digital picture frame.

- Work with classroom teacher or club to schedule student development of booktalks.

Two to Four Weeks Before

- Share digital picture frame samples with students. Communicate acceptable format and file types.

- Have students select a book, giving two weeks to read it.

- Coteach students how to use a reader's notebook or sticky notes to keep track of important thoughts, ideas, events, inspirations, and quotes while reading.

During the Project

- Based on a preplanned schedule, meet with the class or club to teach and create digital picture frame booktalks.

- Preview student products and have corrections made before publishing.

After

- Load final files onto digital picture frames.

- Mount digital picture frames onto preselected walls and set to loop student final products.

Booktalk Screen Savers

A simple and inexpensive alternative to booktalk digital picture frames is booktalk screen savers. Students often wonder what to read next, the next great read, and what others are reading around the school. A fun book promotion that takes very little time is book screen savers. Students and staff create homemade screen savers to promote a particular book or series of books. Each screen saver takes a few minutes to create with graphics and text, then set up school computers to loop as screen savers.

New Books Club

Librarians and educators often struggle with how to promote new books. As the new books come in, students need to notice them. "New books" displays and conversations with individual students only work for the short term. It doesn't keep the books flying off the shelf after the initial persuasive conversation. To work toward resolving this problem, create a New Books Club. Students attend the New Books Club meeting with the promise of being the first to borrow the book before it even hits the library media center shelves. In exchange, students agree to post a book review online for other students to use. In this way, students are writing book reviews that fellow students read. An unexpected and interesting by-product is that students not only write reviews, but if they read a book they like, they feel personally committed to passing it on to peers. This creates a whole new version of the common practice of bringing a friend down to the library media center to share a recommended book. Slowly but surely, new books no longer get one checkout before seeing the shelf. Instead, the selections that New Books Club members like take on a life of their own with little or no "shelf life."

Cost: $

Use paper products already available at the school and the new books recently added to the library media center collection. An option is to use printer label sheets for bookplates.

Planning Time: One Month

Each meeting takes one month of minimal effort to plan, prepare, and host.

Planning Involvement: One Person

This club is very easy to run and only needs an activity planner to prepare, host and maintain.

Suggested Supplies

- Books: new library books

- Create: admission pass, book review and posting instructions, publicity and promotional materials, sign-up or registration, calendar

- Optional: snacks

- Paper: printer label/sticker sheets

- Technology: library media center circulation system capable of posting book reviews or an online review Web site, Microsoft Word or other program with label templates

Instructions

Before meetings begin, prepare new library books for circulation. Instead of circulating or displaying the new books, set them aside for the New Books Club. The first time a meeting is hosted requires a bit more planning and promotion, but after that, it should take on a life of its own with word of mouth and normal student curiosity. At the first meeting, review expectations: participants will check out a new book before it reaches the shelf, read their books between meetings, write and post a review before or during the next meeting, and check out the next new book after posting a new books book review.

Prepare initial training for how to post online book reviews and follow-up, smaller trainings, or peer-led trainings for new members. Throughout the year, unless the club is maxed out, allow interested students to sign up at any time.

Follow whatever schedule formula makes sense for the club, and allow enough time between meetings for reading to be completed, usually two to four weeks. It is easiest on the sponsor and students if meetings have a set pattern. For example, meetings could be held on the first Tuesday of each month. Decide a set time of day that works best for students: before school, lunchtime, recess, or after school.

When creating the necessary forms, such as a sign-up sheet, explanatory promotion bookmarks, a reminder pass, and an RSVP/training bookmark, consider which details are needed for independent and self-motivated participants.

Should the sign-up include space to write in the new book a student has selected to read?

Is a teacher's name needed on the sign-up sheet so the club sponsor later knows where to deliver a reminder pass?

Should the explanatory promotion bookmark include club member expectations so that students can make an informed decision upfront about whether this club is right for them?

Depending on when the meeting is scheduled, should the reminder pass be prepared to pass out the day before (for morning meetings) or the morning of (for lunch, recess, or after school meetings)?

Should there be an RSVP and training bookmark to help students remember what to do, the next meeting date and the next new book selected to review?

It is ideal to use the school library media center online library catalog or book review site that is already supported by the library media center. This could be a homemade Web site, online catalog with review posting capabilities, or the local public library interactive book review site. If these are not available, research and decide the most appropriate national or international Web site for posting the students' book reviews, such as flamingnet.com.

Preplanning

- Place New Books Club meetings on the school calendar.

- Create a sign-up or registration form.

- Create a bookmark explaining the club expectations and inviting students to sign up.

- Create advertisements for the student newsletter and announcements.

- Begin collecting new books as they are processed instead of shelving or displaying them, starting with fiction and narrative nonfiction, reserving them for New Books Club.

Two Weeks to One Month Before

- Make copies, and cut and display invitation bookmarks.

- Make copies of the sign-up form and set out for preregistration.

- Advertise the new club on student announcements and in the student newsletter.

- Share information about the new club with classes and distribute bookmarks to interested students.

One to Two Weeks Before

- Create an admission slip, reminder card or pass, and make copies.

- Review steps for posting book reviews on the selected Web site. Prepare simple training materials.

- Using the label template in Microsoft Word or a similar program, create New Books Club book plates for students to sign and place in highly recommended books.

- Create an RSVP training bookmark.

- Reserve the necessary computers for students to use during the club meeting.

One Day Before

- Make copies of the sign-up form for the upcoming meeting.

- Make copies of bookplates on sheets of printer labels.

- Make copies of the training bookmark.

- Fill out admission passes to distribute.

- Prepare and turn in an announcement reminding students to get the admission pass from their teacher.

- Buy snacks or make dessert, if desired.

Day of the Meeting

- The morning of or day before, depending on club meeting time, distribute admission passes to registered participants.

- Set out the reserved books for the New Books Club meeting.

- Host the New Books Club meeting, including training new members.

  - Have students take turns sharing the title of the book they read, whether or not they liked it, and why. This can be done while eating, if this is a lunch club.

  - For students who consider their book among the best ever read, invite them to sign a recommended read bookplate and place it inside the front of the library book.

  - Distribute the training bookmark and discuss what to include for a good book review.

  - While at computers, train students in how to access the Web page and the process for posting book reviews.

  - Have students select a new book to review, fill out the sign-up form for the next club meeting, check out the book, and fill out a takeaway meeting reminder bookmark for the new book and next meeting.

After the Meeting

- Clean up and store extra supplies for the next meeting.

- Evaluate book reviews and approve for posting.

- Repeat the process as needed for the next meeting.

- If too many new books arrive, move some of the "old" new books into circulation to make room for the club's next selection of new books.

NEW BOOKS CLUB

READING, REVIEWING AND RECOMMENDING NEW BOOKS

Next Meeting:

Sept. 1

Be sure to sign up in advance to attend the next meeting.

READ

P M M S

Library Media Center

IS THIS CLUB FOR YOU?

If you agree, check the box:

◊ Are you looking for a club just right for you?
◊ Do you like to be the first to check out new library books?
◊ Do you want to read new books before anyone else?
◊ Do you like sharing your opinion?
◊ Are you willing to have lunch in the LMC once a month?

If you checked at least two boxes, this club is for you! See Mrs. Preddy to sign up and attend the next New Books Club meeting.

Club Responsibilities:

• Read one new library book every month.
• Attend a club meeting once a month during lunch.
• Share what you have read with other club members at the meeting.
• Write and post an online book review once a month.
• Choose a new library book to read before the next meeting.

An easy way to promote the New Books Club to students is by introducing it to classes and passing out a bookmark to help explain the club's purpose and expectations.

From *Social Readers: Promoting Reading in the 21st Century* by Leslie B. Preddy.
Santa Barbara, CA: Libraries Unlimited. Copyright © 2010.

New Books Club
Book Review Sign-Up

Next Meeting Date (Book Read By): _____

	Name	Grade	Lunch Period	Team	Homeroom	New Title Reviewing
1						
2						
3						
4						
5						
6						
7						
8						
9						
10						
11						
12						
13						
14						
15						

During meetings, invite attendees to register to attend the next meeting. Between meetings, leave **New Books Club** sign-up forms in a designated place in the **Library Media Center** for interested students to sign up. Special things to include are the lunch period, if hosting meetings during lunch; homeroom, or whichever period reminders will be sent out; and the title of the new book being read for review.

From *Social Readers: Promoting Reading in the 21st Century* by Leslie B. Preddy. Santa Barbara, CA: Libraries Unlimited. Copyright © 2010.

Name: _____   Room: _____

New Books Club

PASS *PASS*

Date: APRIL 14

You have signed up to attend today's *New Books Club* meeting.

When your lunch begins, please be sure to bring your lunch immediately to the library media center. If you are buying your lunch, go directly to the cafeteria line & bring your tray to the library media center. Be sure to carry this pass with you to get your lunch and be admitted to the club meeting.

Reservation for Lunch Period: _____

READ

PMMS

If any of this information is incorrect, please let the library media center staff know today.
If for some reason you cannot attend, please let the library media center staff know right away.

PERRY MERIDIAN MIDDLE SCHOOL

Distributing a pass the morning of the meeting can work as a reminder, hall pass and special permission for getting through the lunch line first if hosting during lunch.

WRITING A REVIEW:

Like a TV, radio or online commercial, write the review to talk other students into reading the book, too!

- Keep the ending a secret! Only tell enough to tease the reader into wanting more.
- Tell the book's genre and what type of person might like it. (*If you like to...*)
- Suggest the grade or age of reader you recommend read this book.
- Try to use proper punctuation, spelling and school-appropriate language. Do not use text message or online chat language or spelling.
- If needed, offer a warning or concern for mature themes or content.
- Your review can be anonymous, but if you decide to sign it, use only your first name.
- If time permits, write your review in Microsoft Word. Use spell check and proofread it before cutting, pasting and posting.
-

POSTING REVIEWS ONLINE:

1. Go to destiny.msdpt.k12.in.us/
2. Select our school, then login.
3. Search the catalog for the book. Click on the title.
4. Click on the 'Reviews' folder, then the 'Add Review' button.
5. Choose your star rating, then add your book review to the box.
6. When done, proofread and correct, then click 'Save' to send your review.

BOOK CLUB REVIEWS:
POSTING REVIEWS & RATINGS ONLINE

Writing reviews & recommendations for past, present and future library books.

Sharing Reading Experiences with Others:

Title Chosen:
_____

Book to be Read by Next Meeting Date:
_____

READ

P M M S

Library Media Center
pmms.msdpt.k12.in.us/imc/index.htm

Passing out a bookmark at each meeting helps as a friendly reminder for the next meeting, a guide for writing an effective review, and a place marker for the new book being read.

2010-2011
New Books Club
This book recommended by:

Perry Meridian Middle School

2010-2011
New Books Club
This book recommended by:

Perry Meridian Middle School

2010-2011
New Books Club
This book recommended by:

Perry Meridian Middle School

2010-2011
New Books Club
This book recommended by:

Perry Meridian Middle School

2010-2011
New Books Club
This book recommended by:

Perry Meridian Middle School

2010-2011
New Books Club
This book recommended by:

Perry Meridian Middle School

2010-2011
New Books Club
This book recommended by:

Perry Meridian Middle School

2010-2011
New Books Club
This book recommended by:

Perry Meridian Middle School

2010-2011
New Books Club
This book recommended by:

Perry Meridian Middle School

2010-2011
New Books Club
This book recommended by:

Perry Meridian Middle School

Using a labels template in Microsoft Word or similar program, create bookplates for students to sign and place in the front of books highly recommended by participants.

From *Social Readers: Promoting Reading in the 21st Century* by Leslie B. Preddy.
Santa Barbara, CA: Libraries Unlimited. Copyright © 2010.

Reader's Theatre/Participatory Read-Aloud

Using Skype or a similar Internet distance learning video tool, actively sharing reading between grade levels or schools is fast, affordable, and fun. While an older group prepares a read-aloud experience for a younger audience, younger students learn the joy of sharing reading and oral interpretation of literature from older students. With reader's theatre, students bring stories to life through voices and gestures. With a read-aloud, students model reading fluency and bring stories to life through oral interpretation of the text.

Cost: $–$$$

By keeping it simple using free video connection software and cameras and microphones already built into computers, costs are kept to a minimum. Optional technology enhancements, which schools may or may not already have, may increase expenses. These might include a document camera, external microphone, and external digital video camera. Experience enhancements, such as a craft connection or giving the partnering school extra copies of the book, also increase the budget. The partnering school will be responsible for any technology expenses on their end.

Planning Time: Four Weeks

Planning requires coordinating and testing technology with the partnering school, arranging the presentation schedule, training and practice time for student readers, and the optional purchase and distribution of craft supplies.

Planning Involvement: Two or More People

An activity planner is needed to coordinate communication and planning between the two schools. An adult contact with the student group and companion school is also necessary.

Your school: This project requires one adult and the desired number of students per book. The quantity of students could range from the use of a club, a specially selected group, or particular classes.

Partnering school: A contact will coordinate the participation within the companion school.

Suggested Supplies

- Books: picture book, poetry, or other book from library media center that is well suited for read-aloud or reader's theatre

- Create: lesson plans, reader's theatre or read-aloud script, schedule

- Optional: craft instructions and enough craft supplies for each student in the partnering classroom, document camera, external microphone, external digital video camera or cameras

- Technology: computer with built-in camera or microphone, Skype or other videoconferencing/distance learning program

- Miscellaneous: partnering school with matching videoconferencing/distance learning technology

Instructions

To begin, research what Web-based videoconferencing tools are approved or currently in use by the school or district. If one does not exist, locate an affordable or free tool, such as Skype.

Consider which book to use. Make a selection based on familiarity, popularity, read-aloud entertainment value, season, and availability. For example, *The Polar Express* may be a good choice for November or December and could be a read aloud or converted into a reader's theatre script.

If doing reader's theatre, convert the book into a script; an online search will produce many free reader's theatre script adaptions. If developing a read-aloud, divide the text into the needed number of narrators. Some of the joy for the audience is when segments are read aloud by multiple voices simultaneously.

When locating a partnering school, distance should not be an issue. The school could be in the school district, neighboring state, across the country, or around the world. A place to post a partner request is the Center for Interactive Learning and Collaboration (CILC; www.cilc.org). Once a partner is found, set up an event day and time as well as one or more pre-event test sessions so you'll have time to work out any technical glitches in advance. Plan for a fifteen- to thirty-minute event, depending on the length of the selection, discussion time desired after the reading, and optional craft time. Prepare for possibilities by setting up extra connection time. Plan extra time before and after the planned event. The extra time may be needed for increased student engagement or technical difficulties.

Partner with a team, club, or class. Develop and present lessons and training materials to help students understand how to orally interpret children's literature. Invest the time needed for students to practice their parts with the technology so that they can work on staging, transitions, and other visual and audio needs. Depending on what works, transition between images from the book and the live action.

An enriching option is to have partnering younger students create a simple craft. This craft relates to the story and is based on the example modeled and presented by the older students. Considerations are per craft cost, number of students in the partnering school, and getting supplies to the partnering school. The supplies could be ordered online and shipped directly to the partnering school, or the partnering school may agree to purchase the supplies themselves.

Preplanning

- Research and download videoconferencing or distance learning software as needed.

- Purchase equipment as desired.

- Make reading selection options.

- Coordinate a partnering educator and his club, group, team, or class.

- Locate a companion craft if desired.

- Schedule event date and time with stakeholders.

Four Weeks Before

- Locate a partnering school.

- Develop or locate training materials and script.

- Students read the selection and begin practicing reading it aloud.

- Order craft supplies if needed.

Two Weeks Before

- Present training and lessons to students.

- Host frequent practice sessions with students and technology.

- Test technology and the Internet connection with the partner school.

During the Activity

- Set up and test the technology.

- Host the event based on a preplanned schedule.

After the Activity

- Pack up and store technology.

- Work with participants to evaluate technology and the event. Make adjustments for future endeavors.

- Send thank you note to the partner school.

Social Networking

Social networking is continually expanding and morphing as young people learn and grow with it. In today's world, it means actively interacting with others through the Internet. Social networking is interacting with others through the Internet. Students are not just viewing material on the Internet; they also contribute to it. For book junkies—and book junkies in the making—this could include book discussions, book reviews, digital commercials, storytelling, and much more.

If the library media center is not already involved with the preexisting social networking tool needed for a project, check with school administration and district policy to learn what requirements, tools, or options exist or need to be considered. The district may have a preexisting tool to access and use, or there may be specific, school board or district policy–approved social networking tools from which to choose. If there is freedom to pick, seek Web tools that require students to use a password/login to post and that needs administrative approval before a student's post is made public.

When diving into social networking, designing social network etiquette is important. It may be a preestablished school board or school district policy. If guidelines do not already exist, develop the school's rules of etiquette with the assistance of the technology committee and administration. In the long run, it will be much easier if the social network etiquette is developed collaboratively and utilized throughout the school.

All social networking projects have certain supplies in common to consider:

- Books: books from the library media center collection

- Create: publicity and promotional materials, social network etiquette document, project-specific training materials

- Student contribution: Internet, library or personal copy of book

- Technology: computer, Internet

Book Commercials

Commercials are a way of life. People are bombarded with advertisements on newspapers and Web pages, in magazines, during television programs, before movies at the theatre, on the radio, and on book covers and jackets. Students know and understand the nuances of commercials better than many adults. A digital book commercial is a promotion for a book, similar to a movie trailer or TV commercial, intended to interest a person to read the promoted material. Taking advantage of people's ability to identify with commercials and technology, their television and moviegoing experiences can be used quite advantageously to create book commercials.

Commercials are shared with the school community through televised announcements, a school's closed-circuit information channel, or the school's or library's Web site. If able to post the commercials online, there is the added benefit of the positive publicity this will give the school as the student creators direct their friends and family to the link for viewing.

Samples of professional book commercials are available at Scholastic's Video in the Stacks site (http://www.scholastic.com/kids/stacks/videos) by clicking on "Inside the Book." If interested in an alternative that does not require a script or narration, see the end of this entry for the simpler alternative, a Book Trailer.

Cost: $$$

If the school does not already have simple digital production equipment those costs need to be calculated into the budget. Possibilities include, but are not limited to, a digital video camera, digital still camera, USB port audio recorder, background music, and sound effects. Schools can go online to purchase audio from places like www.royaltyfreemusic.com, or use the free songs that come with many programs. If a digital video editor is not currently owned, one may be purchased, or simple programs such as Microsoft Movie Maker and Microsoft Photo Story are free downloads.

Planning Time: Two to Four Weeks

Depending on the time students have available to meet and create, estimate two to four weeks for production after the book has been read. Production includes story boarding the action, writing the script, recording video and audio, editing, and publishing the final product.

Planning Involvement: One or More Adults and a Student Club, Group, or Class

An activity planner and sponsor or classroom teacher train, supervise, guide, and assist students through the process.

Suggested Supplies

- Create: storyboard or graphic organizer, training materials

- Technology: computer and video production program, digital audio recorder, digital still camera, digital video camera, purchased royalty-free music or free downloads, site for posting digital video, USB port headset microphone

Instructions

While researching which programs and equipment to purchase or download for free, seek programs capable of saving in avi, mp, or another standard format for the best flexibility and compatibility of viewers. These formats are compatible with most video production equipment used in students' televised announcements and can easily be posted online for viewing on the Internet. When teaching oneself or preparing training for students, free online material tutorials are helpful. Search online for self-help Web sites and training tutorials specific to the program being used. Some examples are (URLs were accurate as of January 29, 2010):

- "Creating and Sharing Great Movies" (Microsoft Corporation): http://www.microsoft.com/windowsxp/using/moviemaker/create/default.mspx

- "Get Started with Windows Movie Maker" (Microsoft Corporation): http://www.microsoft.com/windowsxp/using/moviemaker/getstarted/default.mspx

- "Microsoft Photo Story 3 for Windows: Make Show-n-Tell Cool Again" (Microsoft Corporation): http://www.microsoft.com/windowsxp/using/digitalphotography/photostory/default.mspx

Preplanning

- Research and purchase the necessary equipment.

- Research and purchase any necessary digital editing programs and download free programs.

- Prepare a collection of copyright-compliant sound effects and background music, or plan to use any that is provided free through the chosen program.

- Plan to use the library media center online library catalog to post commercials online. If the online library catalog is unable to host this, learn how to post the commercials on the library media center Web site or blog. If that is not possible, or if desired, other public sites may be approved by administration, such as TeacherTube.

- Create or locate student training materials.

- Research and practice how to use the equipment, programs, and posting of final products.

- Confirm the final format needed to air on televised announcements and post on the Internet.

- Schedule a class, group, or club of students to create commercials.

- Students select and read books in preparation for commercial development. Teach students how to process reading and make notes while reading.

Two to Four Weeks Before

- Meet with students to begin drafting scripts.

- Teach students how to create and utilize a storyboard for production.

- Help students finalize storyboards and record the necessary images with the digital video and still cameras.

One to Two Weeks Before

- Work with students to download footage into the computer's video production program and create the final commercial.

Day of Airing

- Run finalized commercial on televised student announcements.

- Post book commercial in designated Web site on the Internet.

- Promote Internet access to the commercials through the student newsletter, e-mail, and other means.

After the Airing

- Remove old commercials from Web site as necessary.

An Alternative: The Book Trailer

A simple and quick alternative to the book commercial is a book trailer. With a book trailer, students or staff create a video with Microsoft PowerPoint, Movie Maker, Photo Story, or other visual production software. Using still digital images, text, and simple background music, students set a mood and tone and include content to draw student interest toward reading the book. A simple search on TeacherTube.com will provide examples.

Book Discussion

Using something as simple as a blog or a similar online dialogue tool, virtual book discussions can occur anytime, anyplace. A Web-based book discussion can be held in real time, with scheduled hours for discussion, but it is also effective with this generation for discussions to flow naturally so that students can read, comment, and share in their own way, in their own time. This is how the insomniac or early bird can still participate at the peak hour of his or her cognitive skills. With today's youth, schedules and free time vary drastically from person to person, depending on many variables: family, extracurricular activities, friends, social commitments, emotional stability, family, stress, and even day of the week.

Cost: $

This costs nothing, if using one of the free educator blog or blog-type resources. Check the school district policy to find out if there is a preapproved or preexisting blog tool educators are encouraged or required to use.

Planning Time: Two to Four Weeks Setup, then Ongoing

It may take two to four weeks to set up and promote the blog or other online discussion tool. Monitoring, maintaining, and promoting are ongoing.

Planning Involvement: One Person

One activity planner is needed to coordinate and promote the project and act as the site administrator for the online conversation tool. It is important for the activity planner to consult staff and students while developing online discussion etiquette and discussion page design.

Suggested Supplies

- Create: online discussion page, online discussion etiquette

- Technology: online discussion tool

Instructions

If the library media center or school district does not have a preexisting blog site or similar online communication tool, gain permission to research and select a free blog tool available for educational purposes. Think about how to use the tool for maximum effectiveness.

Should there be multiple discussions occurring simultaneously?

Should the discussion starters be general and broad or very specific?

Should a general genre discussion be included?

Should there be a discussion surrounding a particularly popular author?

Are there specific titles to discuss given their general popularity or because of upcoming awards or special school events, such as an all-school read?

Should there be a range of questions or just one?

How frequently will a new strand begin? How long should a conversation strand remain active?

How will rules and etiquette be communicated to participants?

Preplanning

- Meet with administration to approve the social networking project.
- Do the necessary research to select and register a blog tool.
- Meet with student groups to get advice and feedback on what they would recommend for the blog's content, format, and etiquette.
- Meet a representative group of staff members to get their recommendations for the blog.

Two Weeks Before

- Meet with administration and technology committee to discuss, create, and approve online discussion etiquette if it has not already been established by the school or district.
- Based on feedback from students and staff, design blog layout and post a starter discussion strand(s).
- Draft a timeline for when to update the blog and add or change discussion strands.
- Create promotional materials, including an announcement with login instructions, in the student newsletter and e-mails.

During the Project

- Advertise as planned.
- Approve postings as needed.
- Continue throughout year or as desired.
- Update and post new discussion strands as planned or whenever opportunities arise.
- Re-advertise as new discussion strands start.

After the Project

- Clear discussions and postings as needed.
- At the end of the semester, clean the blog site to prepare for the new semester.

Book Review

Through the Internet, book reviews take on a life of their own outside the classroom. Students can post reviews in a real-world setting for other people to read. To see samples, check out RIF Reading Planet Book Zone (http://www.rif.org/kids/readingplanet/bookzone.htm) for online book summaries and reader reviews. Student book reviews become an engaging, purposeful social activity through the use of

Web sites with tools for posting book reviews. Some of these resources include Flamingnet (http://www.flamingnet.com/) or Young Adult (and Kids) Books Central (http://www.yabookscentral. com), public library patron review pages, school reading blogs, Moodle, or online library catalogs with review posting functions.

Cost: $

There is no direct cost if using preexisting Web tools.

Planning Time: One Week, then Ongoing

It will take one week to create lessons and training materials, then ongoing promotion, reminders, and time to train teachers and students.

Planning Involvement: One Person

This requires one activity planner to take the lead as trainer and promoter, but the more staff who encourage students to participate, the faster word spreads—and the more students who will create and use online book reviews.

Suggested Supplies

- Technology: library automation system with a book review option or other approved book review posting Web site

Instructions

Many students may be familiar with book reviews. Review the section on book reviews in Chapter 3 for further insight. If the library media center is not capable of posting online book reviews through the library automation system or library wiki, check the local public library Web site because many now have book review posting capabilities. You can also do research to locate a valid, student-safe site that is acceptable for your school to use. Check with administration to confirm that posting reviews and the selected Web site are acceptable with district and school policy.

Seek a site where it is possible to for you to review, edit, and approve student posts before they are made public. Considering the need to keep the posting authentic, decide which, if any, grammatical or spelling errors will be corrected. Also decide how students will sign the reviews: initials, first name only, full name, or screen name.

Preplanning

- Do necessary research to select the review site and set yourself up as the review administrator.
- Create or locate training materials or lesson plans.
- Create a book reviewer's guide with a list of tips for what to include and how to access and login to the Web site.

One Week Before

- Share Web site and book review techniques with staff members. Invite them to participate and post reviews.
- Schedule student book review training.

- Create promotional materials for the student newsletter and announcements.
- Create posters, signs, and bookmarks.

During the Project

- Advertise as planned.
- Meet with classes, groups, and individuals to introduce book review techniques and share the process.
- Review and approve book reviews as posted.
- Continue throughout year or as desired and needed.

After the Project

- Revisit and revise etiquette and training materials annually.
- Delete old book reviews when appropriate.

How to write an online Library Book Review:

◊ Summarize the story just enough to make a person want to read it, but do *not* give away the ending or any surprises and twists in the story.
◊ Who would be interested in reading this? Would it appeal to a person with specific personal interests, a certain age group, boys, girls, or both?
◊ What is the genre?
◊ Describe the main character. What is the age, gender, ethnicity, and personality of the main character?
◊ Is there a major theme, problem, issue, or moral raised?
◊ Are there illustrations? Do they help the reader better understand and enjoy the text?
◊ Be expressive. Use descriptive adjectives (avoid boring words like nice, good, poor, etc.).
◊ Be nice. Use appropriate language. Do not be overly cruel or kind.

COMPLETE THE
5 ★ RATING

★ = not recommended
★★ = it is just okay
★★★ = good-it is worth a try
★★★★ = excellent
★★★★★ = the best - everyone must read this!

With a book review, students help each other make informed reading choices.

From *Social Readers: Promoting Reading in the 21st Century* by Leslie B. Preddy.
Santa Barbara, CA: Libraries Unlimited. Copyright © 2010.

Storytelling

Reading cannot be discussed without also discussing writing; the two are so closely linked. The ability to write and to tell a good story is strongly connected to becoming an effective reader. The two should be married whenever possible. Through web 2.0 tools, such as a wiki or Moodle, students collectively write, revise, edit, and rewrite at all hours of the day or night. The stories can take on a life of their own, morphing pieces of amazing, creative genius and ending much differently than the originator could ever have created or imagined alone.

Cost: $

Costs are eliminated by using a preexisting tool that the school district already owns or a free teacher tool that has been approved by the school district, like PBwiki.

Planning Time: One Month

It will take one week to create, promote, and begin the current stories. Use the final three weeks to continue to promote, remind, close, and restart the next month's storyline.

Planning Involvement: One or Two People

This requires one to two people to take the lead as trainer, promoter, and site administrator.

Suggested Supplies

- Create: online storytelling page, storytelling guidelines
- Technology: computer with Internet, online storytelling tool

Instructions

If the library media center does not currently have a wiki tool, check the district policy. If it is not a requirement to use a preapproved Web site, research to locate a valid, student-safe site that is acceptable. If you are free to pick anything, use one that requires students to use a password/login and administrative approval before a posting is made public. Think about how to use the tool for maximum effectiveness.

Should there be multiple stories going at one time?

How frequently will a new story begin?

How long should a storyline remain active?

Should an inactive story remain available for viewing?

For further understanding, go to the Encyclopedia of Educational Technology wikis article (http://coe.sdsu.edu/eet/Articles/wikis/index.htm) and Wikispaces (http://www.wikispaces.com) and review the features and tours for further understanding of a wiki.

Preplanning

- Do the necessary research to select and register for an online interactive storytelling tool.
- Meet with student groups to get advice and feedback about what they would recommend for story starters and project etiquette.

• Meet with a staff group to get recommendations for wiki participation rules and guidelines.

One Month Before

• Based on feedback from students and staff, design the online storytelling site. Post procedures and simple etiquette rules on the site.

• Draft a timeline for when to add new and close old stories.

Two Weeks Before

• Ask staff members to test the online storytelling tool and provide feedback for editing the site before rolling out the project to students.

• Create announcements for the student newsletter and daily announcements.

• Design poster, signs, and bookmarks.

During the Project

• Advertise as planned. Re-advertise as a new storytelling strand begins.

• Approve wiki postings as needed.

• Continue throughout year as outlined in the calendar.

After the Project

• Revisit and revise etiquette and training materials annually.

• At the end and beginning of the year, clean the storytelling site and prepare for the new year.

Appendix

Themes

A variety of reading themes can be adopted by a school for an event, club, program, poster, or campaign. Ideas offered here can be used for those themes or as a springboard to imagine other themes personalized to work for your school.

All-You-Can-Read Book Buffet
Bank Reading Minutes
Best Friend Books
Book Bandits
Book Bash
Book Bonanza
Book Buddies
Book Buffet
Book Cooks
Book Extravaganza
Book Jockies
Book Passport
Bookmark Bunch
Books Build Brains
Books for Breakfast
Books R 4 U
Books R Sweet
Books Take You Places
Bookslingers
Booktalk Gang
Born to Read
Brown Bag Book Club
Capture Reading
Caution: Readers at Work
Celebrate a Good Book!
Celebrate Reading!
Craveable Books

Discover the Magic of Reading
Dive into Reading
Driven to Read
Everywhere—READ—Anywhere
Exercising the Right to Read
Explore the World through Books
Find Friends in Books
Find the Hidden Treasure in Books
Follow the Reader
Free to Read
Get Carried Away with a Good Book
Give a Little Love—Share a Book
Give the Gift of Books
Good Readers = Good Writers
Good Reading!
Hey! What Are You Reading?!?
I'm Booked
If You Like _____, You'll Love …
Ink Eaters
Leaders Are Readers
Leap into a Good Book
Library Lizards/Library Lounge Lizards
Live—Laugh—Love—Read
Master the Art of Reading
New Books Club
One Book, One School, One Author
Open a New Chapter—READ

Pay It Forward—Share Good Books
Radical Readers
Read Alert
Read 2 Me
Read 2 Succeed
Read a Book, Pass It On
Read an Adventure
Read Every Day!
Read Here, There, and Everywhere
Read in the New Year
Read More—Be More
Read to Succeed
Read with Friends
Read—Pass It On!
Reader's Café
Readers and Writers Wanted
Readers Leaders
Reader's Reward
Reading Is Fun!
Reading Makes Dreams Come Alive
Reading Menu

Reading Passport: Where Will You Go?
Reading Riders
Reading Rocks
Reading Rules!
Reading Takes U Places
Reading Wonderland
Reading Wranglers
Reading Writers
Real Men Read
Rockin' Readers
Share a Book You Love
Share Books!
Sink Your Teeth into a Good Book
Spring into Books
U Need 2 Read
U R A Reader
Use Your Imagination—Bring a Book to Life
Wanted: Readers!
What R U Reading?
Yield to a Good Book
Your Key to the World: Reading

References

Gardiner, Steve. "A Skill for Life." *Educational Leadership* 63, no. 2 (October 2005): 67–70.

Greenberg, E., Dunleavy, E., and Kutner, M. (2007). *Literacy behind Bars: Results from the 2003 National Assessment of Adult Literacy Prison Survey* (NCES 2007-473). Washington, DC: National Center for Education Statistics, U.S. Department of Education. http://nces.ed.gov/pubs2007/2007473_1.pdf (accessed September 7, 2008).

Indiana Department of Education. Indiana Standards and Resources. http://dc.doe.in.gov/Standards/AcademicStandards/StandardSearch.aspx (accessed October 11, 2009).

"Learning in the 21st Century: The Role of the School Library Media Program." SLJ Leadership Summit 2006, Chicago, IL, November 2–3, 2006.

Payne, Ruby. *A Framework for Understanding Poverty* (3rd revised ed.). Highlands, TX: Aha Process, 2003.

Planty, M., Hussar, W., Snyder, T., Provasnik, S., Kena, G., Dinkes, R., Kewalramani, A., and Kemp, J. *The Condition of Education 2008* (NCES 2008-031). Washington, DC: National Center for Education Statistics, Institute of Education Sciences, U.S. Department of Education, 2008. http://nces.ed.gov/programs/coe/2008/pdf/20_2008.pdf (accessed August 8, 2008).

Preddy, Leslie. "Social Reading: Promoting Reading in the Millennial Learner." *School Library Media Activities Monthly*, XXV (January 2009), pp. 23–25.

Preddy, Leslie. *SSR with Intervention: A School Library Action Research Project*. Westport, CT: Libraries Unlimited, 2007.

Przeclawski, Gail, and Woods, Christina. "Literacy and Generational Poverty." AASL National Conference Session 1275, October 26, 2007.

Readence, John E., Bean, Thomas W., and Baldwin, R. Scott. *Content Area Literacy: An Integrated Approach,* 8th edition. Dubuque, IA: Kendall/Hunt, 2004.

"Reading between the Lines: What the ACT Reveals about College Readiness in Reading." Iowa City, IA: ACT, 2006. http://www.act.org/path/policy/reports/reading.html (accessed June 6, 2006).

U.S. Department of Education, National Center for Education Statistics. *The Condition of Education 2007* (NCES 2007-064). Washington, DC: U.S. Government Printing Office, 2007. http://nces.ed.gov/programs/coe/2007/pdf/18_2007.pdf (accessed August 8, 2008).

Whitehurst, Grover P. "Archived Information: Evidence-Based Education (EBE)." Office of Education Research and Improvement. http://www.ed.gov/offices/OERI/presentations/evidencebase.html (accessed December 2, 2007).

Index

About the Author

LESLIE B. PREDDY is the library media specialist for Perry Meridian Middle School in Indianapolis, Indiana, and instructs graduate-level courses for Indiana State University and Indiana University–Purdue University Indianapolis. She developed a research model, Student Inquiry in the Research Process, and a reading program, SSR with Interventions. She was the 2009 Metropolitan School District of Perry Township Teacher of the Year. She is a past recipient of the American Association of School Librarians' Collaborative School Library Media Award, Lilly Teacher Creativity Fellowship, and 2010 Indiana State Teacher of the Year finalist. She is a past president for the Association for Indiana Media Educators (AIME), a past general chair of the state's Young Hoosier Book Award (YHBA) program, and recipient of AIME's prestigious Peggy L. Pfeiffer Service Award. She presents at the local, state, and national levels; is a book reviewer for Library Media Connection; publishes a range of articles in professional journals; and has co-created online resources. She coauthored *The Blue Book on Literacy and Instruction for the Information Age* (Libraries Unlimited 2006) with Dr. Daniel Callison and her book *SSR with Intervention* (Libraries Unlimited 2007) was named one of the Best Professional Books of 2007 by *Teacher Librarian* magazine.

Photograph by Lifetouch National School Studios.